Lisbon

Lagos

Sagres

Ceuta

Tangier

MOROCCO

MADIERA IS.

Porto
Santo

Funchal

CANARY Islands

Cape
Bojador

io de Ouro

ARGUIM

Cape
Branco

AFRICA

Senegal River

SENEGAL

GAMBIA

GUINEA COAST

Sierra Leone

Gulf of Guinea

W

E

S

HENRY
The Navigator

HENRY THE NAVIGATOR
Prince of Portugal 1394–1460

*From a contemporary manuscript chronicle
in the National Library, Paris.*

HENRY
The Navigator

THE STORY OF A
GREAT PRINCE
AND HIS TIMES

By Elaine Sanceau

ARCHON BOOKS
1969

G
286
H5
S32
1969

SBN: 208 00681 8
Library of Congress Catalog Card Number: 69-11549
Printed in the United States of America

Contents

[Author's Note:—None of the conversations in this book have been invented by me. They are all translations of words recorded by the chroniclers—principally Zurara.]

I

The Older Generation

WHEN John of Gaunt offered the King of Portugal choice between his two daughters—Philippa aged twenty-eight, or Catherine in her teens—D. João declared unhesitatingly that he chose Philippa.

His reasons were wholly unsentimental. He did not know what either girl was like. He only knew that he wanted a wife without awkward dynastic claims. Catherine was heiress to a host of troubles. Her mother, John of Gaunt's second wife, was daughter of that Pedro the Cruel of Castile whose brother had usurped his throne. Catherine's husband would be in honor bound to vindicate her right to her grandfather's crown. Philippa, being the child of the English Blanche of Lancaster, had no axe to grind in the peninsular imbroglio, and so it was that D. João preferred her to her sister.

D. João did not wish to be committed to indefinite Castilian wars. All he asked was to be allowed to wear the crown of Portugal in peace. The King of Castile, as it happened, claimed that crown for his own wife, and the crushing defeat of Aljubarrota had not yet persuaded him to give up the idea. It was to change his thoughts that D. João had sent for John of Gaunt. If Juan of Castile claimed Portugal for his Queen Beatriz, had not the Duke of Lancaster as good a right to assert the pretensions of his own Duchess against the usurping House of Trastamara?

Convenient though it was to hold the Englishman over his rival's head, D. João was not in a position to profess strict views upon dynastic legitimism. He himself was king by no right but the people's will and that of his victorious sword. He was a bastard son of King Pedro I of Portugal and a certain Teresa Lourenço—a lady whose origin gains luster as the generations pass. To contemporary chroniclers, she is "a lady named Teresa Lourenço"—nothing more—but by the time we reach the sixteenth century, historians have much to say about her genealogy and lofty birth.

Teresa Lourenço's son had passed an inconspicuous boyhood at the court of his brother, the good-natured but feckless D. Fernando, "o Formoso." Neither the handsome Fernando, nor the beautiful minx whom he had made his queen, ever suspected that the little Master of Aviz would one day succeed him on the throne. The idea probably did not occur to D. João himself until Fernando died in 1383, leaving confusion in his realm, and his daughter and sole heiress married to the Castilian king. D. Juan of Castile entered Portugal at once to claim his wife's inheritance, upon which the people rose and refused to accept a foreign lord. The Master of Aviz, after some prudent hesitation, accepted the leadership of the rebellion. He was first proclaimed Defender of the Realm, and subsequently King.

The people's choice proved worthy of their confidence. D. João was not a genius, but he was both able and efficient. He was a brave soldier, an intelligent statesman, and a discerning judge of men. He was fortunate in having some very good ones to support his cause, and—unlike many other princes in history—he never failed to appreciate their worth.

The national cause, which had at first seemed hopeless, triumphed by degrees. Thanks to the military genius of his Constable, Nunalvares Pereira, D. João won some spectacular victories over his powerful adversary, and meanwhile sent a pressing invitation to the Duke of Lancaster to come and take a hand. John of Gaunt was nothing loth. He landed with his family at Coruña, in 1386, proclaiming himself King of Castile and Leon.

In the green province of Minho, near the frontier of Galicia, the allies met, and camped in tents, and feasted one another. The Duke of Lancaster's banquet, Froissart says, was *"grand et bel et bien estouffé de toutes choses,"* enlivened by *"grand foison ménestrieux."* D. João's return dinner, laid out in leafy bowers, was also *"très bel et bien ordonné."* Amid festivities the two princes discussed their plans. They decided to invade Castile together the next year, and that Philippa was to be D. João's queen.

It seems that D. João was in no hurry to assume the married state. He kept on putting off his wedding day, until the bride's father brought pressure to bear. The lady was dispatched to Porto without more delay, and the Duke urged the King to marry her at once. Even then D. João did not rush to meet his bride.

The knot was tied at last, in the cathedral of the ancient city of Porto, on February 2nd, 1387, and D. João left his wedded wife immediately in order to fulfil his obligations to his father-in-law.

There is no need to give details of the campaign. By the end of the summer John of Lancaster had had enough. The enemy would not come out and fight, and to conquer every stronghold separately was very slow. Already the English troops had found that Spanish towns were far too poor, and Spanish sun and Spanish wines too potent for their liking. "Oh, take us back to France," they cried, "where summer heat is not so great, and looting is worth while!" At last the Duke himself fell ill, and so decided to make peace. He gave the Princess Catherine in marriage to the heir-presumptive of Castile, thus repairing the breach between the descendants of Pedro the Cruel and those of Enrique of Trastamara. Then, having settled both his daughters, John of Gaunt went home.

João of Portugal, although surprised, was not unduly grieved to see him go. He did not really care who was king of Castile. He led his armies back to Portugal, and then at last he had the chance to get to know his bride.

If marriage is a lottery, D. João certainly had drawn a winning number. The Master of Aviz was one of those people who are born fortunate, and the wife that Fate and politics had blindly brought him was yet another instance of his luck.

We are not told if the new queen of Portugal was pretty, and the inference would therefore seem to be that she was not, but she was the true daughter of Blanche of Lancaster—a sweet and charming woman—and a worthy granddaughter of Philippa of Hainault, Edward III's admirable consort. "She had," Fernão Lopes declares, "every good quality pertaining to a woman of high estate."

Like all devout persons of her day, Philippa indulged in formidable spiritual exercises. Every morning she recited the Canonical Hours, according to the Salisbury ritual—"no easy thing to do," observes the chronicler, deeply impressed. On Fridays she would speak to nobody till she had said her Psalter through; she fasted frequently, and read the Holy Scriptures "at appropriate times." But Philippa's piety was not an empty formalism. It carried with it a practical and sunshiny goodness that warmed and gladdened everyone around. "There was no spite or malice in her nature," we are told, "but all her works were done in love of God and of her neighbor." She ruled her household with a sweet dignity that yet had not a trace of haughtiness. Queen Philippa was found by everyone to be a very simple friendly person, and though a busy woman, she was not above enjoying games with her young maids of honor.

And she was adaptable. Transplanted from the English court to the throne of Portugal—a land where climate, people, language, everything was different—Philippa won her subjects' hearts completely and at once, and never seems to have been thought of as a foreigner amongst them.

As for her husband, he was a young man aged twenty-nine, of medium height and dark complexion. He had black eyes, a determined chin, and the sort of nose that is described as capable. He excelled in military exercises and was a mighty hunter, with yet sufficient book learning to give him pretensions to culture. Like all his family, D. João could be violent when aroused, but he generally showed self-control, and must have had a pleasant personality, for he was popular with his subjects. In character he certainly was not the equal of his wife, but he was a decent and an upright man, and it is to his credit that he should have been so, for there had not been many elevating influences to guide his youth. But D. João was naturally right-minded and a great admirer of goodness in others. As for his personal morals, Philippa's bridegroom was neither a libertine—as his brother Fernando had been—nor yet a Galahad like his friend, Nunalvares Pereira. In this, as in most things, he steered a midway course. He was generally considered a serious young man, but a certain Ines Pires had gladdened his bachelor days and given him a son and daughter.

Like every well-brought-up young woman of her time, Philippa of Lancaster entered the married state fully prepared to do her duty by whatever bridegroom Heaven and her father had seen fit to choose. And she considered that they had done well for her— "God gave her a husband to her liking," says the chronicler, and being a wise medieval wife, "she was careful never to displease him."

The discovery of Ines Pires does not seem to have upset Philippa. She had seen such things in her own family. Regrettably, men were like that! At the same time, D. João's wife was a woman of character; she had no mind to repeat the rôle of her Spanish stepmother, who had shared both husband and home with the fair Katherine Rouet.

Philippa handled the situation with firmness and tact. Ines Pires had to retire into a convent—there was nothing else that could be done with ladies in her case—but Philippa was not unkind to her defeated rival. Thanks to her patronage, Ines soon became Prioress; the Queen took the whole community under her favor and protection, while the little Afonso and Beatriz were brought up at their father's court.

In all this D. João gave no trouble at all. Perhaps he was already tired of Ines Pires. He allowed his former flame to be eclipsed without protest, and settled down contentedly to the conjugal life.

The marriage was a success. The most ardent romantic could not have pretended that it was a love match, but it developed into something quite as satisfactory. D. João, in his youth, had not had opportunity to meet many good women—the species did not flourish at Fernando's court—so Philippa was a new experience to him, and his admiration for her knew no bounds. The affection that grew up between these two, though based on nothing more exciting than mutual esteem, strengthened and deepened with each year that passed. There was no Ines Pires in D. João's married life. He surrendered unreservedly to D. Philippa, and let her make a model husband of him.

There could hardly have been a cleaner break than that between the reign of D. João I and that of his predecessor. A superficial observer—visiting Portugal under the late Fernando—would have been tempted to say that here was a people in decadence, a nation destined to be swept away. He would have seen there a licentious court presided over by an adulterous queen, a king whose good intentions were frustrated by his evil wife, a self-seeking and grasping aristocracy, and a bewildered people looking vainly for a leader, while close at hand a foreign ruler watched and waited—ready to pounce the moment that the crumbling edifice collapsed.

But this apparent desolation was no more real than that of barren fields in early spring. There were vital forces working underneath. When the crisis came, this nation that had seemed about to die, rose to its feet, and shook off its oppressors.

The struggle was deadly, and in its throes an old order was swept away, and everything made new. The country was impoverished and devastated by war, but its sons were proud and hopeful in their strength that had won them the victory. The bad old days were like a nightmare that had passed. It was a period of moral regeneration. All the laxity and corruption in high places were gone. Instead of the effete Fernando stood the energetic D. João; where the scandalous Leonor Teles once had held her court, the immaculate Philippa of Lancaster now ruled, while the time-serving chiefs of the nobility were eclipsed by the great Constable, Nunalvares Pereira.

Even more than the King and Queen, Nunalvares Pereira was the idol of the people. It was he quite as much as they who helped to bring the new Portugal to birth, and his influence may be traced in all D. João's sons. Nunalvares was as perfect a knight as may be found in chivalrous romance, but with more practical realism, and a much better developed sense of humor. No leader of theirs has ever understood his temperamental countrymen so well or made them bow more cheerfully to discipline. Nunalvares neither blustered nor stormed—"My friend! Is such conduct worthy of a man like you?" was the line that he took, and seldom did it fail to work. The King himself was not so well obeyed. You could not have found anywhere a better behaved army than the one that the Constable led. He even succeeded in banishing all female followers from the camp, while listening patiently and pleasantly to a chorus of angry protests. The men were obstinate, but he was adamant. He was always polite, always good-tempered, and he always had his way.

D. João admired Nunalvares immensely. "The King," writes Fernão Lopes, "was often wont to say that all the good customs there were in Portugal had been introduced by the Constable." It is certain that good customs did prevail during this reign. What with the example of their King and Queen to make domestic virtue fashionable, and Nunalvares Pereira as hero-model for the young manhood of the land, the national life of Portugal was raised to a standard of purity that it had never known. The court, once so corrupt, must have been easily the most moral in Europe.

The reign of D. João I was a period of reconstruction, and at this task he and his consort labored hand in hand. She did not interfere with politics, nor he with the arrangements of her household or the upbringing of their children. Together they traveled up and down their little kingdom, which differed from its European contemporaries in that it was already a united whole. From Moorish Algarve up to Celtic Minho there were no conflicting dialects, no semi-independent provinces, no feudal lords with vassals and rear-vassals of their own. All fiefs were held directly from the King, all castles were Crown property, there were no robber barons. The four great crusading orders of St. John, Santiago, Aviz and Cristo still garrisoned their fortresses, but there had been no Moors in Portugal for them to fight since the kingdom of Algarve was conquered from the Infidels a hundred years ago.

The fidalgos of Portugal did not live in bastioned towers, behind drawbridge and moat, like their compeers in France. Their homes were open country manors, *quintas*, upon which they maintained the usual retinue of squires, men-at-arms, and other hangers-on, in readiness to march at the royal summons. In time

(14)

of peace the gentry farmed their lands, or hunted the wild boar or else the bear for days on end, or traveled round the country visiting each other, to the sorrow of the little towns through which they passed. It was an awful nuisance, the burghers complained, to have fidalgos in their midst, with their servants and their squires and pages, and the servants of their pages, and the pages of their squires! The great man might lodge at the nearest monastery, but he would billet all his personnel upon the citizens—who simply hated it. Those were fortunate towns that, like the city of Porto, held a charter giving them the right to exclude all fidalgos!

The free municipalities, or *concelhos*, of Portugal enjoyed as many liberties as were ever granted in medieval Europe. Portugal has always tended toward local self-government, and in the Middle Ages administration was very much decentralized. The *concelhos* managed most of their private affairs themselves, subject to the approval of the King who, followed by his court, was always on the move from one end of his kingdom to the other. Only two out of João and Philippa's six children were born in the same town.

Not many *concelhos* could boast of a full-sized city for their administrative head. Medieval Portugal was principally a rural land of scattered villages. Its people were soldiers and seafaring men, farmers and fishermen. There were almost no industries, few great centers of urban life, no wealthy middle classes. Even the large seaports, like Lisbon and Porto, were agricultural as well as maritime—the fathers of the city tilled their fields, and sent their ships to sea. The richest merchants financing the external trade were foreigners, mostly Italians. The trade was very active, for Portugal produced more foodstuffs than her scanty population could consume, and imported all the finer textiles from abroad. Out of the Tagus estuary, and the mouth of the Douro, from Setubal, Aveiro, Vila do Conde, Viana and Ponte de Lima, the tiny ships sailed north up the Atlantic coast to Bayonne, Bordeaux, Flanders and the British Isles; or south and eastward to the Adriatic Sea. Medieval Portugal sent wines to England, salt to Ireland, cork and hides to Flanders, and dried fish to the Levant. She shipped the wax and honey from her scented hills to northern Europe, and sent there olive oil, and figs, and almonds, from Algarve. The returning fleets brought bales of English cloth, Irish linen, Flemish broadcloth, and Italian silks. The maritime traffic was so intense that often, we are told, the port of Lisbon looked like a forest of masts, and the narrow streets were thronged with foreigners.

These crowds and bustle of the outside world hardly penetrated beyond the coast. Inland, the sturdy peasants ploughed their fields as the Romans had taught their fathers to do, and irrigated them through the dry summer after the manner of the Moors. They had marched—armed with their scythes and pitchforks—to defeat the Castilian foe, and when the war was over returned to their hamlets lost among the pine-clad hills. The rise and fall of dynasties did not mean much to them. All that they wanted was a king able to keep the alien from their land. Their fathers had fought for it against the Moors, and the Castilians should not rule their sons!

This was the country and the people over which D. João and Philippa were called to reign at a crucial moment in the nation's history. Hitherto, in spite of all their maritime communications, the Portuguese had in some measure dwelt apart. With its independence constantly at stake, the nation had required all of its energies just to exist. The last crisis had almost been the end, but the people's will to live had triumphed. There remained the future to build.

To the dynasty of Aviz was given the task of showing a harassed people the lead that they lacked, restoring confidence, inspiring new ideals. The reign of D. João "of Happy Memory" was more important in the history of Europe than he could have dreamed, for this was the period that prepared Portugal for her great century. And D. João and Philippa of Lancaster did more than that. It is to them that the world owes the man who was to guide the Portuguese down paths no nation yet had trod, and bring a new age to the earth.

On March 4th, 1394, in the city of Porto, Queen Philippa gave birth to her fourth son. He was the Infante D. Henrique—whom future generations called The Navigator.

II

The Brothers

FAMILY affection does not seem to have been a sentiment much cultivated by medieval princes. On every side we hear about rebellions led against kings by their sons, and near relations striving to eliminate each other.

In this respect D. Henrique, his brothers, and their sister were original. Far from being a band of rivals, these young people were a mutual admiration society. They actually adored each other, "and never," says the Infante Duarte, eldest of the brothers, "was there any jealousy among us!" Of course, not being angels but young human creatures, there must have been sometimes a passing breeze, but nothing to upset their friendship. "We put up with each other's peculiarities," our informant declares, and this praiseworthy spirit maintained peace.

As for their parents—if these were not perfect, it was because perfection cannot be on earth! "We felt that we were very fortunate to have such a father and mother!"

Other people thought that the King was fortunate to have such children. You can read, observes the chronicler, of a king having a good obedient son, but to have five sons—all obedient—seemed almost too good to be true!

Obedience is a virtue more admired by that generation than it is by ours, but D. João does not sound like the tyrant that moderns imagine fathers of past ages to have been. "As far back as we can remember," writes his son, "we never had a blow from him in anger, neither a harsh word." Their obedience, we gather, was born of love rather than fear, and so continued when João and Philippa were in the grave. "Their death," Duarte says, "has not parted me from their love. I still desire to serve and please them as when they were alive. I still fear to do those things of which I know that they would disapprove, and take pleasure in doing what they would have wished."

Duarte, Pedro, Henrique, Isabel, João, and Fernando were the names of this united family, not to mention an elder son and daughter who died in infancy. How the two poor illegitimates, Afonso and Beatriz fitted into the picture is not easy to imagine, but perhaps they hardly were required to do so. Afonso, Count of Barcelos, was a grown man when his half-brothers were still in the nursery. After marrying the richest heiress in the land, he went abroad, and for some years the court saw little of him. Neither had his sister Beatriz much opportunity for feeling envious of her father's legitimate daughter. She sailed for England when quite a young girl, as bride of the Earl Thomas FitzAlan, and her tomb may be seen today in the chapel of Arundel Castle.

D. João's six other surviving children were brought up all together in an atmosphere glorified by their mother's mystic piety, invigorated by their soldier-father and his warrior friends, and rendered intellectual by their own passion for books. Theirs was a rich inheritance. They were descended from great champions like Afonso Henriques, terror of the Moors, the two English Edwards, First and Third, and Afonso IV, hero of Salado. Besides these heroes they had for ancestors such cultured princes as D. Denis, the troubadour king, Alfonso el Sabio of Castile, and John of Gaunt, patron of letters. It is not surprising then that all these young Infantes had a natural taste for learning.

Contemporaries say that from an early age his parents considered Henrique the most promising of all their sons. If that is so, they were remarkably discerning, for he did not grow up as a giant among mediocrities. All of his brothers were above the average, and some of them were brilliant.

Duarte, the heir, was a thoughtful, scholarly youth, gentle and painfully conscientious—more cut out for a peaceful academic life than the torment of a medieval throne. He read voraciously in several languages, and his general knowledge was encyclopedic. Yet Duarte was by no means wholly contemplative in his tastes. He blended with his love of learning a keen interest in sport. He jousted with consummate skill, and was the finest horseman in the land.

There was just a year between him and Pedro, the second son, and a love like that of Jonathan and David bound the two. "My brother D. Pedro, beloved and esteemed above all others," is Duarte's habitual reference to him; and "You are the person I love best in all the world," writes Pedro to Duarte.

Pedro seems to have been the leading spirit. He was more practical than Duarte, and possibly even more versatile. He is generally considered more of a statesman than his brother, but Pedro was a dreamer too, a restless, inquiring soul in pursuit of some quest, as expressed by his enigmatic motto, *Désir*. What was the thing that he desired? Nobody knows. Nor if he ever found it.

Both Pedro and Duarte had the same love of study; both followed with immense interest the speculations of the intellectuals of their time; both tried their hand at literature, and they both liked to moralize, philosophize, and give each other good advice.

It is amazing how people of that period enjoyed exhortation. To be counseled and admonished gives us no pleasure at all, but it appears that in the fifteenth century a right-minded person did not feel that way. The quantity of sage advice that these two brothers lavished on each other would certainly have wrecked a modern home. On every great occasion in the other's life, Duarte or Pedro never failed to write some words of wisdom for his brother's benefit: "It is not for me to counsel you," he would begin, and then proceed to do so. The receiver of such a homily, far from taking it amiss, would read it with delight, and have it copied in a book for future meditation. Were they then prigs? Not in the least. They were simply two earnest young men who wanted to do right.

Henrique was fifteen months younger than Pedro, but six years older than the next Infante, D. João. We know less about João than of the others. His was the least eventful, and perhaps the happiest, life. He seems to have been a cheerful, sensible and unambitious person, upon whose judgment all his brothers much relied. He evidently felt that they were right in doing so, for his complacent motto was *J'ay bien raison!*

The brother fated to be most tragically connected with Henrique's destiny was the youngest of them all—little Fernando, whose birth had nearly cost his mother's life, and who himself for many years seemed unlikely to live. Fernando grew up, none the less, a quiet, mild young man whose "angelic conversation" everybody loved. Not having the vitality of his brothers, he did not share their taste for violent exercise; he lived for religion and books. His was "a great and noble library," and his chapel, we are told, was beautifully appointed, "after the manner of Salisbury" —a high standard of excellence, it seems. *Le bien me plait* was D. Fernando's motto—these half-English Infantes evidently thought that mottoes sounded best in French, the language of English society at that time.

As for the "well-beloved sister" Isabel, she came in between Henrique and João. Duarte says that he never knew how much he cared for Isabel until she went away. That was the fate of all medieval princesses—they had to go away! Sooner or later came the time when they must leave their country and their family for ever. Isabel was fortunate in that with her it was late rather than soon. She was quite thirty when she left her sunny hills and luminous horizons for the gray skies and the mud flats of the Netherlands, and exchanged the simple palaces of Portugal for the luxury and the license of the gay Burgundian court. To a girl brought up, as she was, in an atmosphere of earnestness and idealism, marriage to Philippe le Bon of Burgundy must have brought a few shocks! Her husband's courtiers hardly knew what to make of her, or she of them. *Prude femme, et béguine,* was their impression of the Duke's consort, and we find her calling herself a stranger in a strange land still, after nearly thirty years of married life.

But Philippa of Lancaster's daughter made good. She won her husband's deep respect, if not his roving heart, and this descendant of a gifted family made an efficient wife for an ambitious ruler. We cannot be surprised that in her loneliness she idolized —and spoiled—her only son, but none the less the fact remains that all the best there was in Charles the Bold can be traced to his mother.

It seems that at one time Isabel tried to persuade her brother Henrique to come and live at the Burgundian court. Some say he was her favorite brother. There was not quite three years between them, but this would not mean close association in nursery days, for in the fifteenth century boys and girls were brought up carefully apart.

Duarte and Pedro were the companions of Henrique's childhood, and the three were almost of an age. They formed a harmonious trio, and the intimacy that bound the two firstborn does not seem to have left the younger in the cold. Henrique did not go in for intimacies—neither with the brothers that he loved, nor the parents to whom he was devoted, nor the friends and ser-

vants to whom he might be deeply attached. Henrique gave away
his soul to nobody. He has left us no such self-revealing book as
D. Duarte's *Leal Conselheiro*, no expression of his views on any
subject as did D. Pedro in his *Virtuosa Lemfeitoria*. This member
of an articulate family kept his reserve unbroken to the end, and
carried to the grave the secrets of his heart.

If his sister had succeeded in enticing him to Flanders, Henrique would have made a strange companion for his pleasure-
loving brother-in-law. He was a serious and concentrated young
man to whom the gaieties of court life held small appeal, but
who would gladly sit up all night with his books. It was not the
philosophy in which his brothers dabbled that interested him.
Science—mathematics and astronomy—were his delight. Yet, for
all his studiousness, Henrique was a man of active habits. He was
an enthusiastic huntsman, and he had a passion for things military, never tiring of hearing them discussed. He had a soldier's
courage, too. His only fear was sin, Zurara says—and sin was taken
very seriously by all Philippa's sons. Henrique had much of his
mother's type of faith—a mysticism not to be satisfied by everyday practice. It made him fast almost continuously, and wear a
hair shirt nearly all his life.

A contradictory urge, at once to action and to contemplation,
was a noticeable feature of Henrique's character. In his nature
were blended fire and ice—a fierce energy that could make him
ride forty leagues in a day and a night and back again, without
pausing to rest, while at other times he showed a strange slowness
to act, which Zurara thinks was willed deliberately, "in accordance to some end unknown to men." It must be owned that his
brother Duarte saw nothing more mysterious in it than procrasti-
nation, but none of us look enigmatic to our family! To other people the Infante D. Henrique grew to be something of a legend
even in his life. He was very pleasant and polite, all his contempo-

raries agree, but when you met him for the first time you found
him awe-inspiring.

His anger was wholly unnerving. It is true that no one ever saw
Henrique lose his temper—he waved you from his presence when
displeased: "I commend you to God," he would say coldly; "may
you be fortunate!" That was all. You wilted and withdrew. It
was not what he said, but only what he looked! It was not anything that he did either, or was likely to do. Henrique seldom
punished anyone, and has been taxed with over indulgence
towards the undeserving. In spite of his rather forbidding aspect,
he really was a most good-natured person and generous to a fault.
Nobody ever left his presence empty-handed, we are told. On the
whole he was loved, Zurara says, "for he was profitable to all, and
he did harm to none."

Henrique differed in appearance from his elder brothers. Duarte and Pedro were tall, fair Plantagenets. Henrique, also tall,
like all his mother's family, in coloring and features resembled his
father. They say that this is why he was D. João's favorite son,
but the likeness was purely physical. None of D. João's sons were
really like him. In spite of deep love and mutual confidence, between them and their admired father yawned a gulf wider than
that which separates the generations. D. João belonged entirely
to the Middle Ages. None of the pangs of a period of transition
troubled him. He took the world just as he found it, simply and
without speculation. When he read, it was tales of King Arthur's
court; when he wrote, it was some devout psalms or a treatise on
hunting; and feasts and jousts were his idea of recreation. D. João
was a medieval king of the clear-headed, practical and progressive
sort, but always a medieval.

His sons were of the Renaissance. The rays of that still distant
dawn already touched them and filled their souls with wonder
and surmise. They were not born into their parents' simple world.

To them the riddle of the universe was a problem that had to be considered. How much was there unanswerable, how much merely unanswered? Of the accepted theories of their world, what was false, what was true?—always excepting the doctrines of Holy Mother Church. "My reason will not consent to it!" Duarte writes, referring to beliefs in charms and spells, and through him spoke the voice of a new age, an age when theories had to rest upon reasoned foundations. And yet the search for truth had many pitfalls. In that perplexing world in which they lived, one had to own that many things that seemed impossible were true. Who would have thought, Duarte says, if one had never seen bombards, that a little powder could hurl a great stone so far? "And yet we can no longer doubt it." In face of such phenomena as this, the only line a thoughtful man could take was neither to affirm nor to deny, "till we are shown by certain proofs that they are true." Which shows that Duarte and his brothers already were wandering outside that one dimension world of highly-colored light and shade, of fantastic landscapes haunted by angels and demons, in which the true medieval lived unquestioningly. A time had come when men demanded certain proof that things were what they seemed to be, and wanted to know what was really there, and why.

Henrique, more than any of the others, awoke to scientific curiosity early in life. This serious and reserved young man, who cared for study more than for the pleasures of his age, who harbored no political ambitions, and put all thought of love and marriage from his life, pondered unceasingly upon the mystery of the earth. The world was wide, and stretching far to lands unknown, inhabited by races each one stranger than the last, until they disappeared into the night. What a small island was Christendom, with a sea of Islam surging all round, and enigmatic heathen regions still beyond! The torch of Faith had long ago been carried east; was it still burning there, or had the darkness quenched its beams? And to the south—what lay below the Mauritanian deserts? And what was known about the icy north? What really was known of the world at all?

Henrique sought the answer in his books. He found that medieval writers could tell him plenty about Heaven and Hell but little of the earth on which he lived, and to much of what they told him his reason could not consent—any more than Duarte's did to the power of love philters.

Remained the ancients. D. Henrique read Herodotus, and he studied Ptolemy, Strabo, and Pliny. They told him much about the Greek and Roman world, and many peoples now beyond the Christians' ken. They told him of races and customs, of climates and zones, of stars above, and islands in the sea. But always they left off just where he would begin, and trailed away into hearsay and legend. Of the farthest east, and lowest south, they left him guessing as before. Of the frozen north they had little to say, and of the limits of that western ocean beside which Henrique had been born, they could not tell him anything at all.

III

How Spurs Might Be Won

WILL you choose war or peace?" Such was the message that D. João sent to the boy king of Castile, whose reign began in 1402. The Regent gladly gave his vote for peace. The chancelleries of either kingdom got to work; and so, after much bandying of words and effusion of ink, in 1411 the parties optimistically signed a treaty of friendship and non-aggression for a period of a hundred and one years.

"Thank Heaven that the war is really over!" sighed the older people then. "Henceforth we can enjoy our possessions, and sell our produce without let or hindrance. Our merchants may now travel in safety all over Spain. Our frontier farmers will reoccupy their farms, and we ourselves shall lie at ease in bed, undisturbed by any summons to war, or by hearing the moans of women who are mourning for their husbands!" And quite regardless of expense, they all began to celebrate and entertain each other.

For many years the nation had not felt so pleased with life. "Now," cried the Portuguese exultantly, "is Portugal the greatest and the happiest kingdom in the world, for we have all the good things that a prosperous realm can want!" They counted all their blessings, one by one, and were astonished at their number. Had they not fruit and vegetables, and meat, and fish, and corn, and wines "of diverse sorts," and oil and honey more than sufficient for home consumption? "Our neighbors have more need of us than we of them," for "all things grow in our country without much trouble." And export trade was favored by the pleasing fact that "our ports and anchorages are safe in every weather." Truly, theirs was a goodly heritage, and "since we have such abundance of our own, what more can we desire in reason, except peace?"

So spoke the elderly and middle-aged, but their enthusiasm was not echoed by their sons. The young, it seems, had hoped that war would start again, and they considered that their king had been too lenient with his enemy. If he had lost all the best castles in the realm, they said, he could hardly have made easier terms for the Castilians. It only lacked that he should offer reparations! He had shown himself weak, but what could you expect? That is what comes of growing old, concluded youth morosely.

The fact was that the truce preceding peace had lasted for ten years, and a generation had grown up who did not realize what war with one's neighbors could mean. They had not seen harvests laid waste by hostile raids, nor peasants wandering—homeless— in the night lit by the red glow of their burning villages. They had not known the horrors of cities besieged, nor watched the starving men and women of Lisbon scratching like chickens in the dust for a few grains of corn, nor Almada panting with thirst under the summer sun and driving its horses to die outside the walls because there was no water to be spared for the poor beasts, and their owners could not bear to witness their distress.

These tragedies of more than twenty years ago were only poignant still to those who had lived through them. The younger generation had been brought up on tales of the recent wars, but it was the great days and knightly deeds on which their fancy fed. They loved to hear of their fathers' exploits at Atoleiros, Trancoso, Aljubarrota and Valverde, of the lightning capture of Badajoz, of surprises and stratagems, and successful counterattacks. They wanted to be heroes, too, and hoped that when the truce was ended they would get the chance, but now that the Castilians had made peace—who was there left for them to fight?

As for the King's own sons—Duarte, Pedro, and Henrique theoretically agreed with their father that peace with Castile would be a good thing, but when this good thing came to pass it must be owned that they were disappointed. At the time that the treaty was signed, the three eldest Infantes were seventeen, eighteen, and twenty years old, and hoping to be knighted very soon. To attain knighthood automatically, merely because one was a prince and had reached the right age, did not appeal to them at all. One must do something to deserve the honor, they agreed; but what was there to do? That they might help their cousin of Castile to conquer Granada had been suggested as a good idea. The Regent of Castile, however, refused the kind offer with thanks. As he wanted to claim the crown of Aragon, he said, he did not wish for war with Granada just then. He might have added that Castile preferred to keep the conquest of Granada to herself!

Then D. João informed his sons that he had thought of a great scheme. A series of tournaments might be held for every day throughout a year. Invitations would be broadcast in every land that all nations could send up their champions to join the lists. These foreigners were to be entertained and banqueted upon a princely scale, in such a style as none of them had ever seen before, and dispatched to their several homes laden with costly gifts. In the midst of all this gay and gorgeous pageantry, with representatives from every part of Europe looking on, the young Infantes would receive their knighthood. It would be an expensive way of doing things—of this the King was well aware—but all the same he felt it would be grand!

The young Infantes fully understood that it would be expensive, but they did not think it would be grand at all. They listened in respectful silence to their father's plan, and then withdrew to talk it over with each other, and with their half-brother, the Count of Barcelos, who had just returned from foreign parts. Decidedly, all four agreed, it would not do! "Come," said they to one another, "let us speak to our lord and father, and tell him to arrange some enterprise by which it may be possible for us to achieve honor!"

At this point, João Afonso de Alenquer, the King's treasurer, strolled up to join their group. Might he know the subject of such earnest discussion? The young men hesitated, but João Afonso was noted for "the clearness of his understanding." He was a person worth consulting, so with a little persuasion he prevailed upon them to confide in him.

They did not like this tournament idea, they told him. To be knighted on the merits of a sham fight in such an ostentatious manner might be all very fine for merchants' sons, who take their pride in splashing money about, but it was not the sort of thing they wanted. Clearly, the young Infantes felt that their parents' scheme smacked of the *nouveau riche!* They would have to go abroad, they told João Afonso. Their brother of Barcelos had related most exciting tales of distant lands and foreign courts. Since they had no wars of their own, Duarte, Pedro, and Henrique said regretfully, then they must fight for other people.

João Afonso listened sympathetically. He quite agreed with them that tournaments were but a hollow joy, and that the memory of a banquet fades soon after you have eaten! But if they thought about leaving the country, he declared, "I see no reason why you should go to any other place than Ceuta!" He had sent a servant of his there recently to ransom prisoners, and truly it was a fine town—"the most flourishing in Mauritania, and very near to Spain. You might persuade the King to make ready a fleet, and take you with him to invest that city, and there you could receive knighthood with honor!"

The boys eyed him with admiration. Now this was talking! To conquer Moorish Ceuta—the haven of refuge for all Saracen pirates infesting the Straits! Not only would this be a great and useful feat of arms, but a crusading feat, a much more satisfactory one than helping the King of Castile to conquer Granada! "Why do you not tell the King all this," they asked, "and see what he says?"

"I did," the treasurer replied; "but he did not seem to take me seriously. If, however, all four of you would go to him, and tell him what you feel about it, it may be that he will pay more attention to you than he did to me."

They rushed to their father at once, bursting with the new plan. It would be great, it would be glorious, it would be holy to conquer Ceuta! they cried in unison, and each one argued separately "as well as he knew how." And at the end of all their eloquence, D. João laughed!

Depressed, but not defeated, the young enthusiasts withdrew. They talked the matter over with each other "and the more they thought about this thing, the better and more honorable it seemed." Henrique, more than either of his brothers, became obsessed by the idea. Eighteen is to most of us an age of dreams, and this boy's visions came to him from far away. His young imagination did not make an aim and end of conquering Ceuta, it conjured up a train of radiant possibilities to follow. To carry the crusading sword over to Africa would be to open a new chapter in the history of that holy war which Christendom had waged for six centuries upon Islam. Hitherto the Christian part had been but to defend and to recover. The capture of Ceuta might be the starting point of a great new offensive—an offensive that might strike across the world, might flash from Africa to the far East, and bring about the final victory of the Cross. The mystic of Majorca, Ramon Lull, had dreamed of this a hundred years before, and now a young man of a later generation caught the vision. It is not likely that Henrique, at eighteen, had already formed the purpose of his life, but the call of his future destiny first came to him with the idea of conquering Ceuta.

Though not stirred to such depths, Duarte and Pedro were full of ardor. The three boys thought of nothing but Ceuta all day long, and when they went to bed it was only to dream of ships laden with men-at-arms, of pennons fluttering from conquered towers, and to wake up quite exhausted in the morning after fighting Moors all night! All other topics bored them at this time, Zurara says, and most of what he records in his chronicle was told him by the Infantes themselves.

They all conspired to let their father have no peace until he came round to their point of view. D. João might well have wearied of Ceuta as a subject of conversation. Whenever his sons were with him, they talked of nothing else. The King no longer laughed. He frowned. He pretended to be bored with the whole thing; but the more reluctant he appeared, the more persistent they became.

They must have known their father well enough to suspect that much of his indifference was assumed. D. João was, in fact, far more interested than he seemed to be. He had been brought up as a knight of a crusading Order, and the ideal had never lost its charm. All the same fifty-four does not take fire so easily as twenty, and D. João made up his mind that he would not be rushed. "I will ask my confessor," he told his sons at last, "if this would really be a holy war." At the same time he demanded the advice of all the theologians in the land.

The divines replied with no uncertain sound, backed by a weighty evidence drawn from history and legend. "It is lawful for you to make war on the people of Africa," they said, "if done to the glory of God"—which obviously it would be. And the conquests of strongholds from the Infidels could not fail to be pleasing to the Lord. Had He not sent the Apostle St. James to fight for D. Ramiro at the battle of Clavigo? Had not an angel intervened against the Saracens at Navas de Tolosa? Had not Afonso Henriques received direct assistance from Heaven at Ourique and elsewhere? "From these miraculous deeds of other kings, you may learn how great service it is to God to fight barbarians." Of this the theologians had not the least doubt, nor that it was the whole and final truth. The King, they urged, must not give ear "to any other thing that might be said upon this matter—even should it appear to you in the semblance of a heavenly vision—believe it not, for you may understand it is the Evil One who comes to move you from your good and holy purpose!"

D. João, none the less, gave ear to the insinuations of the fiend. "A thing may be good and desirable," he told his sons, "but it does not follow necessarily that it can be achieved." To begin with, he pointed out, where was the money coming from? He had not got it. As for making a levy upon the people, "I don't see how I can serve God by oppressing the poor!" There were other considerations besides finance. "Ceuta is far away. The town is great and populous. In order to surround it, we shall need to reinforce our troops with foreigners; nor do I see where all the ships may be obtained to transport such an army. Supposing, however, that all this can be overcome, what about home defense? What is there to prevent the Castilians from invading our dominions while we are absent?" Finally—and here the theologians would certainly have heard the promptings of the Evil One—"supposing Castile does nothing, and we conquer Ceuta, what good will come of it? The advantage will be rather for Castile. It will make it so much easier for them to conquer Granada! Now what profit would it be to me for that kingdom to fall into Castilian hands? It would rather be my loss, for they have always hated me and my subjects, the more so at the present time when memory of their defeat is so recent. And the more the power of Castile grows, the smaller in comparison will Portugal appear. Now, if any one of you can answer these objections—let him do so!"

No one could, offhand, and a chilly silence fell while the enthusiasts saw their radiant hope about to flicker out. "Certainly," they conceded gloomily, "a prudent prince has to consider everything. But, perhaps if you give us time, we can meet all these arguments."

"Think it over by all means," said the King gravely, suppressing a smile. He liked to teach his sons to tackle problems.

They walked off much dejected. What uphill work it was to move the middle-aged! As they put their heads together, however, their spirits revived, for one by one solutions were devised.

The financial aspect, they told their father, need not discourage him. What about the money he had proposed laying out on feasts and tournaments "and useless things like that." Instead of all this, they suggested an economy campaign, and drastic reduction of court expenses. Then, in order to increase the nation's store of ready cash, they could arrange with foreign merchants to take goods in exchange for copper and silver in bars to be converted into currency. This would give all the necessary money. After all, they pointed out, the King was now far richer than he had been during the late wars, when he had none the less managed to carry on. And as the conquest of Ceuta was a holy war—the theologians said it was—therefore God would provide!

Ships could be chartered from abroad with little difficulty, and men would certainly embark in them to join the enterprise. There were plenty of soldiers at a loose end knocking about Europe, so recruits would not be lacking.

As for a possible Castilian invasion—how could that be? argued the Infantes in the simple faith of early youth, when a treaty had just been signed. After the solemn pledges that had been passed on either side, even an Infidel would be ashamed to break his word! Besides—and this consideration might hold some weight for D. João's more disillusioned fifty years—the Regent of Castile was far too preoccupied about the crown of Aragon to think of Portugal, added to which, "the Lady Queen, our Aunt, would not approve!" Finally, though the conquest of Ceuta might make that of Granada easier for Castile—surely a Christian prince should not object to that!—the profit to our Holy Faith would counterbalance any loss to Portugal.

But it was just this question of Granada that seems to have weighed heaviest on D. João. He had a private talk upon the subject with Henrique, upon whose judgment he already felt he could rely. "It seemed to me the other day," he said, "that you had more to say about it than your brothers. Now, tell me what you really think!"

Henrique answered with that becoming diffidence expected from a well-brought-up young man when speaking to his lord and father. "Excuse my youth and ignorance, Sir," he said, "but at the time when, by the grace of God you were made King, you only had a small part of this realm, and all the power of Castile was against you. Now that you rule the whole of Portugal, what difference will it make if Granada is added to Castile?" Henrique did not believe that the Castilians were irreconcilable foes to Portugal—not like the Moors. "The Infidels by nature are against us, but the King of Castile only by chance." And the conquest of Ceuta would add to Portuguese prestige. The Castilians would be impressed. "The greatness of this deed would show them the courage and strength of your subjects." And the friendship of the strong is always courted.

Then D. João threw hesitation to the winds. After all, it was not the first time that he had taken risks. His bid for the throne in his youth had been a great gamble against heavy odds—why should his sons not be allowed to take their plunge? Beaming with smiles, he threw his arms about Henrique's neck and blessed him. "That is enough, my boy!" he cried, "I want no further answer. I have decided, with the help and grace of God, to undertake this deed and to achieve it!"

Henrique, overwhelmed with joy, dropped on his knees and kissed his father's hands, thanking him fervently. He flew to break the glad news to his brothers, and all of them rushed back to D. João to hear the glorious fact confirmed from his own lips.

It was a great moment. The King himself "felt no small happiness within his heart." What fine lads were his sons! "At ease on horseback or afoot, agile to run and jump, or throw the bar, or lay a lance in rest, and well-trained to bear armor." Their father had looked forward to showing them off before the foreigners at his projected tournaments, but it would be even more interesting to see how they would bear themselves in battle.

From that day D. João set about studying Ceuta with all the circumspection of an old campaigner. Before any preparations could be made, he told his sons, it would be necessary to reconnoiter.

This could not be done openly of course. An embassy to Sicily formed the pretext. A marriage once had been discussed between the queen of that island and D. Duarte. The King now ordered his two finest galleys to be appareled with costly draperies bearing the royal arms, and attired all their crew in "very noble liveries with his motto and device." He appointed to command the expedition one of his most trusty counselors, Afonso Furtado de Mendonça, and sent Alvaro Gonçalves Camelo, Prior of St. John, with him as co-ambassador. These two would visit the Sicilian court in magnificent style, and suggest to D. Duarte's proposed fiancée that she might like to have Pedro instead.

It all went off without a hitch. The lady answered "very simply," we are told, that she had always meant to marry D. Duarte. If he was making other plans, she would remain unwed! The ambassadors bowed and withdrew, expressing their polite regret. They had not really expected another answer.

"Nobly canopied and beflagged," sounding "rich trumpets, the blast of which rejoiced all hearts," the galleys sailed back into Lisbon harbor to the admiration of the Sunday crowds that loitered in the streets, and those on board the foreign ships that filled the port. Men and women gathered on the roofs and towers to appreciate "the sweetness of the spectacle," while the foreign merchants marveled, and said to one another, "Truly this King of Portugal is great in all his deeds, and everything he does is in grand style!"

Happy to cause such a sensation, the envoys disembarked. They rode immediately to Sintra where, at their palace in the chestnut woods, the royal family was spending the summer.

The King received his two ambassadors in public audience, and showed himself conspicuously annoyed that the Queen of Sicily should turn his offer down. But he did not speak of the Queen of Sicily when he called the envoys to a private conference with him and his sons. "What do you think about Ceuta?" was the first question that he asked Afonso Furtado.

Afonso Furtado looked meditative and mysterious. "It has a good port," he said vaguely, "and a good anchorage. Whenever you embark upon this enterprise, by the grace of God, Ceuta will be yours."

"Please God that may be so!" echoed the King; "but I want more details."

Afonso Furtado did not appear disposed to give them. He gazed into space and told a tale of fifty years ago, and a prophecy that he had heard when, as a child, he visited Ceuta with his father. As he stood outside the crenelated walls, watching the Arab horses drinking from a fountain by the beach, an ancient Moor had wept and told him how a King of Portugal would one day rule African lands, and bring his steeds to water at that very fountain. "My spirit will have left this mortal body then," the old man had said, "but I mourn the sorrows that will fall upon my race!" Afonso Furtado had never forgotten these portentous words, "And so I am convinced, Senhor, that you will take Ceuta!"

D. João laughed rather impatiently, and turned to Alvaro Gonçalves. "Senhor, I can say nothing," said the Prior impressively, "without two sacks of sand, a ball of tape, half a bushel of beans, and a basin."

"Do you think that the Captain's prophecies are not enough?" replied the King, still laughing. "Leave off joking, and tell me what I ask." But Alvaro Gonçalves only repeated his request.

D. João began to find the pair exasperating. "Did you ever hear such nonsense!" he exclaimed. "I don't know what to make of these two men. One comes and tells me old wives' fables, and the other takes it into his head to practise magic! I am beginning to wonder why I sent them to Ceuta at all."

The Prior smiled. "Senhor," he said, "I am not given to joking with Your Highness, but even if I would, I could not answer you without those things."

The Infantes, bursting with curiosity, begged their father to let the Prior have his sand and beans. Alvaro Gonçalves then shut himself up quite alone for a long time. "Now you can see my magic!" said he, opening the door at last, and there before the fascinated eyes of D. João and the Infantes lay a relief map of Ceuta bay, modeled in sand. The hills behind the towns were piled up skilfully, the beans were used to represent the houses at their base, the tape ran round like the encircling walls, and the hills of Algeciras and Gibraltar were shown opposite. "Now," said the Prior, pointing proudly to his work of art, "you can ask me

(38)

anything you like, and I can demonstrate my answers!" and so he made a full report. The ambassadors had anchored in Ceuta harbor, both coming and going. They had examined every rock upon the beach, and sounded all the depths by night from a small boat, without arousing the suspicions of the Moors.

The Prior's sand castles settled it. The King decided that Ceuta could and must be conquered.

A last objection still occurred to him—a question that has frequently been voiced by many another family man: "What will your mother say to this?" D. João asked his sons. "The Constable must also be consulted," he added, "for if he disapproves, you know quite well that everyone will be against the enterprise."

The young men groaned in spirit. It had been bad enough to bring their father to the point—was all to be begun again, first with the Queen, and then Nunalvares? They feared some opposition from these two. Their mother was expected to object for obvious reasons; as for the Constable, strange though it may seem, Nunalvares Pereira, the hero of his generation, the terror of whose name alone had made Castilian armies fade away, was no militarist! "A just war to obtain peace," had been his definition of the fight to which he had devoted all his younger years, and when that peace had been ensured, he gladly sheathed his sword. Would he agree to this new enterprise? Of course, this was a holy war, and if the Queen gave her consent, the Infantes assured their father, then "the Constable will not oppose it."

They tried their blandishments upon their mother first. The crafty youngsters did not tell her that their father had already approved of their plan. They begged her prettily to use her influence with the King that they might be allowed to embark on this holy enterprise, and so win their knighthood with honor.

Philippa took it very well. Whatever her feelings may have been, she did not show them. The granddaughter of Edward III, and niece of the Black Prince, understood that her boys must be allowed to win their spurs.

"It is quite true," she said when they had finished, "that I love you as much as any other mother loves her sons, but for such deeds as these I will not oppose your wishes, but rather help you all I can. I shall take this matter up at once in such a way that, by the grace of God, your desire may be fulfilled." And she sent word to D. João to ask if he were disengaged and could receive her, to which her husband answered gallantly that he must wait on her, not she on him!

"My Lord," said Philippa, "I want to ask you something that a mother does not often request for her sons. We usually beg their fathers to keep them from dangerous undertakings for fear that they may come to harm, but I am begging you to turn them aside from games and amusements to face peril and labor. Our sons have told me all about Ceuta, and asked me to intercede for them with you. Since God in His mercy has made them fit in mind and body to perform such deeds, I would not for the world that they should fail to do them?"

"Lady," replied the King, "this is really quite embarrassing. It is I who should have been the first to make such a request of you!" But he also had a favor to ask, "of a like nature." Since it was settled that their sons should go, would she allow her husband to go too?

Philippa was dismayed. "It will be difficult for me to consent with my heart to such a thing!" she said. She had assumed that D. João would stay with her. There was no need for him to go! He had seen all the fighting that anyone could wish for in his youth. His honor as a valiant knight had been firmly established long ago. Why should he seek for more?

"Your reasons, Lady," said the King, "would be worth consideration if I were only moved by the desire for honor, but that is not the case with me. I only recollect that I have stained my hands with Christian blood. To fight the Infidel would wash them clean. And think what service it would be to God to cause His holy name to be adored in a town where now they serve and worship that of Mohammed, whose soul is buried in the lowest depths of Hell, as it deserves to be!"

"If it be a question of serving the Lord God," sighed his wife, "I have no more to say."

The meeting with the Constable required stage-managing. Nunalvares was not often at court. To send for him would have been very easy, but then people would have suspected that something unusual was brewing. In spite of the absence of newspapers, the movements of public characters were noted and discussed as much then as today, and their comings and goings were never inconspicuous, owing to the households that followed in their wake. There was, however, one pretext that might take a man anywhere—one occupation that was so natural and universal that it excited no more comment than a modern politician's round of golf—that was the chase. D. João sent his two sons, Duarte and Henrique, to organize a mighty hunt in Alentejo, near the Constable's estates.

"Your brothers," observed the King to Pedro, when they had been away a few weeks, "imagine that what they do not know of hunting is not worth knowing! You young men always think that you know more than we do. Let us go to those preserves where I have often found many great boars and, see which of us are the better woodsmen!" Followed by his delighted court, D. João traveled south, towards Montemor-O-Novo, near Evora.

"Since my Lord the King is but three leagues away," remarked Nunalvares, who had received a secret message, "it would not be seemly for me not to go and salute him." And he also set out.

The King and the Constable walked side by side in the cork

woods, while D. João told the companion of his youth what he proposed to do. He felt compelled to fight the Infidels in Africa, he said, and so cleanse his soul from the guilt of Christian blood.

Nunalvares listened in silence. He, more than anyone, would understand what was in the King's mind. Was it really the blood of his country's enemies shed in fair fight upon the battlefield that weighed on the conscience of D. João? Rather it must have been the memory of a December evening thirty years ago, when a stiffening corpse lay stretched upon the palace floor—pierced by his dagger.[1] The dead man was a scoundrel undoubtedly, and his assassin the avenger of a brother's honor; but, all the same, if D. João felt oppressed by blood-guiltiness, it is more likely that this murder haunted him than the death of his foemen at Aljubarrota.

D. João told the Constable that he would win Ceuta for the Christian faith. Nunalvares remained a moment deep in thought. "Do you know what it seems to me?" he said at last. "This idea did not come from you or anybody else. It was revealed by God!"

The oracle had spoken! Since the Constable had given the project his blessing, the three Infantes felt that all was well. Approval by the royal council was a foregone conclusion, for Nunalvares promised to see that none of his colleagues should raise objections. "Only let me speak first," he enjoined the King, with the confidence of one whose lead has always been followed.

At Torres Vedras, shortly after, D. João laid his plan before the white-haired councilors, all sworn to secrecy upon the Gospel.

The Constable rose to his feet. "As I have served you in all things," he said, "so will I serve you in this one, with the greater good will that it is better and more profitable!" He knelt and kissed the sovereign's hand. "I do you this homage," he declared, "to thank you for this opportunity of serving you in that office of knighthood to which God in His mercy has called me."

[1] João Fernandes Andeiro, lover of the Queen Leonor Teles, had been assassinated by the young Master of Aviz shortly after King Fernando's death.

Duarte was not slow in taking up the cue. He stepped forward at once. "Since the Constable who has shared in so many glorious enterprises, and has gained so much honor, thinks your purpose is good—what can I say, who never yet have been in any dangerous undertaking? I can only rejoice in having the chance to earn distinction, and I thank God and you for having pleased to ordain an enterprise in which I can serve Him and you, and so increase my honor!" He kissed his father's hand on bended knee, and his brothers followed enthusiastically.

After that—what could anybody do? The King might safely press his counselors for their candid opinion of his plan, nobody felt that he could decently object. As the liveliest veteran of them all cried out when asked to speak: "I don't see, Senhor, what else I can say, except—Forward, Grayheads!" And the council broke up amid a roar of laughter.

Youth had won.

IV

The Mystery Expedition

B EFORE proceeding further with this matter," Henrique
entreated his father, "I beg you to grant me two things!
When God pleases that we arrive at Ceuta, let me be
among the first to disembark, and when your scaling ladder is
put to the wall, may I be the first person to climb up?"

D. João laughed at the earnest young face. "Bless you, my boy!"
said he, "I can't promise that yet. At a more fitting moment than
the present, I shall give you an answer."

The present moment was hectic. All Portugal was humming
like a vast workshop, and every class was busy. The Secretaries of
State were taking a census of all able-bodied men, and sending
far and wide the royal summons to arms; in every port all ships
had been inventoried and retained, while the King sent to England, Bretagne, Biscay, and Flanders for still more. Trees by the
hundreds were laid low, all carpenters in Portugal were requisi-
tioned, and soon the dockyards of Lisbon and Porto were "beautiful to see," Zurara says, crowded with ships of every size, under
repair.

The beauty of the picture must have been somewhat marred
by the carcasses of cattle strewn beside the shore, where teams of
men working at all hours were flaying, carving, salting meat, and
packing it in barrels.

Fishermen and their wives were hard at work. Thanks to their

(44)

efforts all the sun-swept spaces up the coast reeked to the heavens of drying fish. Every cook in the country was baking biscuits and preserving food; the coopers all were busy making casks and barrels; every artificer was devising artillery; and in the Mint no man could hear another speak for the sound of hammers beating ceaselessly beside the furnaces that roared both day and night.

All knights and squires were polishing their armor well; and every tailor, it appears, was cutting out new clothes. Each man was anxious to arrive before his King in style, though no one knew why he should have been summoned. To have no idea what the bustle was about made things still more exciting. D. João had only given out that the Infantes Pedro and Henrique would command the fleet. He gave no inkling of its destination, and every day a new story went round. One knowing person had it on good authority that the Infantes were sailing for England. A marriage had been arranged there for their sister Isabel, and all these ships were her escort. The objection that armaments do not figure in a bridal train was easily disposed of. As soon as the happy event had taken place, the Infantes, with their cousin the English king, would cross the Channel to fight France!

Not England, others had reason to believe, but Naples was the destination—and the marriage was not for the King's daughter, but his sons. A queen for each might be picked up among the little kingdoms over there, and such an expedition would make a good show.

The marriage theory might find favor with romantic souls, but others turned it down. Some foresaw an attack on Bruges; others who knew some history suggested that the King was out to conquer Normandy because his great-great-grandfather had been Count of Boulogne! And finally there were pious people who said that the Infantes were bound for Jerusalem to collect holy relics. The only man who happened on the truth was a certain Judah

(45)

Negro, of the Queen's household. This Hebrew sent a poem to D. Pedro's squire, declaring that the fleet was sailing for Ceuta. Nobody paid attention at the time, and later it was said that he had guessed the secret by astrology, "which he frequently practised."

If speculation was enjoyable at home, abroad D. João's preparations were viewed with alarm. The King of Portugal was arming —against whom?

Castile was the first to take fright. The Portuguese were designing a *coup* on Seville, cried the panic-mongers, and "let us fortify before it is too late!" A wise man of the royal council calmed them with soothing words of common sense. "It is reasonable to assume that our peace treaty will be respected," he said. "God forbid that good faith should ever be abandoned among rulers, for if that came to pass great evil would arise!" To silence apprehension, an embassy was sent to D. João, suggesting that he should ratify his oath.

Their fears were wholly set at rest. The King of Portugal received the Castilian envoy with open arms. He housed them sumptuously, and feasted them upon fresh fish—a delicacy not often enjoyed in Castile, it appears—he gave them all the guarantees for which they asked, and expressed his eternal friendship for their king.

Castile was reassured, but Aragon then grew uneasy. By this time D. Fernando, former regent of Castile, was in peaceful but unpopular possession of the Aragonese throne. Did the King of Portugal propose to back the claims of the rival pretender, the Count of Urgel? So D. João had yet another embassy to soothe. He was the King of Aragon's good friend, he hastened to affirm, and if he could have told his secret to a soul, then D. Fernando would have been the chosen confidant!

He showed himself polite but colder with the envoys from

Granada, who came next. The Moorish king was really in a fright. "I cannot see," said D. João, "the cause for agitation." These armaments were not designed against Granada, he gave them to understand, but he refused to sign a non-aggression pact. The Moors were more alarmed than ever; and, tactless if well meaning, tried to gain their end by offering bribes to the King's family. They promised Philippa a dazzling trousseau for her daughter, and D. Duarte anything he liked to ask, if they would use their influence with D. João. "My daughter will not lack a trousseau for her wedding," said the Queen haughtily; "and you should approach the King my lord direct for anything you want!"

"In this country princes do not sell their favors," Duarte told them with equal hauteur. "They would deserve to be called merchants rather than lords or princes if they did such a thing. The King of Granada, your master, has no just reason to be nervous."

But the Moors thought that he had. They returned to Granada quite convinced that their kingdom was the objective that the King of Portugal had in view. They started feverishly to fortify the coast.

D. João did not like this. True, he had no designs on Granada, but Ceuta was too near not to be infected by the panic. Some excuse for his military preparations must be found, or by a process of elimination the truth would be discovered. He decided to spread the news that he was planning to make war on Holland —none of his neighbors would mind in the least what happened over there. He went so far as to dispatch an embassy to carry his defiance to Count William. The object of this mission was ostensibly a secret, but those about to embark for the North were careful to divulge it confidentially to people who were sure to pass it on—in strictest confidence, of course!—to all their other friends.

The envoys really sailed for Holland, and there they had a private conference with the Count. The King of Portugal sent him his hearty greetings. He did not mean to fight Holland at all, he said; but would Count William be so kind as to play up to him and pretend that he believed there would be war?

The Dutch prince was amused at the comedy, and promised to oblige. In public audience the ambassadors complained of piracy against the ships of Portugal on the high seas. They declared war on Holland in their King's name, and the Count took up the challenge with apparent wrath, saying that he was ready! The performance went off without a hitch, and shortly after the envoys set sail, enriched by presents from the Count, and bearing his affectionate—but private—greetings to their King. The Dutch were startled by this sudden challenge from so far away, but not wholly surprised. There really had been acts of piracy, Zurara says, but from this date on they were discontinued. By which we may conclude that D. João was not so simple as he looked!

Having turned foreign curiosity on to a false scent, and set his neighbors' minds at rest, D. João pushed on preparations still more vigorously. He saw to it that his sons did their share. After all, this was their expedition, and they must put the shoulder to the wheel. Each youth was allotted his special task, and none of these were sinecures.

Henrique was detailed to gather troops in the province of Beira and the North. He was to concentrate them all at Porto, and supervise their embarkation in the fleet that he himself had to equip and organize.

Pedro would do the same in Alentejo, and bring his forces to Lisbon where another squadron had to be prepared. The two fleets were to sail together when Henrique came down from the North.

As befitted the eldest son, Duarte's was the hardest task of all. It also was the dullest for, in order to be free to superintend and organize the expedition, the King turned over to his heir the whole administration of finance and justice. This was fine training for a future ruler, but a heavy burden for an inexperienced youth, the more so that the conscientious Duarte went to it with a zeal and thoroughness that brought him to the verge of a nervous breakdown. He gave up outdoor exercise and relaxation of all kind, working for over sixteen hours a day, and then he was surprised to find a black depression settling on his soul. Such melancholy must accompany increasing age, concluded this young man of twenty-two. "I supposed that everybody felt like that," he wrote, and so he said nothing to anyone, but simply carried on.

D. João's sons were not spoon-fed. "I leave it entirely to your discretion," said his father to Henrique, when the boy asked for written instructions of what he had to do. "You will only take a letter from me, like the one that I am giving Pedro, to order all men to obey you as their commander. Go off to Porto at once, and get your fleet under way as quickly as possible. Only be prudent," he added, remembering that an epidemic brought by the foreign ships was raging already in every port, "don't enter the town more often than is strictly necessary."

Henrique started gladly for his native city, sure of a hearty welcome there. The Portuenses took possessive pride in their Infante, and all were very fond of him. They backed him up on this occasion enthusiastically. Of all the towns in Portugal, none responded to the royal summons with a better will. The whole district was soon agog with preparations—all roads congested with ox-wagons and trains of pack-mules laden with provisions for the fleet, all sailors and dock hands working beside the river day and night, and all the citizens living on tripe that every ounce of meat from all the cattle slaughtered could be salted for the ships. "You really are *tripeiros!*" jeered some disagreeable person—from Lisbon perhaps. "We like to be *tripeiros!*" said the Portuenses stiffly,.

and *tripeiros* they have called themselves up to the present day.

The pestilence was raging in the city all the while, but nobody had much leisure to think about it. Even the victims of the plague, they say, met death regretting nothing quite so much as the fact that they would never see D. João's enterprise achieved. What it might be, of course, nobody knew, but they had proofs that it enjoyed celestial favor. A monk of São Domingos, praying before the altar at cockcrow, had seen a vision of his King kneeling before the Virgin Mary. D. João's hands were lifted up to Heaven, whence a glorious being was holding out a shining sword. The good monk told the vision to his friend the sacristan, who spread the tale throughout the city, and all wondered at the sign.

In such a fervent atmosphere, Henrique had no difficulty in raising his troops. From Minho, Tras-os-Montes, and the far-off frontier mountains men for the fighting forces kept on pouring in. The trouble was not who should go, but who would stay behind!

Among the first arrivals the Infante was amazed to see the knight, Ayres Gonçalves de Figueiredo—a picturesque figure, ninety years old. Erect and gallant in his coat of mail, he rode before his squires and men-at-arms, and dismounted to kiss the hand of his young prince.

Henrique smiled. "It seems to me," he said, "that a man of your age should rest from all his labors!"

"I know not if age may have weakened my limbs," responded the old warrior proudly, "but my good will is no less today than when I served your father in the past. I desire no better honor for my funeral rites than to take part in this enterprise before my days are ended."

A like spirit was shown by two old squires of Bayonne who had fought for the King in the late wars. The pair had been retired on a pension, but when Henrique came to Porto, both presented themselves.

"I think you have done quite enough," he said. "I am grateful for your good will, but it seems to me that such labors are not for your age." The valiant Gascons were indignant at the suggestion. On no account would they consent to stay—the Infante would have to take them with him!

"How can that be?" he asked. "The weapons that I had, have all been given out, and I have no arms left for you."

That did not matter in the least, said the old fighting cocks. "No man is any good who sells his arms whatever be his need. We have sometimes been hard up when our pension was in arrears, but we have never parted from our arms! Only pay us our maintenance according to your regulations, and never worry about weapons for us!" Needless to say Henrique took them on, and gave them a generous reward.

The brave men of Bayonne were not the only foreign volunteers to swell the native forces. There was the wealthy London citizen, named Mundy—a resident in Porto, it appears. He offered four ships to Henrique's fleet, which he accompanied himself together with a number of archers and men-at-arms, maintained at his expense. A French knight, Antoine de La Salle, of literary fame, with two Picards, Messire Henry d'Antoing, and Pierret Bataille, and the Norman Gui Le Boutiller, came with their retainers to join the expedition; so did a German baron. A German grand duke would have gone too if D. João had told him where it was to be, but that the King would not disclose, and so the duke backed out.

Besides accepting these spontaneous offers, it appears that the King sent to England for recruits. There are two letters signed by Henry V, authorizing João Vaz de Almada to raise several hundreds of lances in his land. Whether they reached Portugal is not

(51)

so certain, for war broke out about this time between England and France. The fleet that the Earl of Arundel had promised to send his father-in-law could not sail for this cause.

D. João hardly needed it. Henrique's fleet was beautiful to look at as it lay between the steep banks of the Douro in the May sunshine. Seventy ships equipped and manned, all new and shining with gilt and fresh paint, with flags and pennons waving to the breeze, bearing Henrique's motto: *Talent de bien faire. Talent* meant desiring, and as the Infante surveyed the result of three months' endeavor, he could feel truly that he had *bien fait*.

The Portuenses were delighted too. Their Infante did them credit! Who would have thought that one so young and inexperienced could have organized all things in such short time. "He received great praise for this marvelous deed," and he had well deserved it. Of course, the citizens of Porto observed to each other, gazing complacently upon the splendid ships, this could not have been done elsewhere. As they informed the Cortes later on: "We do not know of any other town that could have turned out such a fleet as that!"

The day of sailing was the happier because everybody was wearing new clothes, "which always brings increase of gladness to the heart," explains Zurara feelingly, "especially to the young." Henrique, being young enough to appreciate this pleasure, had caused new liveries to be made for all his followers and—finding it interesting to depart from the established rule—he dressed the men of low estate in silk, and gave suits of fine woolen cloth to those of higher rank!

To the cheerful sound of trumpets, each ship crossed the Douro's narrow bar and sailed down the Atlantic coast towards the Tagus, out of which the Infante D. Pedro swept all the galleys and small craft of the royal fleet to meet his brother. The reception was spectacular, for "if the fleet from Porto was well canopied and beflagged, that of Lisbon was not less so, all with the bearings and motto of the King."

Henrique's ships sailed up in beautiful formation. The smaller units came first, then the big ships, and finally the galleys with his own vessel bringing up the rear. At the mouth of the river they assembled and spread out to the delight of all beholders from the shore. This maneuver made the fleet look very impressive and still more numerous than it really was.

Curvetting and circling round like prancing steeds, with all their bugles sounding, the ships were brought to anchor at Belem, and the Infantes disembarked. Their other brothers and most of the court turned out to meet them and admire Henrique's lovely fleet, and none stinted their praise. But better far than all their compliments were his father's congratulations when the Infante came to Odivelas, where both parents were.

"My son," D. João said, "you have fulfilled the charge I gave you in a manner far beyond what might have been expected of a man of your age. They tell me that your fleet is very well equipped, as by one who desires to serve me and increase his honor. You can even say that you have been more diligent than we, for you were ready first!" It was the proudest moment he had known in his young life.

The only cloud upon the bright horizon was hearing that his mother was unwell. But it was nothing serious, they assured him.

V

Three Swords

THE alluvial flats of Sacavem steamed in the summer sun, beside the glassy river-bed and green hills turning brown. The plain of Ribatejo lost itself in translucent mist, and westward the plague-stricken city of Lisbon shimmered under a haze.

In the cool dimness of Sacavem church Queen Philippa was praying. She knelt there every day from early morning till midday, and she returned there in the afternoon and prayed till late at night. The summer days were slipping by, the fleet would soon set sail, bearing her husband and three eldest sons to fight the Moors. "I would not have you fail to do such deeds!" the Queen had told them once. She meant it then, she meant it still; she would not keep them if she could, but all the same the burden of it was breaking her heart.

Philippa had not been strong for many years—probably not since 1402, when she had nearly died in giving birth to her last child. D. João knew that she must not be worried or distressed, and so he had not talked to her again about his own departure. She rather fancied that he had given up the idea. It was not known officially that the King proposed to accompany the expedition, nor was it given out that Duarte would go. Pedro and Henrique were held before the public as the commanders of the fleet, and the general supposition was that neither D. João nor his heir would leave the country. It seems that Philippa had been buoyed by the hope that it was deemed advisable for both to stay behind. During those busy months she can have seen but little of her husband and her sons, and there would be no opportunity for private conversation. It came, therefore, as something of a bombshell when D. João—while they sat talking in her room one day—announced that he had quite decided to sail with the fleet. Their sons, he said, would need his guidance and advice. And poor Duarte could not be left behind. It would not be fair on the boy! "He is of age, and so anxious to try his strength. Therefore, God willing, I intend to go, and take him with his brothers."

Philippa had feared as much, but now the blow had fallen. At the stricken look that came into her face, the two ladies-in-waiting who were present burst into sympathetic tears. The Queen, however, soon recovered her serenity.

"It is true, my Lord," she said, "that I myself asked you to send your sons about this deed, though I told you then that it seemed reasonable for you to stay. I quite see that Duarte has to go, and however much I mind, I would not show it; but I cannot hide what I feel about your going! But, since you think it right to go, may God please that it redound to His service, to your honor, and that of your sons, and the good of your realm—— You need not cry, my dears," she added, turning to the two ladies who still sniffed and sobbed in unison, "it does not help at all! Let us rather play our part, which is to recommend this thing to God. Let us pray unwearyingly and do good works, that God may hear our prayers. That is better than shedding tears."

She begged her husband one thing only: "Will you knight your sons before you embark, with the swords that I shall give each one of them together with my blessing?" D. João promised gladly, and Philippa found some comfort in ordering from Lisbon the three most beautiful swords that could be made there.

Then she gave herself up entirely to prayer and fasting. For a long time she had been forbidden to fast, but, at a moment like this she felt that such a prohibition could not hold. She was far too absorbed in her devotions to take much notice when the pestilence from Lisbon spread to Sacavem. "Such an old woman as I am should not fear the plague!" she said, when D. João urged her to remove to Odivelas without delay. "You go, my Lord, and I shall follow after this morning's services." D. João went, leaving his wife in church where, that same morning, she was taken ill.

Her husband was alarmed, fearing the plague, but she arrived at Odivelas later in the day, looking much better than he had expected, and three days after, when Henrique joined them, her joy was such that she seemed almost well.

Duarte arrived with him—poor Duarte, released at last from his arduous and arid labors, and no longer obliged to pretend that he expected to remain behind! None of the fun and bustle of the preparations had been shared by him—he could not even get his own things ready, or the secret would have been out. No wonder that Duarte came to Odivelas as joyful as a creature let free from a cage.

It was a cheerful family party that gathered there during the next few days. Their mother did not seem very ill, and she was so glad to see her two boys happy, and so proud of Henrique's recent success, that she could neither think of, nor show, her suffering.

They all concluded that she was weak and run down by abstinence, and would be better soon. When Henrique returned to Pedro, who had stayed with the fleet, neither expected to receive an urgent message from Duarte the next day saying that their mother was very ill.

This time there was no doubt. It was the pestilence, whatever that infection may have been—medical science of that day was vague in diagnosis. The two little brothers were sent away from danger of contagion, while the others, with their sister and their horror-stricken father gathered round. Poor D. João was frantic. He neither ate nor slept, and it was his children who looked after everything. Duarte seems to have been almost like a daughter. It was he who took command in the sickroom. He saw to all the medicines, we are told, and it was to him that the doctors reported.

Philippa was very quiet and resigned. She did not expect to recover. "God knows," she told her sons, "how I have longed to see you knighted by your father! I had prepared three swords for the occasion, but God has not seen fit to grant me such joy in this world. Were the swords ready yet?" she asked anxiously, and hearing that they were not, she sent orders to Lisbon that they should be finished and brought at once.

Meanwhile, she broke a wooden cross into four parts, and handed one to each son, keeping the fourth for her husband. "I had wanted to give you the swords today," said Philippa, "but since they are not here, I give you now the buckler of defense that is the wood of the True Cross. I entreat you, my sons, to wear it always, for you never know the day and hour of peril." Each young man took his fragment reverently, both as a holy relic and a dying mother's gift, and each one wore it on his bosom till he died.

The swords came the next day, shining and beautiful, and Philippa sent for her three young knights. She gave the longest sword to Duarte.

"My son," she said, "since God has chosen you among your brothers to be heir of this realm, I give you this sword. May it be a sword of justice to rule over great and small! When God please that by your father's death you govern this kingdom, I commend its people to your care. I beg you to defend them with all your power, and maintain them in right and justice. And, son, when I say justice, I mean justice with mercy, for justice without mercy is called cruelty. I beg you to be knighted with this sword. I had them made that the King my Lord should knight you and your brothers in my presence, but God has willed otherwise. Take this one with my blessing, and with that of your ancestors from whom I descend. I know that knights do not care to receive arms from women's hands, but my desire for your honor is such that I do not think that mine can do you harm."

Duarte knelt and kissed his mother's hand, and promised to remember her words all his life.

She called Pedro. "Since you were a small boy I have always seen you honor and defend the ladies, which is the special duty of a knight. I have commended the people to your brother, and I commit the ladies of the land to you that you make them your charge." So saying, she gave him his sword.

It was getting almost more than they could bear, though by a struggle all three remained calm. Philippa looked at their drawn faces and her heart smote her for her children. To relieve the tension she smiled very brightly.

"Come here, my son!" she said cheerfully to Henrique. "You saw the swords that I gave to your brothers? This third one I have kept for you—I believe it is as strong as you are! I have commended the people to one of your brothers, and the ladies and damsels to the other, so I shall commit to your special charge all the nobles, knights, gentlemen, and squires of this realm. I know that the King has care of them, according to each one's estate, but they will need your help that they may be maintained in right, and receive reasonable reward. You have always been fond of them, so I chose this for you. I give you this sword with my blessing, to be knighted with it."

Henrique took it, on his knees. That sword, he said, would be his greatest treasure. His mother smiled again, and raised her hand in benediction over his head.

"Look after all your brothers," she enjoined her eldest son. "Treat them as such good brothers deserve, and do not put others before them. Remember always that they are my sons, and those of your father, who both love you so much." She also commended their future king to Pedro and Henrique. "Since you have to be subjects," their mother pointed out, "you should be very glad to be those of your elder brother, who is so good and who loves you. You ought to be more satisfied with any small thing that he can give you, than with great riches from the hand of any other prince. I hope that you will always serve and love him with good will."

Philippa's lucidity never failed her as the illness ran its course and she had more things to say to her children before leaving them. She begged them to remain the united band of brothers that they had always been. "I have never seen you quarrel," she said, "and if you love each other in the future as you have done in the past, all will go well with you. Take the example of an arrow," added this daughter of the land of archery. "In our country there is a story illustrating how, though one by one they may easily be broken, to snap many together needs great strength."

They promised, and a silence fell. Only the strong sea wind, moaning beneath a summer sky, swept clouds of dust across the plain, and whistling in the keyhole, shook the doors. "What wind is that?" asked Philippa, and they told her that it was from the north.

"That is a good wind for your voyage," she said. And, "Is it not strange," she went on wistfully, "that I, who so looked forward to seeing you knighted, and sail should be the one to hold you up. And now I know that I shall never see it!"

"You will, please God!" cried Duarte, trying to put conviction in his voice. "Other people have been worse than you are, and God restored their health."

"I think," said his mother gently, "that God has deprived me of so great a pleasure in this world that I might have it in the next, where it will be more profitable to my eternal welfare. I shall see you from above, and my illness shall not prevent your departure. You will sail by the feast of St. James." Her sons looked at each other wonderingly. That meant in a week's time!

Philippa's peace only deepened as death drew near, but her husband was in such a state that their children resolved that he must not be present at the end. It would be too painful for both. "How can I abandon a wife who has been my companion for so long?" sobbed D. João. "I will not leave her! I would that God in His mercy were pleased to take me with her to the other world!" When, however, Duarte pointed out that he was only making it harder for Philippa, and all his councilors pressed him to go, he bade his wife a heartrending farewell, and rode away.

So Philippa was left with her four eldest children, and in their presence she died painlessly next day, with a smile on her face.

Her death spread blank dismay throughout the land. Queen Philippa had been adored by high and low and rich and poor. This was the end of everything, the people said. The expedition simply could not sail! The Lord had shown Himself against it by repeated signs. On June 7th there had been a terrifying eclipse of the sun. The pestilence had ravaged all the summer and—last and worst of all—the Queen was dead. Surely it would be tempting Providence to proceed!

The Infantes buried their mother at Odivelas that same night, and dressed in coarse white cloth of mourning, rode to the King at Alhos Vedros, just across the river.

"What are we to do now?" they asked.

D. João was bowed down with grief. "My sons," he answered

brokenly, "I can think of nothing but my loss! I leave it all to you. Speak to the councilors, and let me know what you decide."

The councilors were as much shaken as everybody else. Seven of them said that the expedition ought to be called off before a worse thing happened. The plague was raging still. On board ship the danger of infection would be greater—and they no longer had the Queen to pray for them!

The remaining four, and with them the Infantes, declared that having gone so far they must proceed. The Queen's death was a personal grief, but could not affect the military aspect of the expedition one way or another. And think how foolish they would look before the eyes of all the world if, after such elaborate preparations, they did nothing at all!

Opinions being equally divided, the matter had to be decided by the King. The Infantes went to report to their father, with three members of the opposition who wanted to make certain that their views would be expressed.

D. João by this time had pulled himself together, and gave his full attention while the fair-minded Duarte began by setting forth everything that had been said against the execution of his cherished plan. "Is there anything else that you would like to say?" he asked with heroic restraint before launching upon his side of the controversy, and they admiringly replied that he had put their case far better and more clearly than they could have done themselves!

D. João, however, was in that frame of mind when anything seems better than to stay at home under the burden of one's sorrow. He did not need to hear Duarte's glowing defense of the expedition, nor did he require to be gingered up by the exhortations of the Englishman, Mundy, who having heard a rumor that the fleet was not to sail, arrived to protest in a fluster of indignation. D. João said that he would embark immediately. His wife in

Heaven could pray for them far better than was possible on earth —"that is perhaps the reason why the Lord God has been pleased to take her from us!"

"But you are not prepared to go yet," the opposition argued. The Queen's illness had upset everything, they said. The fleet could not be ready for at least a month.

"And your fleet?" asked the King of Henrique, "is it so unready as to require all that time to be set in order?"

"The unpreparedness of my fleet is such," Henrique said complacently, "that you can join it and get underway whenever you choose! The greatest delay will be the weighing of the anchors and the trimming of the sails!"

"In that case," declared the King, "I shall not linger after Wednesday. Let those follow me who can! Go to your fleet, my sons, and hasten preparations. And because feats of arms are not compatible with tears and sadness, discard your mourning, and dress in your best clothes, and make everyone do likewise. We can keep our mourning for a more appropriate time."

His command was obeyed. The white of mourning was exchanged for colored dress. The ships were decked with flags, and to restore the morale of the troops every trumpet on board was sounded merrily.

The people hastened to the shore to gaze and wonder, and many shook their heads in disapproval. The King was flying in the face of Providence in spite of every warning, and a pretty father he was, so to risk his sons! His sinful pride in them was such that it had turned his head, some wiseacres commented. Others opined that the fidalgos were to blame; the majority, however, finally agreed that it was really the Infante D. Henrique's fault. He had insisted that his fleet was ready, and his father spoiled him.

Such were the murmurings of the mob, but when on July 24th

the great fleet sailed majestically across the bar out to the open sea, the people wept for joy to see so fair a sight. What love the Lord had shown to Portugal, they cried, to give them such a king!

Dipping their sails in reverence to the relics of St. Vincent, the ships sailed round the windswept cape and into Lagos bay. There the secret of the expedition was at last revealed in a learned sermon preached by Brother João Xira to the court and listening crowd. The speaker published a Crusading Bull, and fulminated the idea that mourning for the Queen should thwart this holy purpose. Had not the Romans discarded their mourning shortly after the battle of Cannae in which the flower of their manhood had died? If the Romans did this "when they knew that those souls had gone straight to Hell, how can we weep the death of her who is now with the blessed saints?"

This argument was quite unanswerable. The Romans all were roasting down below without a doubt, but certainly they had been knowing fellows! In view of their example nothing more was said of the indecency of pushing on the expedition, but D. João need not have troubled to announce its destination. So many false rumors had circulated that the truth was met with the blank stare of unbelief. "Tell us another!" the people murmured, on hearing that their King was sailing to Ceuta. "Last year he was going to Holland. Tell him to think of a better story this time!"

Commending himself devoutly to the Virgin, for he was a lamentably bad sailor, D. João led his fleet across the summer seas.

VI

Knighthood with Honor

THE rugged outline of Cape Spartel loomed dark against the
evening sky. The ships hung back and hovered like a flock
of birds over the waves from which the last sunbeams had
died. When night fell, they spread their wings again, and glided
through the darkness towards the Straits of Gibraltar.

It was a fortnight since the fleet had sailed from Lisbon, and
it had lain becalmed off Faro for a week. What a long and tedious
voyage, already men said to each other—men whose grandsons
would sail patiently half round the world, and lose all sight of
land for months on far more desolate seas!

The time had not yet come when every fidalgo of Portugal was
born a sailor. The cramped spaces of small overcrowded ships
were new to most of them. The heat below was terrible, the unaccustomed diet of salted food gave everyone a raging thirst, and
worse than that, there were cases of pestilence on board.

Duarte found his galley to be permeated by a nasty smell—
"due to its goodness," one writer says surprisingly—another version which appears more probable is that the sanitary arrangements were to blame.

Whatever may have been the cause, when Duarte could endure
it no longer he fled to spend the night on board Henrique's ship,
and there the two young men might have been burnt to death.

Duarte, as he lay dozing on deck, solacing his afflicted nose by breathing the night air, was suddenly aroused by cries of "Fire!" A lantern had burst into flames, and the conflagration seemed likely to spread. Duarte's first thought was to rush below and wake his brother, who was in the cabin fast asleep. Henrique, jerked out of his slumbers, did not turn a hair. He came on deck, and quite coolly picked up the burning lamp in both his hands, and threw it into the sea. Buckets of water stopped the fire from spreading further, so disaster was averted just in time. Henrique's hands were badly burnt, however, which filled him with dismay. Supposing they blistered so that it would be impossible to wield a sword? Try plunging them in honey, someone suggested, and that person proved right. Although the burnt hands peeled in a few days, they did not blister much.

To add yet further incident to the short voyage, Henrique's comptroller of household, Fernandalvares Cabral, was seized with violent delirium one night, as he lay on deck, sleeping upon a table. The Infante was attacked by Moors, he kept on crying out, and "there is nobody to help him!"

"This is a touch of pestilence," said the physician to Henrique. "As his medical adviser, I should ask you to go and quiet him by your presence—as yours, however, I say don't go near!" Henrique promptly went, and soothed the invalid, but later Fernandalvares grew worse, and had to be landed for treatment at Tarifa.

Like phantom ships looming in a sea mist, the fleet appeared off Algeciras bay, striking terror into the hearts of the Gibraltar Moors, and delighting Martin Fernandez Portocarrero, who was warden of Tarifa for the Castilian crown.

Magnified by distance and the fog, the vessels appeared numberless. "If all the trees of Portugal had been sawed into planks," observed the watchers on the beach, "and all the men turned carpenters, they never could have made so many ships!" This was no navy built by human hands, they whispered to each other, but an apparition from the spirit world.

But Martin Fernandez believed his eyes, and expressed admiration for the King of Portugal. "When I think of the deeds of this man," he exclaimed, "it almost seems to me that I am dreaming!" Such enthusiasm on the part of a Castilian might appear unnatural, but Martin Fernandez, they say, had Portuguese connections.

The Straits of Gibraltar proved difficult to navigate. A thick fog stretched from coast to coast, and when the pilots, groping through the whiteness, found Ceuta, only the smaller craft could anchor near enough to shore not to be swept over to Malaga by the swift current that was running. Then, when at last they did assemble in Ceuta bay, a furious windstorm rose, and blew all back to Algeciras.

The Moors, who had been panic-stricken, breathed once more, and rejoiced. Light-heartedly they begged their ruler, Sala-ben-Sala, to send away the Berber tribesmen who had been called in to help defend the town. Such wild allies were as bad as the enemy, the Moors declared, and foolishly Sala-ben-Sala granted their request.

At Algeciras, D. João held council with his captains and his sons. What would now be the wisest move? he asked.

Opinions were divided. Why must they take Ceuta? some people demurred. Would not Gibraltar do instead? Ceuta would be very difficult to conquer, for though they could blockade it from the sea, it had the whole of Africa behind. And if the King once laid siege to the town, he could not raise it without loss of prestige. Gibraltar was conveniently to hand. Why not be satisfied with Gibraltar?

Neither Ceuta nor Gibraltar, answered more disgruntled souls. The best thing to do now was to go home! A siege of Ceuta might last for years, and where would supplies and material come from? And it was no good talking about Gibraltar. The King of Castile would take that amiss. "He refused your offer to assist him with that conquest, and he would say that you had captured Gibraltar to spite him!" The King's purpose had been to serve God, had it not? The Almighty, these councilors assured the King, would take the will for the deed.

But D. João meant to achieve the deed. So did his sons. Therefore it was the third opinion that prevailed, and this was to go straight back to Ceuta, and get on with the attack.

"My son," said the King, beaming at Henrique, "I have not forgotten what you begged me when we were near Lisbon, and now the time has come to give my answer. You wished to be with the first landing party, and I will have you go with them as their commander! Tonight, God willing, we shall anchor our fleet before the town, while you with your squadron go round to Almina. The Moors, seeing the greater force upon the other side, will conclude that there we are to disembark, and most of them will concentrate there. When you hear my signal, land as quickly as you can, and when you have taken the beach we shall move our fleet over to your side, and follow you."

Henrique kissed his father's hand ecstatically. The moment for which he had longed and worked during three years would be tomorrow! Three years to a young man of twenty-one seem a good slice of life. He hastened back to his galley in an exalted mood, to find his ardor greeted there by a cold douche!

While their superiors sat in council with the King, the lesser men on board ship had been talking too. They had been talking far too much. The fact was that, what with calms, and fog, and storm and current, and secret councils of the higher ranks, there had been so many comings and goings, and deliberations and delays, that men were losing faith in their commanders. They

(67)

doubted that the King meant to take Ceuta at all. He was merely
casting about for some way of retiring gracefully, and quite prepared to sacrifice a number of his men if necessary to save his face.

"We are all quite sure," two of his squires informed a thunderstruck Henrique, "that the King, your father, feels that he cannot take Ceuta as he hoped to do, and does not know how to
withdraw in a manner that looks well. He therefore means to lead
the fleet against the town, and land the smaller men with the
lesser captains, while he and you, and the other great ones stay
with the fleet. Then he can say that he tried to land but found it
impossible. If that is so, Senhor," they concluded in indignant
tones, "you know it is too bad! Your father ought to find some
other excuse, for we shall simply be cut to pieces on the beach.
Consider if it would not be well to tell your father what we feel
about it!"

Henrique recovered his power of speech. "It seems to me," he
answered in white scorn, "that while the King, my lord, held his
council ashore you held your own on board! You think that we
do not take proper care of all your lives. You oblige me to tell
you what I had wished to keep secret—namely, that tomorrow,
please God, I shall be the first one you see walking down my
galley plank, and," he added witheringly to the two spokesmen,
"neither of you need follow me. I will send for two men from the
other ships—you can do what you like. And let nobody move till
you have seen me land!"

Henrique knew his men. Stung to the quick, their *volte-face*
was instantaneous. "You shall not go without us!" they both
shouted. "There is no one here who would not rather die than
to endure such an affront. We will all land with you, or throw
ourselves into the sea!"

"Not another word!" said the Infante grimly. "It shall be as I

(68)

say." So the squires held another indignation meeting between themselves—this time of quite a different nature.

Illuminated by a thousand candles set in every window, door, and slit, the city of Ceuta shone out through the night. The hostile fleet swinging at anchor in the bay stabbed the black water with its shafts of quivering fire. From sea to land the rival flames challenged each other until the stars died, during a night in which nobody slept on board the Christian ships or in the Moorish town. Such was the young Infantes' first armed vigil.

"How are your preparations getting on?" called the King to Henrique at dawn, arriving in a boat alongside his son's galley. "As you see, Sir!" cried Henrique, stepping forth fully armed, and pointing to his men equipped and ready.

His father was delighted. "Did I not tell you," he remarked with immense pride to his companions, "that my son would be quite ready early in the morning? At such a time he does not mind losing a whole night's sleep. Now, my boy," he added, "you know what you have to do. Go ahead, with God's blessing, and mine!"

Duarte, on his father's galley, buckled his armor on with joyful and impatient hands. Perhaps that is why he scratched himself in the process, and so drew blood. An omen! cried some superstitious person, "you should not disembark today!" This made Duarte laugh. "You have not read the augury aright," he mocked. "What can it mean except that by the grace of God I shall shed so much of the Infidels' blood that, by the strength of my arm, they will fly before me from the town!"

This cheered the pessimists, and all the young squires fell to discussing the mighty deeds each hoped to do that day to win his lady's love—"and you, Senhor," declared Duarte's page, "will achieve something great for your lady!"

"If you remind me of her," said Duarte cheerfully, "at a time when there is a chance of doing something really spectacular to win her favor!"—from which the chronicler infers that the young man was fancy-free.

Henrique, commanding the landing-party, was in no humor for such frivolous talk. Like a racer waiting for the starter's word, he stood beside his galley plank, and his young men hung breathlessly behind. The chaplain, Father Martim Paes, filled in the time profitably by a stirring address. He had time to finish his sermon, he made the warriors kneel and say a General Confession, he blessed them all—and still the signal tarried. On the Almina beach some Moors began to show themselves in menacing and jeering attitudes.

One fidalgo, on board the Count of Barcelos's ship, could endure the tension no longer. He flung himself into a boat and waded ashore. This was too much for Henrique. Signal or no signal, he leaped into his boat, and bade his trumpeters to sound the charge. A helter-skelter rush followed, while each man strove to be the first to reach the shore. As for the recalcitrants of the other day, they were so eager not to stay behind that literally they threw themselves into the sea! They jumped all into the same boat with such vigor that the boat promptly capsized. Their armor and their gallant plumes "lost all their beauty" in the water, we are told, but all the same it was a most refreshing bath upon a scorching day.

Duarte, watching from his father's galley, felt that he must join the fun. D. João, still in his small boat, was inspecting the fleet, and before he came back again, the young man slipped away to join his brother. Their father laughed when he discovered the defection: "My son could not wait for me," he said, "for fear that an old man like myself might disembark too late, or else I might not run and jump so lightly as he can!"

Duarte found Henrique fighting hard upon the beach. "Let us

push the Moors towards the door," he said, "that when they enter we may follow them, or at least prevent them from closing it behind them."

The Moors put up a tough resistance—one terrible dark warrior especially. "The aspect of this Moor," Zurara says, "was fearsome. His body was black as a raven, his teeth were white and long, and his lips were very thick."

The negro giant flung stones to right and left of him as easily as he might toss a tennis ball. At last a certain Vasco Martins de Albergaria ran a lance through his naked body, and the sight of their Goliath's fall put all the Moors to flight. It was this same Vasco Martins who followed them first through the gate. "Here goes Albergaria!" he cried lustily. Henrique's standard-bearer got through next, and the Infante, followed by five hundred men, hurtled into the town.

Those who were waiting on the ships of the King's fleet fumed as they watched the sight. Would the King never let them go? The Infante Pedro, as chief commander of the heavier ships, had been unable to abandon his post and join his brothers with the landing-party from the galleys. He possessed his soul in patience, like the philosopher he was, but other young men grumbled. It was not fair! they said. What was the fun of landing now, when Ceuta had already been entered?

They found plenty still to do, however, when D. João judged the time opportune to land with all his force. The outer ramparts had been taken, but there was an inner circle of defending walls yet to be captured, and the castle. The King's army arrived to find fierce fighting in the outer town, of which the Infantes had only seized a few strategic points. All threw themselves furiously into the fray, and scattered right and left along the narrow streets.

The treasurer, João Afonso—original promoter of the expedition —came upon Duarte and Henrique in possession of the highest eminence, which as it happens, was the city rubbish heap. "My lords!" he cried out joyfully, "what do you think of this festival to celebrate your knighthood? Are you not happier where you are than in the cool halls of Sintra?" And the Infantes, standing upon the odorous mound, perspiring in the sun, agreed with all their hearts.

Others felt that way too. Henrique's two old squires of Bayonne were in great form, enjoying every minute of their day. "Is not this better," they called to the Infante in exultant tones, "than remaining at Porto, where Your Worship would have left us?" As for the nonagenarian Ayres Gonçalves de Figueiredo, he carved his way about like a young man.

The Infantes cast off their armor, and fought hard. Henrique, with a few followers only, charged so far and furiously that he was lost to view among the tortuous streets. For two hours nobody knew what had become of him, and rumor went about that he was killed. "That is the common fate of warriors!" observed his father stoically, but apprehensions presently were laid at rest. The Infante was found at last by Garcia Moniz, who used to have charge of him when he was a small boy. Henrique had chased the Moors up to the castle ramparts, and forced them through a door, which he had closed behind them. With his handful of men he now guarded this door, and none of his companions would leave him alone in such a dangerous place to fetch help.

Garcia Moniz fixed his former pupil with a sternly disapproving eye. What right had Henrique to cause so much anxiety? "You want to attempt things that are beyond the powers of men!" And if he was expecting reinforcements, well—he could expect! "Don't you imagine that your men are still bent on fighting Moors? All that interests them now is plundering the empty houses! Your brothers and the other captains are scattered about the town, and meanwhile the Moors of the castle may sally forth, or those still in the town may try to escape through this door, and would count it a stroke of luck to find you here and take their vengeance in your blood. I beg you, come away where you can achieve honor with a better chance of survival!"

The voice of Garcia Moniz still carried authority. Henrique was constrained to leave his door. As he turned to retrace his steps, a fresh crowd of assailants surged from a side street and surrounded him. The Infante might have been killed if his faithful servant Vasco Fernandes de Ataide had not borne down to his rescue, scattering the enemy, and losing his own life.

Duarte, who with Pedro, had occupied the mosque, sent word to Henrique to join them. "Tell him," Henrique told the messenger, "it would be better if he came to me." But Duarte was firm. The town was taken all except the castle; Henrique must come to his elder brother and the captains in the mosque, to discuss how they were to storm the citadel.

The sun already was declining, and fighting in the streets had mostly ceased. The Moors had fled into the castle or out of the town, leaving behind their dead. The angels of darkness had worked hard that day, Zurara says with gloomy satisfaction, "tearing out the souls of these unfortunate wretches, and carrying them with great joy into eternal captivity!" It was comfortable to feel so certain that your enemies were children of the devil.

In the great mosque where the captains were assembled, Duarte received his brother with open arms. Henrique flung himself down on the floor to rest from the exertions of the day, and as it was too late for further action, a guard was set to watch the castle walls until the morning when the Moors could be finally dislodged.

The dark shape of the tower stood sharply silhouetted on the silver evening sky. No sign of life showed in between the battlements—only a flock of sparrows retiring noisily to roost, fluttered and chirped around the wall. "Those birds seem very much at ease," observed one watchman to his companion as they approached the tower. "May I be slain if the Moors have not gone away, and left the castle empty!"

This was reported to the King. "Then take the flag of St. Vincent," he said, "and plant it on the highest tower."

Already they were battering in the door, when two figures appeared upon the wall. "Don't trouble to break the door," called a voice in Castilian. "The Moors have gone away, and we are here alone. We will open the gates for you as soon as you like." The speakers, one a Biscayan and the other Genoese, then let the Portuguese into the castle. Within its walls was found the richest spoil, for here Sala-ben-Sala kept his treasure.

So was the castle occupied that very evening, and on the strength of that success Duarte sent his standard-bearer to carry his own banner to what was called the Tower of Fez, upon the ramparts of the town, facing inland. This was not such an easy matter, for the Moors made their last stand below those walls. A sharp skirmish dislodged them notwithstanding, and the Portuguese were left in undisturbed possession of the town.

The King, surrounded by his warriors, listened with pride to their recital of Henrique's deeds. He sent a messenger to fetch his son. "As a reward for your valor," said D. João embracing him, "it is my pleasure to knight you here and now!"

On no account would Henrique steal a march on his brothers. "I thank you, sir," he answered, "but I beg you not to do that. God brought us into this world one after the other, and I should like this honor to be given to us in the same order." Which D. João had to admit was only fair.

Night fell, and a thin new moon shone down upon the corpses in the narrow streets. The lamentations of the vanquished sounded from without the city walls, while through the mosaic courts of the deserted homes rough soldiers roamed and plundered at their will. After victory, the sack! All fifteenth-century armies took this as their right, and the sack of Ceuta was worth while. Its citizens were wealthy, and their beautiful tiled houses were replete with gorgeous Eastern embroideries, Indian muslins, Persian carpets, Moroccan brasswork, and silver and gold. The gardens were dug up, and yielded buried treasure, the wells were plumbed and dragged for submerged hoards. The looters ripped up sacks of cinnamon and pepper and then beheld to their dismay the precious contents spilled. An acrid scent of scattered spices filled the hot night air, while cloves and ginger in the street mingled with mud and blood.

The streets of Ceuta were horrible to see. Henrique asked his father in dismay, what could be done with so many dead bodies. It seems that this more hardened warrior had scarcely noticed them! Since Henrique had raised the question, he replied, they might as well be thrown into the sea. This was done the next day.

Some skirmishing still continued outside the walls, but nothing of importance. The only noteworthy event, Zurara says, was the death of an Englishman whom he calls Inequixius Dama! The bearer of this amazing name broke from the ranks and charged the Moors so recklessly that he was killed. Such minor actions took place almost every day, but there was no serious attempt to drive the Portuguese out of Ceuta.

D. João considered that his victory was complete, and lost no time in transmitting the news to Tarifa. Martin Fernandez, he suggested, might like to let them know about it in Castile!

The crowning moment was still to come. "On Sunday, if God please," said the King to Brother João Xira, "I would hear Mass in the great mosque."

The priests then set to work to prepare the building for consecration. They found the beautiful tiled floor buried below layer upon layer of old praying mats. The Moors never removed these mats, it seems, they merely spread new ones above. The Christians therefore had to rake out whole cartloads of rotting straw before they cleaned up everything and erected their altar. Henrique searched the town for two church bells that Moorish pirates once had carried off from Lagos. These bells were discovered at last and joyfully restored to Christian worship.

On Sunday morning, in the presence of the King and all his court arrayed in their most brilliant clothes, the mosque was purified with salt and water.

"The house of the Lord is founded on the heights," chanted the priests, *"to it shall all the nations come, saying Glory be to Thee, Oh Lord!"*

Solemnly they draped the curtains round the altar, and signed it with the sign of the Cross in holy water. They sprinkled the four walls that once had looked upon the "evil and abominable" rites of Islam. *"This is the house of the Lord,"* they sang, *"founded upon the Rock. Arise, Oh Lord, and let Thine enemies be scattered! and let those that abhor Thee flee before Thy face!"* They spread upon the altar a fair linen cloth, and placed the Host upon it; they hung a rich frontal before, and as all candles and torches were set ablaze, they sang the *Te Deum.*

The great deed was accomplished. The Moslem stain was washed away. D. João, joining in the hymn of praise, rejoiced to feel that he had conquered for the Cross in his old age, and young Henrique gazing at the shining lights of this first Christian church restored to Africa, had visions of still greater triumphs to be won.

When Mass was over D. João knighted his sons—three tall young warriors in shining armor, each wearing—proudly girded to his side—the sword that his mother had blessed.

Duarte stepped forward the first, and knelt before the King. He drew the precious sword and kissed its blade before he passed it to his father, who gave him the accolade. In this same manner Pedro and Henrique were made knights.

The three boys had obtained their hearts' desire—knighthood with honor. Their dream could not have been more perfectly fulfilled than in a mosque converted to the Christian faith, in a town conquered by their maiden swords. Other triumphs would come to them in later years, but never one like this. The conquest of Ceuta remained for all three the greatest moment of their lives —a pinnacle forever lighted by the glamorous sunshine of their youth.

D. João only lingered at Ceuta such days as were necessary to select and equip the garrison. The valiant Count D. Pedro de Menezes volunteered to take command of the defenses of the town, and other fidalgos offered to remain with him. The rank and file who formed their troops, it seems were more reluctant. To hold a fort that commanded the passage from the West to the Levant, to man a garrison destined to be a thorn in the side of the King of Fez, was a post of honor and of danger that a knight could fill with pride, but less attractive to the common people. The peasant soldiers, who were longing for their simple homesteads and their tiny farms, wept when the fleet set sail and they were left in a strange town in a strange land, with Infidels all around. They vented their feelings on these same Infidels, however, by fighting them heroically and fiercely.

The homing fleet, meanwhile, with trumpets and rejoicing, sailed triumphantly toward the coast of Algarve. When they anchored at Tavira D. João called his sons. "All services demand reward," he said, "and since, besides being my sons, I find that you have served me well, I want you to receive some recompense. I don't know what honor I can bestow upon my son Duarte beyond that which God has given him of being my first-born and the heir to my kingdom. He can take what he likes of my lands during my lifetime, but I will make dukes of you others."

There never yet had been a duke in Portugal, so D. João was striking a new line when he ordained that Pedro should be Duke of Coimbra, and Henrique of Viseu. Beyond this, Henrique was to be the Lord of Covilham, "for the greatness of his effort, not only in equipping the fleet at Porto, but also for the peril he incurred on the day that we conquered the town." It is evident that Henrique was his father's favorite son, but neither Duarte nor Pedro seemed to mind.

With pomp and ritual D. João invested his sons with their new titles, then he addressed the other knights and gentlemen who had helped him to conquer Ceuta. He thanked them for their loyal service—"Let each one come and ask me what he will," he said; adding, "I thank the Lord for calling me to reign over such people!"

All Portugal rejoiced to welcome home its King. The two little Infantes, who were at Evora with their sister, rode out to meet their father and their elder brothers. A great crowd followed them on horseback and on foot, while the women of Evora swept and cleaned all the streets, and hung their richest cloths from every window. The children of the city turned out, too, singing to greet their king as he proceeded to the palace where his daughter waited eagerly, surrounded by the noblest ladies in the land.

It was a homecoming of triumph tinged with pain. D. João and the Infantes came back to the bereavement they had left, and among the ladies of the royal household a mother mourned her son. This was D. Mecia Coutinho, intimate friend of the late Queen, and mother of Vasco Fernandes de Ataide, who had been Henrique's preceptor and companion, and died defending him. The young man could not bear to face D. Mecia on his return, and fled into his room before the news was broken. "Forgive me, for God's sake!" was all that he could say when, later on, he met the stricken mother. "Because of me you have lost your good son!" His distress was so pitiful to see, that D. Mecia, serene in her grief, spoke brave words to console him.

The army disbanded in Algarve and Alentejo, and each man traveled overland back to his home. All had fine gifts to take to their delighted wives, and—satisfactory ending to a successful enterprise—they say that many a man arrived in time to do his vintage!

The conquest of Ceuta was acclaimed by the nation with pride. Abroad, it was admired as a brilliant crusading feat. To public opinion both national and foreign, the capture of a Moorish town in Africa was a pious and spectacular performance, adding luster to the performers' fame as valiant knights, and enhancing their merit as good Christians. That was all. Few saw in it much practical material value or far-reaching consequence.

They could not guess that the conquest of Ceuta would be a turning point in Universal history.

VII

Earth's Enigma

THE longed-for golden spurs had been worthily won. The three Infantes felt that they had started their career. The path of life before them wound alluringly, by unknown ways, for unknown years. All the secret planning and exciting preparations with which their manhood had been ushered in had culminated in a few triumphant weeks—and now, what next? Not much for the present, it seemed. Life in Portugal was quiet.

Duarte, in his simple serious way, settled down to the whole-time job of chief assistant to his father. The apprenticeship of future ruler might be an arduous one, but so long as a few leisure hours remained for him to practise horsemanship, to read his books, and cover pages with reflections of his own philosophy, Duarte was quite happy.

The speculative Pedro was more restless. In his father's small, well-governed kingdom there was less for him to do. Pedro was anxious to see other lands and other men, to know how life went on in other parts of Europe. He planned a tour of visits to the different foreign courts, beginning with that of the Emperor Sigismund in the far-off romantic realm of Hungary.

Meanwhile, there had appeared to be a chance of some more fighting at Ceuta. In 1418, the kings of Granada and Fez united to besiege the town. The King of Portugal prepared to send Henrique with a fleet, accompanied by his young brother, the Infante

João. Nothing was said about Pedro, however, and he suspected that his father did not mean to let him go. Pedro decided that it might be wiser not to ask, but just embark incognito, disguised as someone's servant. He managed to reach Lisbon unobserved, and his plan might have worked out very well if he had not made his confession first, as a pious warrior should. The friar who absolved him preached a crusading sermon to the citizens next day, and tactlessly commended the Infante Pedro to their prayers. That was the end of Ceuta for poor Pedro. He had to interview his father after that, and though Duarte went with him to back him up and help him out, in spite of every persuasion still the King said no!

There never was any attempt to hold Henrique back. It always seems to have been understood that Ceuta was Henrique's special concern. A few months after the conquest, in 1416, the King had signed a document appointing the Infante Governor of the town. This meant that it would be Henrique's task to see that the defenders of the garrison lacked nothing in equipment or supplies. He saw to it conscientiously, and the gallant captain Pedro de Menezes did the rest. Ceuta, constantly besieged, kept the flag flying, and brilliant sorties answered each attack. Only in 1418, when the nephew of the King of Granada arrived with overwhelming force, had the brave count consented to write asking for help from home.

Henrique had his fleet underway with dispatch and delight. His brother João came hopefully, expecting to do mighty deeds. But when the two young men arrived in Africa, the worst was over. The Moors had just attacked and been repulsed. The beautiful nephew of the King of Granada lay with his yellow ringlets in the dust, when D. Pedro de Menezes—a grim figure straight from the battlefield, grasping a naked blood-stained sword—met the Infantes on the beach. He would have knelt to kiss the princes' hands, but they admired the hero far too much to permit such a gesture. All the same, it was sad that he had left them nothing much to do!

The Moors faded away on the arrival of Henrique's fleet, and though the brothers remained at Ceuta for three months, there was no more excitement. Henrique then proposed to cross the Straits and conquer Gibraltar. His counselors demurred. Gibraltar was the lawful prey of the King of Castile, they pointed out—if Henrique were to butt in, there would be trouble. Besides, it was winter! Henrique said that he must go and see what could be done, and set sail with the fleet, but a wild storm arose and scattered all his ships. The young man would have tried again—the opportunity for such a deed seemed far too good to miss—but his aspirations were nipped in the bud by a peremptory message from his father: Henrique and João were to come straight back home at once, ordered the King, and not embark on any new adventures! Reluctantly, Henrique brought his brother home. All prospect of fresh deeds of arms was off for years.

Pedro, fully convinced of this, set out for Hungary without more delay, escorted by his traveled friend, Alvaro Vaz de Almada, and cautioned by some pages of Duarte's good advice. Duarte hoped that Pedro would not let his household fall into bad ways while in foreign parts. Be careful about drink especially, he urged, "for this vice is much more common abroad!"

So D. Pedro rode east to see kingdoms and men. Henrique had no wish to follow. Henrique was absorbed in problems of his own. He was not interested in politics or states—it was the cosmos that intrigued him. The riddle of the universe, he felt, could not be studied in the feverish haunts of men. Henrique at the age of twenty-five was not the recluse that he became in later years. He still found pleasure in the company of his kind, and did not flee from social functions, but there were moments when he felt the need to be alone. There were times when he had to get away, far from all towns, far from the court, far from his father and his brothers even. Then he would travel to the furthermost southwest point of Algarve, where on the barren rocks of Cape St. Vincent, with Portugal and all Europe behind, he faced infinity across a boundless sea. Upon this windswept promontory, above the stony shores of Sagres bay, was isolation undisturbed by echoes of the world. Only a scattered fishing population shared the solitude. This end of all the earth became Henrique's haven of escape, and a modest house in the village of Raposeira a few miles away was the place where he betook himself to study and to think.

Under the clear Algarvian skies he read his great-grandfather's treatise on astronomy, he watched the heavenly bodies coursing through the night, and on his bed he dreamed of stars and continents and seas. He heard the boom of the Atlantic swell, rolling from half around the world, crash into foam on Sagres rocks. He pondered on that waste of water stretching west, stretching to no man knew what distant shore, below the far horizon beyond which no ship had sailed. He thought of the intriguing coast of Africa that ran on southward for unmeasured miles beside this unknown sea. What he had seen of that great continent was but its outer fringe. Henrique's visits to Ceuta had stimulated his curiosity, like oil thrown into fire.

Those countries where Pedro was traveling were interesting, no doubt, but they were not mysterious. Their boundaries were clearly defined and well known, there was no doubt of what might lie beyond. But Ceuta left you wondering. There, on the edge of an unknown continent, East mingled with the West, and spices from the Orient were brought down to the western ocean. Those sacks of pepper and those bales of cinnamon that he had seen the soldiers squander in the streets so recklessly had reached Ceuta from the far ends of the earth by trade routes through the heart of the unknown. This enigmatic Africa, crossed by the Arab caravans, extended eastward to the Ancients' Erythraean Sea. And southward? No one knew, for none had ever been right to the end; only the Moors told tales of land, and yet more land.

The Moors had told Henrique things that he had never learned in books. They spoke to him about the hinterland of Morocco and Fez, and the wild Bedouin that roamed on the outskirts of the great desert. They told him of the vastness of the Sahara, stretching into the heart of Africa, and of the Berber tribes dwelling upon the confines of the negro realms in the green jungle. Henrique heard of gold brought down from Timbuktu, and ivory from the distant land of Guinea. That was the farthest point of Moorish penetration to the south, but their trade routes ran eastward to the shores of the Red Sea.

Henrique pondered on the problem of the East, and all the fascinating lands lying that way, Tunisia, Egypt, Tartary, India, Ceylon, Cathay—alluring names adorning travelers' tales, but places which some Europeans had really seen! Some traders, and some missionaries, from time to time had crossed the eastern steppes and visited the court of the Great Khan. Reports of those regions beyond had reached the western lands, but true accounts were mingled with legend and fable. Few could distinguish the false from the true, for the eastern hemisphere as known to the medieval Christian world was like a landscape in a drifting mist. Sometimes the clouds parted and showed a glimpse of the beyond, and then the fog rolled back again, and all was lost. The veil had lifted for a while when Asia was ruled by the race of Genghis Khan, but dropped conclusively when the Mongols were converted to Islam.

The western infiltration had been tentative and slight, but such as it was, it had once raised hopes. The early fourteenth-century Franciscans had visualized a day when China should be turned from Confucius to Christ, and all the Khans of Tartary embrace the Christian faith. But the dream of a few devout souls was premature. The tide of Islam soon surged back. In the Infante D. Henrique's time all Christian penetration into Asia had been stopped for the last fifty years, all central Asian routes were closed —from Egypt to the shores of the Black Sea the Crescent reigned supreme and barred the way.

Henrique, a true son of Philippa of Lancaster, thought sadly of the conquests of the Infidel over the Christian. It seemed that Moslem rule extended throughout Asia, and Africa as well. Nothing remained except the land of Prester John. Somewhere, lost in the dark mountains of Africa, there was a Christian kingdom. Black monks from a mysterious land above the Nile could be met at Jerusalem—sometimes they even had traveled to Rome. Was there a sea route to the land of Prester John? Henrique wondered. What was the best way to get there? Could not a western people allied to Prester John take up the challenge of Islam in the East? How were Christians to get back to the East again—to those enchanted lands described by Marco Polo? Every land route was closed; there remained but one other way—untried, unknown, but possible.

"The sea beyond the Pillars of Hercules, which is called the Atlantic, and the Erythraean are all one and the same sea . . ." wrote Herodotus some two thousand years ago. "As for Libya," the Father of History further stated, "we know it to be washed on all sides by the sea, except where it is attached to Asia." A legend told that the Phœnicians once had sailed around Africa from Egypt, through the Indian Ocean to the Atlantic. The Carthaginian Hanno made an attempt from the western side, and how far he succeeded no one knows. That such a feat of navigation might be possible had been suggested more than once by different theorists. But few thought it a practical idea, for no one knew the shape and size of Africa, how far its coast ran southward toward the Pole, or what rivers flowed from its hidden heart into the unknown sea. The Arabs had something to say of the east coast. They knew the ports upon that side from Zanzibar to Sofala and Madagascar; but the western shores of the great continent were as mysterious as the ocean on which no man sailed that surged on its forsaken beaches.

The Arabs were great travelers by land and sea. Their caravans traversed tremendous distances across north African and central Asian deserts, their sailors navigated Levantine and eastern seas. Their corsair galleys ploughed the Mediterranean from the Dardanelles to Gibraltar, their djelbas sailed the length of the Red Sea, their dhows were borne across the Indian Ocean by the rhythmic, recurring winds—but neither Moor nor Arab dared face the Atlantic. "Green Sea of Darkness," it was to them—a moving waste ruled by uncertain winds, with no inhabited country beyond, a shoreless abyss in which a ship might drift on everlastingly through treacherous mist and fog till she was lost. The Atlantic, Arab theologians laid down, was not a navigable sea—any man mad enough to try should be deprived of all his civic rights!

Western geographers were not much more encouraging. The missionary, Marignolli, had traveled widely overland, but he said that God did not mean the human race to sail around the world! It would be of no use to try in any case, he added, for "sure experience" had taught him that half the surface of the ocean was unnavigable.

Such few ventures as had been made by western seamen off the accustomed routes seemed to bear out Marignolli's assertion. The brothers Vivaldi, who had sailed from Genoa in 1291, hoping to find a way around Africa, were never seen again. Those Catalans who had set out in 1346 to seek for the River of Gold had vanished forever behind the veil that shrouded the Dark Ocean. No one seemed to get further than Cape Non, from which the proverb said "he would return—or not!" and although better informed persons might not believe that the sea really boiled within the tropics, and only the unlearned considered the risk of falling over the edge of the earth, still all medievals were agreed that to sail south of the Moroccan coast was harebrained madness.

None the less tradition, legend, speculation united to allege that there must be a way around Africa, so why not seek till it be found, Henrique mused, and having found it, make it certain for all time? That was exactly what no one had yet attempted. All ocean exploration heretofore had been spasmodic and sporadic. The Vikings had defied the northern seas and reached some fertile lands beyond, but then they had forgotten all about them. The Phœnicians may have sailed round Africa, but it seems that they never sought to repeat the performance, and the route was lost. The Genoese had tried and failed, but only once, and so quite possibly had several others. Nobody had persevered. Those isolated voyages never followed up were no more than a wild goose chase. Henrique was a dreamer, but no chaser of wild geese. He was a man of action. He who would penetrate the secret of the far horizon line must be prepared to seek, and seek again. He must arm himself with careful study, earnest thought, and above all, infinite patience. The riddle of the universe would not be solved by haphazard adventure or by lucky hits—only slowly, systematically, and bit by bit, might the mystery be elucidated for all future generations.

So the Infante D. Henrique mused in his retreat beside the sea through the short summer nights.

The stars had died. The morning sun shone on the waves. Henrique arose from his bed full of a new resolve. Enough of wondering and of speculation—he would know the truth! Henceforth the purpose of his life was fixed.

(87)

To those around it seemed that their Infante must have seen a vision. For without discussing, or explaining, that same day he ordered two ships to be equipped, with as much diligence "as if that night he had been told that without more delay, nor inquiry of what he had sought to find out, he should send to discover."

VIII

The Islands of the Blest

IT MUST have been about this time—1419 or 1420—that two squires, João Gonçalves Zarco with a young friend, Tristão Vaz Teixeira, sought the Infante D. Henrique. If he had any enterprise in hand, they said, they were his men! All that they asked was for some honorable employment—because, they added virtuously, it seemed to them that time was wasted when they did no work.

They might have added that they were hard up. João Gonçalves was a poor man with a rising family, and Tristão Vaz was anxious to acquire some wealth. Besides this, they were bored. The adventure of Ceuta had been an appetizer provoking the desire for more. After the spiritual uplift of crusading, and material joys of loot, to settle down at home was rather dull.

Henrique listened sympathetically. Had not the dying Queen urged him to be protector of the fidalgos of Portugal? It was a charge not always easy to fulfil. Ever since peace had been made with Castile, this class had been suffering from what would be described today as the post-war depression. The petty aristocracy lived mainly by the sword, and when there was no enemy to be despoiled its members were faced with financial ruin. What could be done with them at home in times of peace was a perpetual problem to the King. This is no doubt one reason why D. João gave his full support to the schemes of his son, for since the land could not provide, there still remained the sea.

Henrique had his two ships ready. They were small clumsy vessels of a type then known as *barchas*, for the caravels, in after years so famous, had not come into being yet. These *barchas* had a capacity under a hundred tons. They had one mast and one square sail, and were not of a kind—the experts say—that can be made to sail into the wind. Henrique offered the command of these to João Gonçalves and to Tristão Vaz. How would they like to take them down the coast of Africa? he asked. They could fight any Moorish corsair that they met upon the way, and try to sail as far south as the land of Guinea.

This suited both admirably. João Gonçalves hailed from the fishing village of Matosinhos, and probably had been a sailor all his life. Tristão was a spirited young man anxious for adventure. Each one embarked on his respective cockleshell and put to sea, and just how far down the Moroccan coast they reached remains uncertain. All accounts of their voyage are fragmentary and vague. We only know that they returned with much to say about a storm, and of an island.

The wind and waves had been terrific, it appears. The tiny ships had been borne far away to sea. Tossing like driftwood on the swell, driven before a wind that blew them ever further from the coast towards shoreless infinity, João Gonçalves, Tristão, and their men began to feel their appetite for adventure losing its edge. Already they had given up all hope of seeing Portugal again, when at long last the wind began to die, and they found themselves within the shelter of an island.

It was a little island, rather bare, with rocky peaks above a bay of snow-white sand. Porto Santo was what they called this haven of refuge in which they brought their battered ships to anchor.

A pleasant spot it seemed to João Gonçalves and to Tristão Vaz —not many trees indeed, but splendid pasture in the hollows and upon the crumpled hills, and sweet resinous plants scenting the slopes of grass. The air was health-giving and fresh, the soil seemed good and might produce much corn, while dragon-trees and junipers flourished upon the mountain side. No trace of human habitation could be found, neither any wild beast. The island was a little sunlit garden, all abandoned to the sea and sky.

Henrique's squires were so delighted with their discovery—or re-discovery, as it seems it was in truth—that they lingered there only for three days, and then struck out for home, with specimens of island plants to show to the Infante.

He was decidedly interested, we are told, and very pleased, but it is doubtful if he was surprised. Medieval geographers seem to have been aware of the existence of Atlantic islands, for they peppered them with varying accuracy about their maps. What historians have not established yet is just how far this knowledge was experimental. So few authenticated documents are found bearing upon the subject, the question is so entangled with legend and surmise, that all research has ended in blind alleys, or left the seeker wandering in a maze.

Who first saw the enchanted islands of the Ocean? Their early history might be written in sea mist. These fragments of a lost Atlantis, glamorous as fairyland, that rise before the vision of seafarers like a mirage from the waves, or disappear in a blue haze beyond a wake of foam, have haunted European legends since the earliest times. Hesperides, the Islands of the Blest, St. Brandon's Island of the Birds, the Fortunate Isles—they seem to have been lost, and found, and lost again, at intervals during more than two thousand years. So near to Europe or North Africa that a storm-tossed coasting ship might easily be driven to their shores, and yet so small, and so cut off by leagues of uncharted sea that an unskillful mariner who happened on them once might never find his way back there again.

These islands hovered thus for centuries on the fringe of European ken, until the group of the Canaries, being relatively near to the mainland, was the first of them all to drift from legend into light. Exactly when or how this came to pass is vague, but by Henrique's time they had been known to several generations—nearly as well as we today know the more isolated archipelagos of the Pacific Ocean.

Might João Gonçalves' new-found Porto Santo count as one of the Canary Islands? This was a question giving food for thought. For many years the Canaries had been the subject of a standing argument between the kingdoms of Castile and Portugal, though owing to the distance of these islands from all normal travel routes the interest of such discussions had hitherto been mainly academic.

The debate opens in 1344, when the Pope granted the islands to the Castilian prince, D. Juan de La Cerda, and Afonso IV of Portugal protested to the Holy See: The Canaries should rightfully be his, he wrote, for his subjects had found them first, as everybody knew; Afonso had designed to conquer the islands himself, he said, and convert all the natives, as soon as he had time, but the Castilians and the Moors had so far kept him busy!

This protest, it seems, was made on principle. Afonso IV was not really keen on the Canaries. Neither, we gather, did Juan de La Cerda do much with them, for as late as 1402 the islands still remained unconquered and their natives unconverted. At this date, says the chronicler Zurara, a "noble and catholic French gentleman," Jehan de Béthencourt, with his friend, Gadifer de La Salle, obtained leave from the Castilian king to try their luck, "being desirous to serve God, because they knew that these islands were heathen."

They also knew that these islands were far away! "The Sieur de Béthencourt, and Messire Gadifer de La Salle have sold up all their property, saying that they were off to conquer the Canaries —and no one knows what has become of them." So King Charles VI informed the English delegates who had complained of acts of piracy done by these pious gentlemen, which throws some light upon the kindling of their missionary zeal.

Assisted by men and munitions from Castile, Jehan de Béthencourt had gained possession of Lançarote, Forteventura, and Ferro—the three smallest islands of the group—and when after a few years he returned to France, he left his nephew Maciot in command, to enforce order as well as he could. It seems, however, that Maciot could not. This far-off feudal appanage of the Castilian crown was on its way to becoming a nest of pirates and adventurers, with rival captains squabbling for the power.

Henrique followed the process with interest and some disapproval. That was not his idea how islands should be colonized! If they could be ceded to him, he felt that he could have made better use of the Canaries. He suggested as much to the Castilian king, who did not jump at the idea. Henrique wanted islands that might serve as base for exploration of the Guinea coast; he therefore welcomed João Gonçalves with his news of Porto Santo. Whether it belonged to the Canary group or not, the Infante made up his mind to have it fully occupied before his cousin of Castile should look around and inquire.

D. João backed him up. For strategic reasons he objected to Castilian settlements off the Atlantic coast of Africa. He therefore gave Henrique leave to go ahead and plant and populate his desert island to his heart's content.

João Gonçalves and Tristão Vaz were willing to go back. Another fidalgo, Bartolomeu Perestrelo, proposed himself as their companion. Three ships were then equipped, the colonists took plants and seeds of diverse kinds, and a friend of Perestrelo's gave him a doe rabbit in a cage by way of a parting present.

He took her cheerfully, nor when she produced a litter of small rabbits on the voyage was he seized with misgivings. The settlers built themselves shacks upon the island, and Perestrelo gaily let his rabbits loose.

Porto Santo proved to be everything that the colonists had hoped. The climate was agreeable and the soil, though rather dry, not unfertile. Their plantations might have done very well had it not been for Bartolomeu Perestrelo's rabbits.

If the settlers found the country healthy, so did the rabbits! All that they planted grew and would have multiplied—only the rabbits multiplied still more. There were not any beasts of prey to hunt and decimate them, and they found quantities of food to eat. The more the settlers sowed, the more the rabbits ate, the more they ate the more they reproduced and flourished. Everyone must have grown quite sick of rabbit pie, and however they might persecute and kill the little brats their numbers never seemed to grow the less.

After two years the men were thoroughly discouraged. It was all the fault of Bartolomeu Perestrelo! João Gonçalves and Tristão would have been more than human had they failed to point this out. It seems, however, that they rubbed it in rather unnecessarily, which brought about a bitter quarrel, ending in bloodshed. Utterly disgusted, all three decided to go home, and leave the island to the rabbits.

Henrique listened to their tale of woe, but he was not the man to suffer defeat at the teeth of rodents. To him each island occupied was an outpost upon the long sea route he planned to conquer. With all his vision the Infante was no romantic dreamer. He had set himself to seek the far ends of the earth, but he embarked upon the quest without impetuosity. Hot-footed enthusiasts had started out before, he knew, and either lost themselves or lost what they had found. Henrique meant to achieve permanent results, and so he was contented to go slow.

He did not reproach João Gonçalves and Tristão for their defection. He only urged them to go back, and if they did not care for Porto Santo, let them look for a better island, for it seemed that there was land of some kind very near. Had they not told him that from the south coast they always saw a cloud on the horizon? João Gonçalves had often wondered what that cloud might be. "Why wonder?" we can hear the Infante saying to him—"Don't wonder, go and see!"

So the companions put to sea once more in early June of 1424 or 1425. They found their rabbit-eaten island quite unchanged, and the intriguing cloud still low on the horizon. They watched it several days attentively, to make quite sure it never lifted, nor dispersed. At every hour it could be seen—a blue or violet shadow by daylight, and a dark mass in the rays of the moon. They weighed anchor on Sunday, July 1st, and sailed towards the shadow before dawn.

All day they drifted towards the cloud, and still it did not lift. Still they could see no beach ahead, only some black crags rising from a wall of mist that hung down to the sea, while in their ears the surge of unseen breakers crashing upon hidden rocks thundered menacingly.

Cautiously, for fear of shipwreck on the submerged reefs, the ships drew near, while the mist melted in the sun, and they beheld a lovely land of mountains clothed in forest sweeping to the sea.

Here was a better island in all conscience! A fair exchange for

(95)

rabbit-devastated Porto Santo. By evening the ships anchored in an ample bay, beside a sandy beach with precipitous wooded slopes towering above. The seamen danced and sang, and hardly could compose themselves to sleep till morning dawned, enabling them to go ashore.

They were not disappointed. The island was as beautiful as Paradise, bathed in sunshine that warmed but did not burn, watered by crystal streams that bubbled from the hills, caressed by scented breezes. But it was difficult to penetrate inland, for everywhere the mountain side was clothed in a forest as dense as that which screened the palace of the Sleeping Beauty.

They struggled into the enchanted shade, and slashed their way from shore to shore, and everywhere the same green canopy spread overhead, while underfoot the fallen leaves of countless years piled up a carpet of unmeasured depth. No serpent was found in this Eden, nor any wild beast, nor any noisome insect. It was the kingdom of the birds, that undisturbed since the creation, built their nests and sang their songs in the deep woods, and never having known a hunter, showed no fear of man.

In all the scented wilderness they found one trace of human passage. Beside the bay where they first disembarked there stood a ruined shanty. On a giant tree close by a wooden cross had been erected, with a rudely carved Latin inscription declaring that "here came Machin, an Englishman, driven by the tempest, and here lies buried Anna d'Arfet, a woman who was with him." So says a much-repeated story, and here we are befogged in legend once again.

It is so hard to strip the veil of myth from these bewitching islands and flood them with the cold light of facts! We look for dates and documents, and they elude us. We feel for clues, and they melt in our hands. The mirage mingles with reality, and

(96)

when we try to stand upon firm ground, we find that we are sinking in quicksands.

What truth is there in the sad tale of Robert Machin and the hapless Anna d'Arfet? Historians have brushed it aside with scorn. Yet surely Zarco's men did find a grave and an inscription, for it is mentioned in one of the earliest records. There seems to be no reason why it should have been invented. Whether the detailed and romantic tale that has come down to us is substantially true is quite another matter. It seems to have been first told in a Moorish prison by one captive to another, who was ransomed later and so passed the story on.

It is a melancholy love-lorn tale, quite in the taste of late medieval fiction. The hero, Robert Machin, was an amorous squire, who lived in England during the reign of Edward III. The peerless Anna d'Arfet requited his love, but her cruel father refused his consent and forced her to marry another. Robert and Anna then decided to elope, and embarked at Bristol on a ship sailing for Spain. Owing to bad weather, say some, because their pilot was a poor navigator, according to others—for both reasons, no doubt —the ship never reached Spain at all, and the first land they sighted was Madeira. Poor Anna, who was terribly seasick, begged to be put ashore for a few days. Her Robert disembarked with her, of course; also some of their companions. Meanwhile the ship made off, one version says on purpose, others say that it was impelled by weather.

Anna d'Arfet had not the spirit of a pioneer! To find herself marooned upon a desert island filled her with such dismay that in a few days she was dead. Thereupon Robert Machin died of grief—as a romantic lover should—while his more practical companions left the island in an open boat. In time, they drifted to the Moroccan coast and there they all were captured. So it was

that by devious ways, and after many years, the tale reached Por
tugal and Spain. It could be true, it may be false—historians do
not take it seriously. They cannot say it is impossible, but it is
quite unproven.

Whoever may or may not have preceded him, João Gonçalves
took possession of the island for his king. Madeira was the name
given to it, because of the abundance of its wood. A priest sprinkled holy water on the ground and in the air, to exorcise the evil
spirits of the wilderness, after which he set up a cross by Anna
d'Arfet's grave, and celebrated Mass. According to Henrique's
orders, they collected samples for him to see of island earth, and
diverse woods, and water from the different springs. With all these
things they then returned to Portugal in triumph.

They were particularly welcome. Henrique, who still hankered
after the Canary Islands, had recently dispatched a fleet to try
and gain possession of the largest of them all. The captain, D
Fernando de Castro, had found, however, that the inhabitants
were far too numerous and ferocious for a peaceful settlement
and he had not the necessary provisions for a prolonged war. So
he returned to Portugal, reporting no success. As the venture had
cost the royal exchequer 39,000 doubloons, it was not an experi
ment that could be easily renewed. Added to this, it gave rise to
diplomatic complications. The King of Castile, though his sub
jects had never gained a footing on the Grand Canary, was inclined to be querulous about the incident. The archipelago was
his, he said, and even if he did not conquer the islands himself
he still would count it an unfriendly act for anybody else to do so
D. João had no wish to pick a quarrel with Castile, and so he let
the matter drop.

The arrival of João Gonçalves with news of the splendid island
that he had found could not have been more opportune. Madeira
was a gift! Here were no natives to pacify, and if action were taken

at once, no fear of Castilians butting in. Henrique set to work immediately, with the collaboration and complete approval of his father.

João Gonçalves Zarco volunteered to take his family to live on the island, to which Henrique heartily agreed. He made him hereditary captain of one half of Madeira, and gave the other half to Tristão Vaz.

Three ships were prepared with all dispatch. They carried seeds and plants and domestic animals (no rabbits, we presume!), and the King further gave João Gonçalves kind permission to clear out all the inmates of the state prisons, and take them with him. João Gonçalves, however, weeded them carefully. He would have nobody whose condemnation was for treason, or for theft, nor for any offense against religion. Supported by this band of honest and right-thinking criminals, he sailed from Portugal at last, with D. Constança, his wife, their son aged twelve, two little daughters, and his servants.

Henrique saw them go with hope and satisfaction. He felt that there was nothing lacking for the settlers to make good. It must therefore have been a nasty shock when, not long after, the same ship returned, with the announcement that the island was on fire! Yes, the whole island! Blazing merrily! Everything was burnt up. And what about João Gonçalves and his family? Living precariously in improvised shelters by the shore, and every time the wind blew from the burning forest all they could do was rush into the sea, and camp upon the rocks.

No doubt the tale lost nothing in the telling, but what happened must have been pretty bad. It all resulted because when the settlers had wished to till the soil, they could not find it. The earth was buried deep under decaying vegetation centuries old. Burn it! ordered João Gonçalves airily, and soon the virgin forest was ablaze. No one could extinguish the flames. They licked up the dead wood of ages past. They roared beside the beach, and raged over the Funchal valley. The settlers narrowly escaped a fiery death.

It cannot be said that the Gonçalves Zarco family lacked grit. They sent the ship back home for assistance, but they themselves remained. They set their teeth, and fought the flames, and lived on birds and fishes till the ship returned with help.

Henrique sent them back fresh supplies of everything—of plants, and animals, and yet more colonists both men and women. They found the Funchal valley all burnt out. Tradition has it that the fire went on smouldering here and there for seven years, but still the worst was over. They ploughed the virgin soil, all newly cleared and carbonized, and everything they sowed there yielded fiftyfold. João Gonçalves traced his city of Funchal, and parceled out the land among his followers.

This was Europe's first serious colonial venture of modern times, for the haphazard and spasmodic occupation of the Canaries hardly counts as such. The island never became at any time a vassal kingdom as the Canary Archipelago was to the Castilian crown. Its hereditary captains were not independent feudal princes, but subjects with restrictions to their power. Under the mother country's direct supervision and fostering care, the infant settlement grew up and flourished. In less than two decades Madeira could boast of rising towns and prosperous villages, surrounded by plantations of all fruits and vegetables known to European or Moorish agriculture. The less fortunate Canaries at that time were little more developed than when first discovered. The handful of adventurers living there made no attempt at cultivation. They lived precariously upon the native produce of the soil, and passed their time in quarreling with one another. "They have neither wine, nor wheat," observed the Venetian, Cadamosto, who visited the islands in 1455, "except that which is brought hem from outside—little fruit, and hardly anything good."

Madeira by that date, and long before, was exporting its produce. "The whole island is a garden!" the same Venetian exclaims
apturously. The planting of this garden had been Henrique's
labor of love. Every month his captains had to send him news of
their progress, and how to make the most of the island had been
his earnest study. We know that samples of earth, wood, and water had been brought him by the first explorers of the land, but
he demanded more: "Send me specimens of wood from all parts
of the island," he wrote to João Gonçalves, "and branches of the
trees—tell me what are their names, and what the fruit is called.
Send me pieces of stone . . . and a sack of earth."

This practical visionary studied the possibilities in that spirit of
scientific investigation that he brought to bear on everything. The
timber was found to be of a superior quality—here was a valuable
export all ready found—the earth and water could be made to do
the rest. Hearing that Madeira had many streams, Henrique sent
for sugar canes from Sicily to plant upon his sunny island, and
contracted the services of experts in the art of making sugar.

Grapes should do well in that climate, he supposed, and considering what kind ought to be best, Henrique ordered malmsey
vines from Cyprus for Madeira.

The colonists were not left short of anything needful to life
or work. Every year the Infante sent them shiploads of iron, steel,
and tools, and seeds and animals from Portugal, and in that Island
of Blest all turned to gold. Corn yielded sixtyfold, cattle fattened
and multiplied, the vines bore almost more bunches than leaves,
with large sweet grapes in clusters two feet long, and Madeira
wine grew famous in a few years. Honey and wax were sent abroad,
and the island sugar was considered the best in the world.

Much of the beautiful forest had been consumed in the great
fire, but much fine timber still remained. There were iron woods

that did not float on water, and dye woods such as brazil; there were magnificent woods for marquetry, and reeds that made the loveliest white baskets anyone had seen. There was also good hard wood for building ships. Some say that the first caravels were built from the Madeira forest. This type of ship came into use from 1430 on, so it may well be so.

With all this Henrique did not neglect his first-found island of Porto Santo. It seems that Bartolomeu Perestrelo, having got rid of his companions, allowed himself to be persuaded to return and face the rabbits. He brought out colonists with him, and though they could not cultivate the soil with any great success, they made quite a good thing of cattle breeding. Zurara, writing after thirty years, describes the multitude of rabbits as "almost infinite." Bartolomeu Perestrelo none the less was satisfied with everything, they say. Being sole master of the island was evidently what made all the difference!

The co-captains of Madeira did not quarrel with each other. There was plenty of room for both on each side of the mountain range. The captaincy of Tristão Vaz was smaller, but he added to it that of the Desertas opposite. These islands, as their name suggests, were too dry for human habitation. Instead of colonists the Infante sent out cattle—sheep and goats—all of which flourished there, as also did peacocks, and partridges, and guinea-fowls.

Tristão Vaz built his capital on the shore of that lovely bay where he and João Gonçalves had first landed. Machico was the name he chose for it.

Did he call it so in memory of the ill-starred Robert Machin, as some writers affirm, and have we here a circumstantial proof to support the sad tale? . . . Not quite a satisfactory one, it seems. There had been Machicos in Portugal, and the late king, D. Fernando, had had a pilot of that name. Some people think that this Machico must have been the first discoverer of Madeira, fifty years before João Gonçalves' voyage. An island of similar name is shown in almost the right place on some maps of that time. Might it not have been added at a later date? others suggest—and so once more we wander in the mist.

Who first discovered the Enchanted Islands? Nobody knows, nor is it likely that anybody will before the end of time. Of one thing only are we sure—the islands that Henrique's navigators found were never lost again.

IX

Cape Bojador and the Lost Islands

FIFTY leagues south of the Canary Islands, the blunt head of Cape Bojador projects out of the barren coast to the forsaken sea.

Here was the end of the medieval world—the limit beyond which no ship might navigate, the boundary marking where all habitable land was lost in burning deserts. Men felt that it would be but tempting Providence to try to force a passage where Nature had barred the way. Who could venture to journey over endless sands; and on the shoals and sandbanks of the shallow sea what ship could live? Miles from the beach the waves might be heard breaking on the rocks; a treacherous current ran beside the shore; for six months of the year the sand dunes of the long low coast were veiled in a mist of Sahara dust, and the wind that blew almost unceasingly from the northeast whipped up gigantic rollers in deep furrows right across the ocean.

To pass Cape Bojador, sailors agreed, would simply be to court disaster. It was believed that there was no navigable sea beyond. The ocean ended in a sort of hideous swamp, where water steamed under the tropic sun which sucked the sea-bed dry in places and which burned a white man black. Horrible serpents writhed in the depths of these turgid pools, marine monsters walked in the salty wastes, the suffocating air was fetid—even poisonous.

Tales such as these were told of the Dark Ocean by the Moors

—and the Moors ought to know it best, for they lived farthest south! Besides them, there was Ptolemy. The Greek geographer had said that man could not live in the equatorial belt, and how was a mere modern to reject what the Ancients affirmed?

Iconoclasts might have been found to challenge Ptolemy; adventurous souls and curious minds might have been tempted to investigate the legends, but there was yet another obstacle, and it was physical and real. A bold seaman might sail around Cape Bojador, borne by the wind and the Canary current—with luck he might avoid the alleged shoals—but how was he to get back home again? In the teeth of that northeast wind, upon a sea whose waters ran to the southeast, no ship could make way up the coast from Bojador. The only thing that could be done would be to abandon one's craft and return overland! And that would mean trekking for months across the desert, and final capture by the Moors.

Clearly, such a voyage was impracticable, as was proved by the fact that nobody had made it! Do not tell us, said Henrique's contemporaries, that in a world that has produced so many heroes in the past, if this thing had been feasible one would not have achieved it! What was the use of trying, anyhow? The continent of Africa obviously trailed away into the desert. What object could there be in sailing around Cape Bojador, since there was nothing on the other side?

Henrique was treated to arguments in this same vicious circle for twelve years, but every year in all this time—from 1421 to 1433—he sent out ships regularly, with orders to sail south of Bojador.

His men thought that their Infante had got a bee in his bonnet. The island explorations they could understand—islands were profitable and worth cultivating. Raids on the coasts of Barbary were also good—you could get prisoners for ransom; but nosing

about desert shores and empty seas was merely chimerical. They
went to please the Infante, but it appears that many captains
did not take their mission very seriously. They sailed perfunc-
torily south, but before reaching Bojador or the Canary current,
they turned their helms around again and made for the Gibraltar
Straits, to change the arid task of explorer for the brave life of
a corsair in the Mediterranean. Once they had had a good scoop
off the Moors, then they went home to exhibit their prizes to
their master.

He was very patient with them. He rewarded them for any useful work they may have done, and he accepted their excuses for
what they had not attempted to do. But every time he said: Go
back—go back and go farther!

They were not all amateur pirates. Among Henrique's seamen
there were earnest seekers like himself, and in the course of so
many repeated voyages some things were found out. This navigation of the coast of Africa was not a simple problem. Discounting
all the mythic bogeys of the south Atlantic, a return voyage within
reach of the continent would still remain almost impossible
against that wind and current. The only solution would be if they
could sail outside the islands on the open sea, if they could somehow skirt the northeast trade, and sweep a semicircle home. To
find out how this might be done, ships must be sent far out of
sight of land to study the Atlantic winds.

It sounds simple enough to us today, but it meant to the early
fifteenth-century mariner complete revision of the science of navigation. The time-honored process of navigating by landfall, pick-
ing up points along the coast, and following the compass in between, had been quite adequate for sailing on an inland sea like
the Mediterranean. The Genoese and Catalans drew beautiful
portulanos showing accurate coast outlines; with charts like these
a seaman could make any port. The wind and waves might throw

you off your course, but with land never far away, you hardly could get lost. Atlantic coasting voyages had more risk, but if you missed your bearings you could always turn in and strike land. It seemed now that such methods were no longer good enough. Henrique's pilots had to learn how they might sail into infinity for days and weeks, and not be swallowed up between the sea and sky.

The answer to this problem obviously was written in the heavens. From ancient times astronomers had known how angles might be drawn from any point on earth to the Pole Star. If mariners would have the freedom of the trackless seas, they must learn how to measure the position of their cockleshell in moving space. The compass had been brought to Europe by the Arabs long ago. The astrolabe was nothing new—Henrique's learned ancestor, Alfonso X of Castile, had owned one. The quadrant was already known to medieval observers. Henrique, with the mathematicians and astronomers that he gathered around him, studied how instruments like these might be perfected, simplified, and adapted to use at sea.

Much has been said and written of the Sagres school for pilots. The truth appears to be that there was no such thing. Henrique never founded a regular school—but his court was like a congress of experts in constant session. The Infante collected men of science all his life, nor was it ever difficult to lure them to his side. For Henrique was generous—almost too generous we gather from the fact that however much his revenues increased, he never seems to have had enough money! All those who worked for him received a rich remuneration, and no one ever left his presence, we are told, without some gift. That being so, his presence naturally was sought by many, and what more ideal patron could a sage or craftsman desire than such a munificent prince who was also a fellow worker and a fellow enthusiast?

Henrique, therefore, burned the midnight oil with a company of cosmopolitan physicists and cosmographers—most of them Jews. One of his principal collaborators was the famous Jaime of Majorca, a recent convert from the Hebrew faith. Jaime Ribes, or Jafuda Cresques—to give him his pre-Christian name—was son of the great Abraham Cresques, designer of that Catalan Atlas which may still be admired today in the Bibliothèque Nationale of France. Protected by the enlightened kings of Aragon, father and son had perfected their science and their art. Abraham worked for King Pedro I, while Jaime became cartographer to his successor, John—a learned prince and enthusiastic bibliophile, who enriched the royal library by confiscating any book he fancied from the collections of his vassals!

When the erudite but predatory John had died, a new dynasty reigned in Catalonia, leaving the aging Jaime of Majorca without his life-long patrons. Exactly when Henrique secured his services can only be surmised. It is generally supposed to have been soon after the discovery of Madeira. Jaime of Majorca was an acquisition worth having. He probably possessed copies of his father's famous maps. He had studied with that master craftsman, and no man was more skilled than he in drawing those exquisite works of art that were the Catalan coast maps.

Jaime was, moreover, an expert maker of compasses and other instruments, added to which he may have brought with him some very useful books. It seems that as a youth he had purchased part of the library left at Majorca by a Jewish physician from Greece. Jews were among the most distinguished of medieval scientists— all that survived of classic learning had remained in Greece— physicians then were usually astronomers as well—therefore the dead practitioner's collection would certainly include some works of great interest.

Altogether, Jaime of Majorca was a man after Henrique's heart.

The elderly sage and the young scholar studied nautical problems side by side, and assisted by kindred minds, with the practical experience of seamen to elucidate their theories, a new science of navigation gradually evolved. And as it grew a new species of technician was formed—those mariners expert alike in theory and in practice, the Portuguese pilots who, in the fifteenth and the sixteenth centuries, were teachers to all Europe of the science of the sea. Since the Phœnicians they were the first to sail deliberately and with assurance out into mid-ocean, to set their course with full knowledge of the prevailing winds, to find their latitude by sun and stars far out on the Atlantic, and to fix the position of their ship when leagues away from sight of land.

There must have been a number of experimental voyages. Since the high road to the far ends of the earth lay through the ocean, it was necessary to learn its mysteries well. But the problems of navigation were by no means the only difficulty. We should remember that these were tiny ships, and the Atlantic was the Great Unknown; it was impossible to calculate how long a voyage might take. Weather and wind might be unfavorable, supplies of all kinds might give out, and wooden ships may well be broken in a storm. If those desolate western reaches of the ocean had some port of call—some haven of refuge where sailors might rest and ships repair—that were indeed a blessing. This may have been the reason why Henrique sent his ships—in 1427 probably—to look for the "Lost Islands."

For it was generally surmised that there were more Atlantic islands than those which the Infante's navigators had already fixed upon the map. No one is certain how Europe became aware of the existence of a group of islands west of Finisterre, for no record of them is found in history. All that the Middle Ages knew of them figures in floating legends, maybe the echoes of a memory of Phœnician voyages long ago: Antilia, Island of the Seven

Cities, the Island of Sea Ravens—alluring names like these of visions seen and lost, are repeated in more or less fantastic travelers' tales. We may find them marked in the Catalan Atlas, and other maps of the same period, though not where any island really is. Oddly enough, the old cartographers place them much nearer Europe than are the Azores, which makes some historians believe that they are mostly guesswork. If anybody really had been there, such writers argue, he would be far more likely to exaggerate his voyage than reduce it to one-third of its length.

However that may be—and the mystery of the islands is not likely to be cleared up upon the evidence available—Henrique obviously had reason to believe in their existence, for he sent Gonçalo Velho Cabral to find them.

Gonçalo Velho was a noble knight, a valiant warrior, and experienced seaman. He had fought successfully ashore, in Africa, and done much useful work at sea in studying the Canary current. He struck out boldly towards the unknown west, and found the missing islands right enough, though nobody is certain how or when. The earliest known map to show the Azores in their proper place was drawn in 1439, and labels them as discovered in 1427. Tradition has it that the date was 1432, but not till 1439 can we find any document referring to the islands. From a royal grant signed at this date, however, we gather that by then they had been known for several years.

That is as near to certainty as we can reach. No contemporary writer records the discovery. These far-flung fragments isolated in the western sea have their first history veiled in even deeper fog than that which clouds the sister groups of Madeira and the Canaries. All that we have to go by is tradition gathered after many years, with the alternate versions and discrepancies that seldom fail to mar oral records. That Gonçalo Velho found the island of Santa Maria appears most probable, but some say that it was only upon a second voyage. The first time he set out he got no farther than those rocks which he named the Formigas, because they somehow made him think of ants. It must have been a misty day, for no island was anywhere in sight—nothing but reefs of barren rocks, between which hissed and boiled the breaking surf. Gonçalo Velho concluded that the island story was a myth—some traveler's exaggeration. He told the Infante as much, but Henrique smiled. "There is an island there," he said with conviction; "go back and find it!"

Gonçalo Velho went—so far is only tradition, but now we come to facts. He found a green and leafy island, uninhabited, almost as fair and fertile as Madeira. There were beeches growing thickly there, and cedar trees; there were laurel bushes, different kinds of heather and much pasture-land; there were streams of water flowing from the hills and, as at Madeira, no wild beasts but multitudes of fearless birds. "Gonçalo Velho's Island," his contemporaries called the place, but Santa Maria was the name that he chose for it.

This was the first of the Azores to be reclaimed from sea and solitude, and just how soon after was found the twin island of São Miguel is vague, and that there still were seven more islands, scattered much farther west, was probably not realized at once. Tradition has it that the group was named after the thousands of falcons found upon them. They may have been there at the time of the discovery, writes the Azorean, Gaspar Fructuoso, at the end of the next century, "but there are none today!" Which is quite in keeping with the general contradictoriness of everything connected with island records.

Henrique did not colonize immediately. So isolated as these islands were out in mid-ocean, there was little fear of another power stepping in. None but a Portuguese would be able to find them, anyhow, so Henrique could take his time. He chose to ship cattle there first—cows, sheep, and goats, as well as poultry. All could run free and multiply, and flourish on those pastures where no wild beast stalked. It was not until 1439 that Gonçalo Velho was authorized to take out colonists. Meanwhile, the animals upon the islands must have been useful to ships homing from the Guinea coast.

These sailings were increasing every year, for at the same time that Henrique found the islands, he broke the barrier of the South Atlantic by conquering Cape Bojador. Gil Eanes of Lagos did the deed. His first attempt was made in 1433, and it was unsuccessful. He got as far as the Canary Islands and turned back—exactly why is not explained. Perhaps because he could not override the inhibitions of his crew. Men did not hesitate to sail into the endless empty west—but then no one had ever said the west was anything but empty. It was not demon-haunted like the south!

Gil Eanes brought back some captives from the Canary Islands, and excused himself, but Henrique was getting tired of this. He had a quiet but serious talk with Gil Eanes before sending him back again. "You know," he said, "that I brought you up as a small boy, and how much confidence I have in you. That is why I have chosen you to be captain of this *barcha!* I want you to pass beyond Cape Bojador—if you do nothing more than pass this Cape, I shall be satisfied." As for the Bojador myth—that, he added, was absurd! "I am amazed that you should all have got such an idea in your heads about something which is so uncertain! I would not blame you if these things had been told by anyone who had the least authority. But you have nothing to go by but the opinion of a few sailors, who, if you take them off the Flanders run, or other ports they know, can neither navigate by compass nor by chart! Just you go, and never mind what they say, and make your voyage from which, by the grace of God, you can derive only honor and profit."

Gil Eanes, put on his mettle, vowed that this time he would not return without success, and it was many days before Henrique saw his face again. When he arrived he brought no captives with him. He bore no spoil of any kind. He came with the light of triumph in his eye, and with some withered herbs held in his hand. Yes, he had rounded Cape Bojador, and sailed beyond! It was not difficult at all. He found calm sea by the African coast, and on the shore there was nothing but sand. He landed in a boat—there were no trees in sight, nor sign of human life, only the silent desert stretching far away. The only living thing beside that stricken coast were some low-growing plants whose dried remains he showed the Infante.

"Because it seemed to me, Senhor," said Gil Eanes, "that I ought to bring you some token of the country since I landed there, I gathered these herbs which I present to Your Worship. Here we call them Roses of Santa Maria."

Henrique took the faded trophy from an arid no-man's-land. These shriveled desert flowers were the symbol of a triumph and a victory. The passage of Cape Bojador, Zurara says, was really a small thing. If its achievement had not been so long delayed, it would have passed almost unnoticed. But then Zurara writes when Bojador, and many capes beyond, had been left far behind. Viewed from a distance that first step looked very short, but there was more in it than its face value. The passage of Cape Bojador was the end of medieval geography, the triumph of experience over hearsay. From that time faith was shaken in theories built on tradition alone, and preconceived ideas became open to ques-

(113)

tion. Never again would purely mythical obstacles stand in the way of man's expansion all over the globe. Henceforth the perils to be overcome were only physical.

As everybody knows, no real danger can be so terrible as the imaginary. Once Gil Eanes had returned unscathed from south of Cape Bojador, there was no hesitation in pursuing the discovery of that coast. He himself returned there the following year, with Afonso Gonçalves Baldaia. They sailed for fifty leagues beyond the cape, and found traces of men and camels in the sand.

"Some settlement cannot be far away," Henrique said, "unless they be men upon their way to some seaport to sell their merchandise. Therefore I will send you back again in this same ship. . . . Go as far as you can, and try to bring news of these people. Capture one of them, if possible. To me it would be no small thing to have some man to tell me of this land!"

They did their best to gratify his wish. They reached the Cape, and sailed a hundred and twenty leagues farther south. They anchored their ship in a sheltered bay, and two young boys under twenty were sent inland on horseback to explore.

These lads rode seven leagues across the sandy waste before they caught sight of a group of nineteen men, all carrying spears. With the recklessness of their few years, the two young warriors charged. The risk, however, turned out to be slight. Their first sight of a European face so terrified the desert dwellers that they scuttled to the rocks. The boys pursued, and skirmished there until sunset, and then they returned to their ship to report the day's work.

Next morning, Afonso Gonçalves sought the men in vain. They had vanished into the desert and the distance, and the only living creatures to be captured were a multitude of sea lions at what seemed to be a river's mouth. Rio de Ouro, they named it, supposing it to be the River of Gold which Moorish travelers called the Senegal. But nothing golden justified the name. The coast was arid and quite empty—only a little farther down they found some beautifully woven fishing nets made of birch bark. That was all. Afonso Gonçalves sailed home again with nothing except those nets and sea-lions' skins.

Beyond this, all they brought were questions and conjectures. Who were those elusive desert men, and where their home? What manner of life did they lead? Were they Moslem or pagan? Henrique, looking from Sagres towards Africa across the sea, thought of the unknown races spread over an unknown world. His followers had failed to make contact with the mysterious strangers who had only shown themselves, and disappeared like wraiths in the Sahara rocks. The dark continent kept its secrets still inviolate, but already the time had come when one by one they would be brought to light. It was only a question of going on. The end might be far off in time and space, enormous trials and hardships might attend the way, but with the passage of Cape Bojador the first step had been made upon a trail that was to lead across the world to India.

X

Family Interlude

WHILE Henrique colonized the desert islands of the ocean and pondered on the mysteries of the deep, his brother Pedro wandered all around Christendom. Nine years passed before he came home—the most traveled prince of his age and generation.

How far his wanderings took him is uncertain. Tradition has it that he visited the Holy Land, Syria, and Egypt, and documentary proof remains of an extensive European tour. We know that Pedro spent some years in Hungary fighting for the Emperor Sigismund, who vested him with the title of Margrave of Treviso. He subsequently journeyed to Paris, it seems, and some say that he visited the King of Denmark. He went to England certainly, and there in 1425 was "honorably received and feasted" by his cousins.

Although they made him welcome, Pedro did not stay with them long. England was not a happy realm just then. The visitor found his relatives at daggers drawn over the cradle of their hapless infant king. They say that Pedro did his best to reconcile his uncle Beaufort with the Duke of Gloucester. The Protector and Bishop, however, could not agree, so Pedro left them to their squabbling and embarked for Flanders.

He spent Christmas at Bruges, as may be gathered from the archives of that town where the visit of "Dom Pierre, fils du roi de Portugal" is on record. A tournament was held in Pedro's honor by the citizens, and their young duke, Philippe of Burgundy, gave a hunting party for him at Wynendale Castle.

Pedro lingered a year or more with his future brother-in-law, and from the Netherlands he wrote Duarte some instructive letters. In spite of separation Duarte and Pedro continued to be each one the other's oracle, and at his brother's request the traveler sent home some pages of advice upon administration. "I know," writes Pedro in conclusion of this letter, "that through my absence you and the Lord King are more burdened with work, but if God bring me safely back again, I hope I may relieve you of that which you bear on my behalf, and I will help you in every way I can."

On the strength of this praiseworthy resolve, Pedro started for home, traveling via Italy where he arrived in March of 1428. The Lords of Venice gave him a magnificent reception, turning out to meet him with a fleet of gondolas. Venice, close to the gates of the Levant, was the emporium of medieval Europe, and the terminus of trade with the forbidden Orient, now all but closed to Christian penetration. In Venice Pedro certainly made observations for Henrique's benefit, and there he gathered at the same time some valuable mementos of his visit. The Venetians offered him a Latin version of the Book of Marco Polo, besides a fine map of all parts of the world then known, compiled from information supplied by Arab traders who traveled to the lands of spices.

Bearing these gifts for his brother's delight, Pedro went on to Rome, where we find him in May. After a short stay at the pontifical court, the Infante set sail for Spain. He visited the kings of Castile and Navarre, and then at last reached Portugal in September and so was able to be present at Duarte's wedding.

It was time that the heir to the throne should take himself a wife. So far, the only married member of the family was the younger Infante, D. João, who four years previously had been united to the daughter of his half brother the Count of Barcelos —a charming girl of about João's own age.

Neither Henrique nor Fernando seem ever to have been upon the marriage market, but Duarte's prospects had given rise to discussion from time to time. Neither he nor anybody else seems to have taken very seriously the question of betrothal to the Queen of Naples, but Duarte really had a fright in 1411 when it was suggested to cement the peace with Castile by marrying the heir of Portugal to the small Castilian Infanta. Poor Duarte had protested vigorously. This marriage was impossible, he said. He could not have a wife of four years old, when he was twenty! Duarte's father showed himself more considerate than many another kingly parent of that period. He did not insist on sacrificing an unwilling son to politics. It seems that he did not bring pressure to bear on any of his children, and at the age of thirty-seven Duarte was a bachelor still.

By then he was ready to change his state. The chosen bride was Leonor of Aragon, a sister to the reigning king, and the marriage was celebrated at Coimbra. The bridegroom's brothers all were there. Pedro arrived just in time, as we have seen; João and Fernando came too; while Henrique, turning his back for once on his cartographers and his astronomy, left all to join the family for the joyful occasion. For some reason—illness perhaps—their father was not present, to his profound regret, no doubt, but greatly to our gain. It is to his absence that we owe a full description of the wedding, written by Henrique for his father's benefit.

There is not much suggesting the "recluse of Sagres" in this letter. Henrique seems to have enjoyed Duarte's wedding, and found that it is fun to watch your brother fall in love! Duarte lost his heart at once to Leonor, but we gather from Henrique that he was a most decorous lover. During the week before the wedding he visited his fiancée two or three times every day, but— "So far as I know," Henrique writes, "in all this while he never kissed her once!"

The festivities went off with great éclat. There were hunting parties, bullfights, and balls. Henrique tells his father with much satisfaction how he killed a boar, and how two of his pages "slew very skillfully" a little bull.

The bridegroom left these fiercer joys to the heart-whole. He had better things to think about than bulls or boars! His Leonor was wonderful! Duarte felt himself to be a lucky man. "He is very happy," the observant brother writes, "and highly praises the singing of the Lady Infanta, and her playing on the minicord, and her style of dancing."

The bride was staying at the convent of Santa Clara, which held the sacred relics of her kinswoman, Saint Isabel of Aragon. People felt that the saint was thus sponsoring the wedding, for it seemed, Henrique says, that Leonor "was marrying from the house of Queen Isabel."

On September 22nd she became Duarte's wife, in a church all hung with crimson and brocade. The happy couple knelt upon a hassock of cloth of gold, before an altar resplendent with silver. The tall athletic figure of the bridegroom was set off to best advantage by a costly tunic with "his emerald as a clasp." Manlike, Henrique does not attempt description of the bride's attire beyond saying that she was "very richly dressed." Her clothes were more splendid than comfortable, it seems, for by the time the long service was over, poor Leonor "was so exhausted by her mantle which was very heavy, and by the heat of the good people there, besides that of the torches which was great, that when we wanted to lead her away, she fainted. . . ." However, "we dashed water over her, and she came to. . . ." So all was well.

After a short rest at the convent, which she must have badly needed, the bride was fetched away by the Infantes Pedro and Henrique, who led her to her husband's house. She rode across the town on a white palfrey harnessed with gold caparisons which were a gift from the King D. João, her father-in-law. Sixty torch-bearers walked in front, the two Infantes held her bride-reins, and all her ladies came on foot behind.

We do not hear of any wedding banquet being served that night; but there were songs and dances, and a light supper of fruit and wine served to the bridegroom by his brothers who acted as waiters. Then everyone withdrew, leaving the happy pair, and so, Henrique ends his letter to his father, "The Lady Infanta is now wholly your daughter."

D. João's new daughter was a good-looking girl with all the average virtues and social accomplishments. With due respect to Duarte, one cannot say that there was anything remarkable about her character or mind, but in his eyes she seemed a paragon. Duarte, at the age of thirty-seven, approached matrimony with all his ideals quite undimmed and his reverence for womanhood intact. His early adoration of his mother had made him inclined to set all women on a pedestal, and the image of the Temptress that medieval theologians paint so black finds no place in Duarte's philosophy. Women are mostly good, he writes, and "though one may censure those that fail—as we too fail—we should remember that in the majority of cases the first fault lies with us."

Having firm faith in womanly virtue, Duarte cannot understand a jealous husband. "A man may feel," he says, "that there is not much perfection in him to be loved," but a good woman will be true to her husband out of "her own virtue and goodness, by which such women will pass over many faults." In any case, the writer is convinced, where there is jealousy there cannot be true love, for love is based on perfect trust.

Most fifteenth-century moralists have solemn and impressive things to say on the subject of wifely obedience. It was a matter upon which a man felt strongly, but the chivalrous Duarte does not hold one-sided views. If a husband would be obeyed, he thinks, the best way that he can obtain it is by winning his wife's love. "Let him strive to do so," Duarte insists; "let him treat her with unfailing courtesy; let him honor her and cherish her, and study to meet her wishes in everything he can!" The woman who did not give her heart to such a husband would be a strange creature. There is no doubt that Leonor loved Duarte well.

But she made no place in her affection for her husband's favorite brother. Unfortunately for herself and him, Leonor never took to Pedro. Henrique she liked very much. He had the pleasant manners that distinguished all his family, and as he lived in a world of his own—a world that Leonor would never dream of entering—there never was occasion to come up against him. How could you quarrel with a man whose whole interests were centered on things so impersonal as seas and stars, and lands where nobody one knew had ever been? But the enigmatic Pedro—that citizen of the world, who had read so much and seen so much, and looked on life with a detached and slightly disillusioned smile— puzzled and irritated his sister-in-law. Pedro was quite as clever as Duarte, she could see, and much more critical. No doubt Duarte often talked above her head, but then he never guessed it! Pedro, whose eye was keen and not blinded by love, could see her limitations far too well, and the fact that he and Duarte understood each other perfectly would not fail to annoy Duarte's wife, who may have felt a little out of it. Leonor was jealous of Pedro's influence over her husband—added to which he placed himself beyond the pale of her regard by marrying the daughter of her father's rival, the Count of Urgel, who once had claimed

the throne of Aragon. It is doubtful if she told Duarte what she
felt upon the subject—he would have been incapable of understanding such a petty spite—but Leonor never forgave Pedro for
giving her this sister-in-law.

Pedro's marriage took place in 1429—shortly before that of
his sister Isabel. We do not know why Isabel remained single so
long, unless it was that D. João had only just awoken to the fact
that his daughter was thirty-two, and still unwed! "I hope that
you will marry her soon," his dying wife had begged him fourteen
years ago. The sorrowing king had promised that he would not
fail to do so, but he was evidently in no hurry to part with his
Isabel. At last the evil day could be put off no longer. The king
was aging fast, and wished to see his children settled in life before he died. Therefore ambassadors from Flanders were welcomed to Portugal, and Van Eyck painted the Infanta's likeness
to show his lord.

Philippe of Burgundy, looking around for a third wife, studied
the portraits of likely princesses with a scrutinizing eye. It seems
that Isabel's picture was the one that pleased him the most, and
so he made proposals for her hand.

The feasts and pageantry that celebrated the Infanta's nuptials
seem to have been more splendid than those held for any of her
brothers. But then Duarte, Pedro, and João had married peninsular brides—such weddings were *en famille* in a way. D. João knew
all about the magnificence of the Netherlands, and did not wish
the foreigners to say that things were not done well in Portugal!
His treasury might crack under the strain, but his daughter must
have a dowry of 200,000 crowns, and the Flemish delegates who
came to fetch her were loaded with gifts, and entertained with
tournaments and banquets quite regardless of expense. Isabel
sailed in January, 1430, escorted by her youngest brother Fernando, and the nation no doubt felt a little flat and dull after two

years of feasts and junketings attendant upon three royal weddings.

The king was perhaps glad to have some quiet. D. João was over seventy and feeling his age. Already his sons did all his work for him, but being both tactful and dutiful, they never let their father feel that he was on the shelf. "The more he advanced in years," Duarte writes, "the more reverence we showed him, always submitting our wishes to him, and following his recommendations. . . ." Thus D. João's declining days were pleasant and peaceful. He could look back upon a strenuous but a satisfactory life. His luck had held from the moment in 1385 when he was proclaimed king until that August day in 1433 when he lay dying in his Lisbon palace with his sons gathered round his bed.

His reign had been half a century of continuous success, and blessings wrested for himself and others. He had saved his country from a foreign yoke; he had brought back peace and plenty to the land; he had given the nation five sons who were its pride; he was respected abroad and beloved at home. He was the first king to plant the flag of Portugal beyond the sea and add to the royal titles that of Senhor de Ceuta. In his old age he had beheld the colonizing of the desert islands of the Atlantic, and seen his favorite son started on a career that was to change the world. Exactly how much did that mean to D. João, who lived to see the dawn of a new age? Perhaps he scarcely noticed it. Ceuta seems to have been nearer to his heart than islands of the ocean of mysterious continents. Henrique—man of science and crusader —embraced in his outlook both the future and the past; his father's face was turned to the crusade alone. It seems he would have crossed to Africa in his old age, and ended his days there fighting the Moors. His sons prevailed on him to stay at home; but he charged them never to forget the holy war.

(123)

There was an eclipse of the sun on the day that D. João died, and all his weeping subjects dressed themselves in white sackcloth. They bore his coffin into the cathedral and laid it before the altar of St. Vincent, and the next day they proclaimed the new king.

Duarte had been governing in his father's name for several years, but he took up his heritage as if it were a heavy burden to be borne for duty's sake. That morning he confessed himself and took the Sacrament before preparing to appear upon the public square. As he arrayed himself in the royal robes, the Jewish physician, Mestre Guedelha, came to his side in great distress. He begged Duarte to postpone his proclamation until after midday— "Please God, it will be for your advantage, and the good of the realm. The hour that you have chosen is unfortunate, and the planets are unfavorable!"

Duarte shrugged his shoulders. "Mestre Guedelha," he said, "I know it is your love for me that causes your concern. I have no doubt that astrology is a lawful science, and that terrestrial bodies are subject to the celestial. But first and foremost I believe that God is over all, and all things are ordered by His hand. Therefore this charge that by His grace I am about to take is His, and in His name and in hope of His help I assume it, humbly praying that He may teach me to govern this His people that He has committed to my care, in such a way as He may best be served."

"God grant it may be so!" replied the Jew. "But what harm would there be in putting off the ceremony for a little while?"

"I shall not do that," said Duarte firmly, "because I ought not. It would appear as if I had no faith in God."

Mestre Guedelha withdrew wrapped in gloom. Duarte's reign would be short and unfortunate, he said. The King was quite unmoved, and at the appointed hour he appeared before the people in his royal robes.

The morning sun lit up a brilliant scene. The vast Terreiro do Paço—Lisbon's historic square beside the river—was all bedecked with draperies and flags. In the center, on a dais, was raised the royal throne, on which the new king took his seat, with his brothers and the great lords of the realm standing around. D. Pedro de Menezes, Count of Viana and Captain of Ceuta, held the Royal Standard furled in his right hand. The Bishop of Evora, splendid in pontifical robes, harangued the people to present them their new king. The heralds ordered silence then, the Count unwound the banner to the breeze, while in a ringing voice he raised the cry of: "*Real! Real! Real!* [1] for Dom Duarte of Portugal, our Lord!" The shout was caught up by the noblemen around the throne, and roared back by the crowd assembled in the square as though the heavens thundered. The Infantes and lords and knights then knelt to kiss their sovereign's hands and do him homage.

The whole show moved Duarte more to melancholy than to exaltation. "Bishop," he said, as the prelate returned to his place, "do you not think that it would be a good thing at the end of this ceremony to burn some tow before me here, as a reminder that the glory and pomp of this world are brief and fleeting?"

"It seems to me, Senhor," the Bishop answered sensibly, "that since you are so fully conscious of this fact, such demonstration is unnecessary!"

The royal *cortège* withdrew into the Palace on the square, while the standard-bearer and the lords rode all around the town, repeating the proclamation in every quarter till they reached the castle hill and planted the Royal Standard on the highest tower.

The court resumed its mourning weeds. The coffin of the late king was carried in solemn state and by slow stages to the monas-

---

[1] This cry, the literal translation of which is "Royal! Royal! Royal!" was raised in every town of medieval Portugal at the accession of a new king.

tery of Batalha, while all the church bells in the land were tolled, and all the nation wept. Beneath the Gothic vault raised by himself in memory of Aljubarrota, D. João was laid to rest beside his queen.

Duarte squared his shoulders and—supported by the usual paper of advice from Pedro—faced his reign.

Henrique, whom neither love, nor life, nor death, could divert from the purpose of his soul, returned to the study of Atlantic winds, a problem that his pilots were just beginning to understand.

XI

Tangier

THE Infante D. Fernando was troubled and perplexed. Since boyhood he had led a quiet and sheltered life. Up to the age of twenty-five his health had been so bad that no one ever thought about a military career for him. He does not seem to have considered it himself. He never even contemplated marriage. He was quite happy in his simple way, administering his properties at Salvaterra and at Atouguia, acting as guide, philosopher, and friend to a small household that adored him, and reading the *Lives of the Saints*, the *Sermons of St. Augustine*, and other such refreshing works collected in his "great and noble library."

Fernando fed the hungry all around. On each birthday he clothed as many poor as were the number of his years, and when he had no money left to give, he explained this to the beggars so sweetly that they went off satisfied! For Fernando loved everyone, and everyone loved him. His powers of persuasion had even converted many Jews and Moors, whose change of heart, we trust, may not be attributed to the fact that subsequently Fernando maintained them.

He had a beautifully appointed chapel of his own, served by a chaplain who had learned at Salisbury to celebrate the holy rites after the manner used in that famous cathedral. There choral Mass was daily sung, sermons were preached on all the festivals, and two on every Sunday during Lent.

All these things made Fernando's life agreeable and interesting. His troubles only seem to have begun when Duarte succeeded to the throne, and made this youngest brother Master of the Knights of Aviz.

This dignity was one of the highest in the realm, and Fernando, accepting it under protest, saw the end of his peaceful unworldly life. The Master of Aviz had to maintain a great household. He must travel in style about the land, with an imposing train of followers. He must work for the glory of the Order and the advancement of its knights, all of whom would expect Fernando to sponsor their kindred.

Poor Fernando—conscientious like all his family—worried dreadfully over everything. When crowds of petitioners waited on him, soliciting what he was unable to give, he was truly distressed. When the men of his retinue, billeted on the citizens of any town, did not behave themselves, he felt responsible and he suffered acutely. When the funds of the Order proved inadequate to meet the expenses of a Master whose private means were small, Fernando did not like to ask his brother to help him out of the royal exchequer.

Above all, Fernando feared for his spiritual life, now that so much time must be devoted to mundane matters. He who would serve God ought not to be hampered by worldly cares—the Holy Scriptures made this clear—and more than anything Fernando wanted to serve God.

He decided that he must leave it all, and go abroad. He thought that if he went to live in England his problems might be simplified. He could count on a welcome from his mother's family, and as Aviz was not an international order, its Master would not be a great man outside Portugal. Fernando felt convinced that he could live there simply, but comfortably, on any pension assigned to him for his services—military services, of course. A prince could have no other kind to offer, and Fernando would not be sorry for the chance to do some deed of arms.

Some deed of arms—this was another matter that had begun to weigh upon his mind. Master of an order of warrior knights, his own knighthood was purely honorary. He had never taken part in any battle. Alone among his brothers, Fernando had never had the chance to win his spurs. It is true that he was never robust, as they were, but all the same his health had much improved of recent years. He seemed to have outgrown most of his youthful weakness, and so he felt ashamed to remember that he had yet had no experience of war.

One day he broached the subject to Duarte, and begged him for his permission to go abroad: "If ever you have need of me at any time," he promised solemnly, "and I should hear of it, though I were Emperor of Germany, or Greece, be certain that I should obey your summons!"

Duarte smiled and shook his head. "Brother," he said, "don't ask me that!" If Fernando were to leave the country as soon as Duarte succeeded to the throne, people would say that they did not get on together. "It would seem as if my rule were so hard and harsh that you could not endure it—or that I wanted the kingdom all to myself for my sons, which God knows is not true!" He wished that he could give Fernando more towards his maintenance—perhaps one day it might be possible—but the kingdom was small, and their father had been obliged to distribute most of its lands among those who had helped him to the throne. But —Duarte concluded on an elder-brotherly tone—"if you would have the blessing of the Queen, our Lady Mother, you should be satisfied with little in this realm rather than seek for more among strangers. She who was so wise, and who loved us so much, advised us so at the hour of her death, and so she would have said to you, had you been old enough."

(129)

"Sir," answered Fernando respectfully, "God knows that I should never wish to displease you in any way, but since you are my brother, and like a father to me, you should desire my honor and advancement. You know that I have never done a knightly deed!" Duarte, Pedro and Henrique had been at the conquest of Ceuta. João had gone there with Henrique later when the city was besieged. Thus all four brothers had obtained their knighthood, "but I alone," Fernando concluded sadly, "though I am older than you were at that time, have not yet earned it, and there does not seem to be a hope!"

Duarte sighed and said that he would see what could be done. This was the third request for leave of absence that he had received since his accession. His nephew, the Count of Arraiolos—the son of their half-brother of Barcelos—had been suing for permission to help the King of Castile with the conquest of Granada. The Count of Ourem, Arraiolos' brother, was also clamoring to go abroad. Besides these, Duarte's sister, Isabel, had written from the Netherlands inviting Henrique to her husband's court. Did everybody want to go away? About Henrique, at least, Duarte felt sure. Henrique would not be tempted so far from Sagres and his beloved islands. It was therefore Henrique whom he consulted on the subject of Fernando's problems. Perhaps Henrique would persuade their younger brother to give up his plan.

But Henrique said that Fernando was quite right! He could not be expected to spend his life doing nothing. But, as the treasurer João Afonso had suggested long ago, Henrique said that Fernando need not seek foreign courts. A new crusade against the Moors would provide ample scope for anyone's ambition. Henrique was ready to go to Ceuta with him, and thence attempt the conquest of Tangier. The enterprise was peculiarly suitable to them who were respectively Master of the Order of Cristo and of Aviz—and both of them were free. "We have neither wife nor hildren to hold us back. Give us leave to cross over to Africa, where with our households and our servants, and the knights of Cristo and Aviz, we can fight the Infidel, and so serve God and you!"

Duarte hesitated. The proposal was not new. The pursuit of he conquest of Morocco had often been discussed during his father's lifetime. In fact D. João on his dying bed had charged it s a sacred duty to his heir. "On this subject," Duarte writes, "were the last words that he was well able to speak to us, and many times he spoke to us in terms that greatly constrained us o continue this conquest." His father's wish had always been Duarte's law. He fully intended to obey D. João's command— his only doubt was if the moment was yet ripe. The first few decades of the fifteenth century were a time of economic crisis and of trade depression throughout Europe. Portugal, emerging from a prolonged war, had not escaped. "The people of my realm," Duarte pointed out to Henrique, "need a period of rest o repair their past losses. My treasury is exhausted by the charges that it has had to meet"—family weddings, in fact, had all but cleared it out!—"and you know what Ceuta costs to keep. Try and quiet Fernando as well as you can, but don't repeat this conversation. He would only get excited and give me more trouble."

Henrique promised, without enthusiasm, to do what he could. He did speak to Fernando, it appears, but it is difficult to carry a conviction that we do not feel. His words had no effect upon his brother at all.

Duarte, on the other hand, was ruminating Henrique's suggestion. Much might be said against it at the present time, but there were certain reasons in its favor. It was true that the people wanted rest and peace, but what about the upper classes? The knights and gentlemen had no use for such tame blessings, and one could not afford to ignore their desires. A number of them

(131)

were at a loose end. Their swords were eating through the sheaths, and if they could not swing them in the service of their king they would seek for employment with a foreign master, and then what would become of home defense? Communications were not such that you could recall your subjects at short notice from any part of Europe. The kingdom was not threatened at the time, but a small country overshadowed by a powerful neighbor can never be wholly carefree. Although the parties had signed everlasting peace, the everlastingness of treaties, as Duarte knew, like time itself, is only relative. The Castilians had not forgotten nor forgiven past defeats, and—writes Duarte—"considering the greatness of their territory, and the multitude of their people, continually behave in a manner that is hard to endure!" Their king was growing querulous of late upon the subject of Portuguese expansion. The Castilians who, twenty years ago, had accepted the conquest of Ceuta without turning a hair, seemed suddenly to have discovered that North Africa formed part of Castile's vital space!

That old bone of contention, the Canary Islands, provoked this attitude. Henrique had tried to persuade the Pope to make over to him all islands of the group that were not occupied. The Holy Father said that Portugal might take them with his blessing, as well as any other territory the Portuguese might discover in Africa upon the sole condition that they instructed the natives in the Christian faith. This called forth bitter complaints from Castile. The Canaries had been bestowed on the Castilian crown in 1344 by Pope Clement VI. Not all the islands had been occupied as yet, but they would be one day, and the King of Castile was just as anxious as the King of Portugal for the islanders' spiritual welfare!

It was a little awkward for the Pope, the more so that he did not really care who had the islands. He sent a vague but soothing Bull to Portugal. He had not realized, he said, that the Canaries were disposed of. He expressed the paternal hope that Portugal would deal kindly with Castilian interests.

The Castilians, however, were growing more emphatic in their claims. At the Council of Bâle, their delegates upheld that the Canaries formed part of the African kingdom of Tingitania which, like Mauretania, might *de facto* be in Moorish hands, but *de jure* ought to have been Castilian. These lands had formerly been ruled by Gothic kings, and the princes of the royal house of Castile were their lawful heirs.

Duarte and Henrique did not like the turn affairs were taking. Did Castile contemplate the conquest of Tangier? If Portugal did not make progress in Africa, there might be complications. A new Moroccan enterprise would combine the advantages of stealing a march on Castile and providing restless spirits with an outlet not too far from home.

It would serve yet another useful purpose beyond that. To have a war of one's own was an acceptable excuse for keeping out of other people's quarrels. In 1435 Duarte had renewed the Anglo-Portuguese alliance and was expecting any day to be invited to send troops to France. Added to this, the King of Aragon, his brother-in-law, seemed to be counting on Duarte's assistance against his foes, and it has never suited Portugal to be involved in European wars. Everything considered, therefore, was not Henrique right? Might not this be the most propitious time for the fulfilment of D. João's dying wish?

Pedro did not agree. It was perhaps the first and only time in which he and Duarte failed to see eye to eye. Duarte's views upon the subject had naturally been colored by years of association with his father and Henrique, to both of whom the conquest of Morocco was of great importance. Pedro, on the other hand, had returned from his long absence abroad cured of his youthful enthusiasm for Ceuta. Henrique's explorations delighted him. Such

enterprise he would support with all his heart, but seizing strongholds in North Africa left him quite cold. They were so costly to
maintain, he said.

Duarte granted him that Ceuta was costly. It figured in his
budget to the tune of 28,500 ducats a year! But that was because
it was an isolated fortress in a hostile country. Let Portugal obtain possession of Alcacer and Tangier, and the position would be
different. The Moors would have no easy base for their attacks,
and the agricultural resources of the country could be exploited.

Pedro continued to affirm that the scheme was unsound, and
that was quite enough to make Queen Leonor throw all her
weight on to the other side. She disliked Pedro, as we know,
whereas Henrique was her favorite brother-in-law, and she was
flattered when he had a talk with her, explaining the desirability
of a new African campaign, and why he was urging the King to
send him and Fernando overseas.

"Brother," said Leonor impressively, "if my feeble understanding does not deceive me, your request is just, honest, and holy—
worthy of such a prince and knight as you! If I can be of any use,
I shall gladly intercede with the King my Lord, for his good and
for your honor and satisfaction." So to this laudable purpose she
used her blandishments.

Some historians are quite convinced that Leonor's intervention
won the day, and shake their heads at Duarte as a weak man.
Others, with equal confidence maintain that it is foolish to suppose that she had anything to do with it. The truth most probably
lies in between. Leonor was an assertive little person, as later
events were to show. That she should join in this debate is quite
in character, but the fact that her views carried some weight with
Duarte does not prove necessarily that he was weak—only that
he was human. If a husband is weak who is influenced in any way
by the opinions of the woman that he loves, then there are no

strong men! It is natural that Leonor's support of Henrique's scheme should help to balance Pedro's disapproval, but at the same time her responsibility ought not to be exaggerated. There is clear documentary evidence that Duarte had been considering a new crusade in Africa for many years—the idea dated from before his marriage. It was his wish to continue with this conquest, and when in 1436 the military and diplomatic situation seemed to favor the enterprise, he sent for his brothers at Leiria and explained his views. The Infantes Pedro and João and the Count of Barcelos were invited to say what they thought. There was no need to consult Fernando or Henrique—everyone knew what their answer would be.

The Infante João would not commit himself. He made a curious speech. War with the Infidel, he said, might be considered from two points of view—that of honor, or that of common sense. "The two do not agree." There clearly was no sense in rushing into war when one was not obliged, and was it really serving God to drag the people off to a crusade? The knights and fidalgos no doubt went willingly, but the common people never liked to leave their homes and farms: "They will go cursing, and reluctantly" —what merit could they gain from slaying Moors in such a frame of mind? "They would be sinning no less than if they were killing Christians." And did God really want one to kill Moors? Could it be serving Him to give the devil all those souls? "If we are to be guided by the doctrines and teaching of Jesus Christ and His apostles it is not certain that He would have us make war upon the Moors. I know that the Holy Scripture enjoins us to convert them by teaching and by the virtuous example of our lives!" If the Lord had intended forcible conversions, He would have ordered us to make them, "and this I have never seen, nor heard that such could be found in authentic Scripture."

The indulgences that the Pope granted to crusaders made no

impression upon João's unmedieval mind: "Just send a thousand doubloons to any cardinal," he said, "for any little charity, and he will get you papal indulgences with even greater blessings!" Nor was he less sceptical about the tales of miracles vouchsafed by Heaven for crusaders' benefit. "One hears of such things," he remarked, "even in wars waged between Christians—and those, whatever way you look at them, cannot be God's service!"

Neither from the point of view of practical business did common sense uphold Moroccan enterprise. The risk was great and the profit uncertain. To be engaged in adventures abroad might lay the country open to invasion by the enemy at hand. What would be the use of gaining Tangier, and Arzila too, if Portugal were lost? Nor was there pleasure to be found in such an undertaking. "I can see nothing in it but expense, toil and care; perils by sea and land; death, wounds, maiming of limbs, sickness, captivity; famine, thirst, cold, and heat!" Such was the case for common sense, concluded D. João.

Having no doubt shocked his hearers by some of his revolutionary ideas, the speaker suddenly came back to his own century. Honor, he said, saw things quite differently from common sense, and he proceeded to demolish one by one his former arguments. The knightly obligation to bear arms, the holiness of war against the Infidels, the text, "Take up thy cross and follow Me"—all these were marshaled in João's exposition of what honor had to say. Even the spirit-shackling question of hard cash was airily dismissed. What was the use of hoarding treasure, which sooner or later was sure to be lost? "Money is mixed with quicksilver," he said, "and just as easily it runs away!"

After thus summing up both sides, João sat down. "I leave the decision to you!" he told Duarte. Perhaps he was not sorry that it did not lie with him. We know too little about this Infante to be sure if the second part of his speech was sarcastic, or if he was propounding a debate that continued in his own mind—questions that might perplex a thoughtful soul in that age of transition.

However that may be, there was no ambiguity in the other two speakers. The Count of Barcelos declared himself convinced by the arguments attributed to common sense. It was a beautiful and very flowery speech, observed the Count admiringly, but the "true flower" was found in the first part. "You should not pursue this war at the present time!"

Pedro spoke quietly with a touch of irony. Why consult them at all, he asked, since Duarte had already made up his mind? Nobody cares to be opposed—particularly kings! All the same, Pedro declared himself frankly against the Tangier enterprise. Think how expensive it was going to be, and "I know that you have no money!" Besides, what was the use of such conquests? "Suppose you take not only Tangier, but Alcacer and Arzila too—what will you do with them? To man them from this poor and depopulated realm would be impossible. . . . You would most certainly lose Portugal and not gain Africa!"

Pedro, in fact, saw all the objections that his father had raised long ago when the conquest of Ceuta was first proposed. It was the son who had convinced the father in its favor then, but now he had arrived at his parent's first point of view. He thought the conquest of Morocco wholly chimerical, and "if your intention in all this is to serve God," he told Duarte severely, "I beg you to consider how you ought to do so, and not what you would like to do or think you can!"

Duarte took the brotherly admonishment in quite good part— he and Pedro would never quarrel with each other. He decided none the less in favor of the expedition, and Pedro helped ungrudgingly with all the preparations.

These did not go as smoothly as might be desired. To begin

with it was necessary to persuade the Cortes to allow the country to be taxed, and this was granted without enthusiasm. Then there was the question of raising men. Duarte calculated that to take Tangier a force of 14,000 would be necessary, and the number was not easy to make up. The problem of transport had also to be solved, for the ships available in home ports were quite insufficient. A messenger was sent to charter ships from England, Germany, Biscay, and Flanders, but all these countries had wars of their own, and most of the vessels were not forthcoming.

At last, Henrique decided to sail with such troops as might be embarked in the ships that he had. The rest could follow when the foreign fleet arrived or, failing this, the men could proceed overland to Gibraltar, where any kind of boat would do to cross the narrow straits.

Henrique and Fernando were both anxious to be gone. The one was quietly happy to embark upon a holy war, the crusade was an end in itself to him—to his brother it was a glorious means towards a still more glorious goal. Moorish Tangier beside Cape Spartel overlooked that Atlantic highway that Henrique hoped to win. The conquest of Tangier would be a new link in the chain he meant to cast around the world—a step towards a greater crusade than man had yet seen.

Each brother made his will, and the two bachelor uncles decided to make Duarte's second son their heir. Henrique went further than this. Already he was godfather to little Fernando, and now he signed a document declaring that he took the boy as his adopted son—"for I have no child of my own, nor expect to have any. . . ."

All the summer of 1437 the kingdom hummed with industry as it had in 1415. This time, however, lacked the atmosphere of mystery that had exercised the popular imagination twenty years ago. Officially nothing was given out, but most people seem to have known quite well that the objective was Tangier. The Moors themselves did not doubt it, and prepared accordingly.

On July 13th the King and Queen, the five Infantes and the court, climbed Lisbon's steepest hill to the Carmelite church where the hero of their youth, Nunalvares, lay buried under a flat stone before the altar. There the Bull of Crusade was read, and a burning sermon urged all men to join the sacred cause. The next Sunday, in the Cathedral, Henrique and Fernando took the Cross from the hands of the Bishop of Ceuta.

With holy relics borne in front, led by the faded banner that Nunalvares had carried to his battles, the royal procession wound down to the river shore where the fleet rode at anchor, all sails ready to unfurl. A knight in shining armor bore Henrique's standard with the crimson cross of his own Order, and Fernando displayed St. Michael on his flag.

The ships slipped down the current to Restelo, near Belem, and lingered there for a few days while the Infantes made their final preparations and their last farewells. The Infante Fernando was ill at the time, and shivering with fever, but he was careful to ignore the fact, for fear that their departure would be delayed.

Duarte heard Mass with his brothers on the last day, and remained with them on their ship until the hour of sailing. Needless to say the usual paper of good counsel was produced—no brother of Duarte or Pedro would be deprived of that! Henrique was cautioned by two such documents, carefully written out in Duarte's own hand. One was devoted to considerations of moral uplift, the other gave detailed instructions for guidance on the campaign. This last Duarte begged his brother to read over many times, and bear all its points well in mind. "Write to me as soon as you reach Ceuta," urged the King, "and I shall make arrangements both by sea and land for you to send me your news every day."

A note of anxiety may be detected in Duarte's admonishments, which may surprise us who are accustomed to think about Henrique only as a quiet and steady man. We remember him principally as a patient seeker and laborious organizer, but it seems that his family saw him in quite another light. Contemporary papers would suggest that they considered him as a firebrand! They had not forgotten his brilliant but dare-devil exploits at the conquest of Ceuta, nor how upon his second visit there his father had to recall him in haste to prevent him from rashly attacking Gibraltar. On no account should the Infante be sent to Africa— Henrique's nephew, the Count of Ourem, had written in 1433— "he would be sure to launch out in some weighty enterprise with insufficient force at his command!" Clearly, Henrique on the battlefield was quite a different man than in his study, and his relations perhaps had good reason to doubt if such a reckless warrior could be a very safe commander.

On this occasion he promised Duarte to be circumspect in everything. The King embraced his brothers, and rowed back to shore, hoping for the best. The ships weighed anchor one by one and crossed the bar. The summer north wind filled their sails and blew them out to sea. Ahead lay Africa, Ceuta and Tangier. For good or ill the die was cast.

XII

The Sacrifice

THE Count D. Pedro de Menezes, already aged and infirm,
after defending Ceuta for twenty years, welcomed Henrique's army to the town.

It was a fine body of men, led by the noblest fidalgos of Portugal, but were its numbers adequate? the veterans of the garrison
suggested. A muster of the forces registered two thousand horse,
a thousand bowmen, and three thousand infantry—did the Infantes hope to take a city like Tangier with only those? It would
be wiser for them to remain at Ceuta, and thence harry the Moors.

Henrique was reminded of the objections raised by his father's
counselors on that occasion long ago when the royal fleet lay at
anchor in the Straits: Better to land a few troops only—Better go
home—Better try taking Gibraltar instead! The dictates of audac-
ity had then prevailed, and brought about an easy and spectacular success. Was the position not the same today?

"I know," said the Infante, "that the men are very few for this
great enterprise, but it appears that God ordains and wills that
we, just as we are, should undertake this labor for His service and
increase of our honor. Be sure that even if I had still fewer men,
I would not remain in this town as you suggest, nor fail to pursue
that for which I came!"

The seasoned warriors of Ceuta had no answer to this. Across

the sun-browned hills via Tetuan, Henrique led his men towards
Tangier.

It was a brilliant and distinguished company. We find among
them all the names that shine in the history of Portugal, borne by
men who were sons and ancestors of heroes.

The Count of Arraiolos, grandson of Nunalvares, led the van-
guard, followed by half a dozen Castros. The Marshal Vasco Fernandes Coutinho was there too, and the Infante Pedro's dearest
friend, Captain Alvaro Vaz de Almada, who had fought for
Henry V at Agincourt and been rewarded by the title of Count
of Avranches. The Menezes line, of past and future fame in the
annals of Portuguese Morocco, was represented by Duarte, the old
count's son, who deputizing for his father as King's Ensign, was
carrying the Royal Standard. There was João Gonçalves Zarco, the
discoverer of Madeira, and Fernandalvares Cabral, whose grandson found Brazil. There were Melos, and there were Cunhas,
Sousas, and Azevedos, as well as Ataidez, and at least one Albu-
querque.

With the lords temporal there came those of the Church. Like
Turpin with the paladins of Charlemagne, the gallant Bishop of
Ceuta rode to war. All his clergy followed behind, their carnal
weapons amply reinforced by an efficacious collection of holy
relics and of sacred images, supplemented by a portrait of the
late King D. João.

The Infante D. Fernando remained with the fleet. Henrique
sent him to Tangier by sea. A boil from which he had been suffering for the last ten days was giving him such pain and such high
fever that he was fit for nothing else but bed. His brother therefore ordered him to stay on board and wait for the army in Tangier
bay.

They skirmished between Ceuta and Tetuan—a ruined town
from which the population had already fled after a recent raid

conducted by young Duarte de Menezes. From Tetuan to Tangier there was no opposition from the Moors. The army, unmolested, reached the Roman ruins just outside the town.

The tents were pitched among the orchards on the slopes of Cape Spartel. All felt happily confident of easy victory. A rumor was reported that the Moors had fled, leaving the city gates wide open!

The more impetuous horsemen would attack at once, and so were disillusioned. The gates of Tangier were securely shut, and though the furious onslaught broke down two of them, they were found to be strongly manned upon the other side. Henrique sent the Count of Arraiolos, with Alvaro Vaz de Almada, to recall the assailants at nightfall, and there was an exciting skirmish just outside the town. Horses were killed, and several men; the Count was wounded by an arrow in the leg; Alvaro Vaz received one in the arm, and there were many casualties among the rank and file. The spread of darkness stopped the fighting for that day, and the firebrands returned to their tents in a more chastened mood. Tangier was not to be pulled off like a ripe plum. And those who were more superstitious remembered uneasily how, when the banners were unfurled to carry to the city wall, a gust of wind had caught the Infante Henrique's flag, and torn it into shreds.

This was no time, however, for discussing signs and omens. Everyone had to lend a hand next day in order to entrench and barricade. D. Fernando, haggard and weak, but full of eagerness to do his share, came ashore with his men. He worked as hard as anyone, and no one but his servants guessed how much the effort cost. After all, he had come for this, and nothing would induce him to back out.

It was necessary to be protected and prepared, for now the fact was plain to all that the men of Ceuta had been right. Tangier was not likely to prove an easy conquest. It was observed to be well fortified, and garrisoned by seven thousand Moors commanded by that same Sala-ben-Sala who had lost Ceuta, and was now panting for revenge.

Even so, the pessimists regained their confidence during the next few days, for there were some well-fought and thrilling battles. The Infante Fernando led his men against one gate, the Count of Arraiolos charged another; the doughty Bishop of Ceuta placed his ladder to the wall, while Henrique led his attack against the castle. The fight continued for five hours. Assailants and defenders performed prodigies of valor. The Portuguese, although outnumbered, repelled every sortie with brilliant success, and attacked in their turn; but still Sala-ben-Sala held fast his town and the army of the Christians stayed without.

Henrique sent to Ceuta for heavy artillery. He called for longer, better ladders (the first ones brought had broken), and for engines of assault. It took about a week to fetch them, and all delay was getting dangerous by that time. Like a flood rising from the hills, an ever-swelling stream of all the tribesmen of Morocco gathered on the mountains round about Tangier. Each time they tried to pour into the town Henrique's army charged and beat them back. As many times as they were driven back, they gathered on the mountain side again.

The morale of the army remained good, if we may judge by a letter written on October 3rd from the camp, two days after an enemy attack some seven thousand strong had been successfully thrown back: "I think," writes Ruy Gomes da Silva, "no man could see anything more beautiful!" No hint of evil omens here —quite the contrary. As the army went forth to meet the Moors, "there appeared over one half of the town a very great cross, as clear as crystal. It was seen by three thousand persons in the camp, who remained on their knees until it faded. . . . May it please God that the True Cross may soon be planted there for His service!" The pessimists, with their torn flag, might well be silenced by a sign like this.

The artillery arrived at last, together with a wooden castle to set up against the wall and to be manned by crossbowmen. There were, moreover, fifty large stone cannon balls, but insufficient powder to fire them it seems, for Henrique sent back the caravel at once to fetch four barrels from Ceuta.

Meanwhile, a new attack was launched against Tangier, and still it was not a success. With burning tar and lighted tow the ladders were destroyed as fast as the assailants placed them to the wall, and half the army had to remain in the rear to hold the seething swarm that harassed from the hills. They drove them back each time with heavy loss, but still their action made it quite impossible to close around the town.

Henrique showed a cheerful countenance to all, but for the first time some misgiving must have chilled his heart. Things were not going according to plan. Supposing God had not "ordained and willed" that Tangier should be taken after all? He dismissed such a thought. Had they not been vouchsafed the vision of the shining cross?

"If after a third attack you cannot take the town," Duarte had written in his instructions, "do not remain before it one day, nor one hour! Withdraw with your men to the ships, and return to Ceuta, where you shall wait for me until next March, for then, please God, I shall join you with all the forces of my realm." Henrique hoped it would not come to that!

He planned a third attack. On board one of the ships there had remained an enormous old ladder, and there was wood with which more might be put together. Laboriously men floundered through the sands, bearing the timber on their backs, and for three days they all worked very hard assembling ladders.

Meanwhile, a few young squires rode out into the field to skirmish with the Moors, and they brought back some prisoners into camp.

What of the Moorish army? the captives were asked. On this subject they had plenty to say. The Christians must expect great peril and hard labor! Sala-ben-Sala had sent for all his allies. The King of Fez was in the field, also the King of Beles. The King of Morocco and Tafilet was on the way, bringing with him a host of Berbers from the southern deserts. Altogether the Moors commanded sixty thousand horse, and seven hundred thousand infantry!

Surely the prisoners lied! They spoke the truth. That very day, lifting their eyes up to the hills, the Portuguese beheld them black with men. From every mountain top, from every valley fold, across the plain, and from all points of the horizon, like an advancing swarm of monstrous ants, the Moslem battalions poured forth.

There was no time to lose. The sailors all were ordered to their ships, the infantry was set to fortify the camp, while the Infantes with the horsemen sallied forth to try and save the artillery outside the city wall from being captured by the Moors.

The horde swept down uttering bloodcurdling cries. In one mad rush it thundered to the wall, dislodged the guardians of the artillery, and seized all the ladders and the bombards. Henrique could do nothing but order his men to fight their way back to the camp, while he remained with the rearguard to cover their retreat.

The action fought was fast and fierce. The Infante counterattacked, and drove the Moors back to the city wall. His horse was slain beneath him, and he himself would have been killed if a page of his brother Fernando had not given him a horse.

All reassembled in the camp at last. The Moors bore down again in force upon them, but still were beaten back with heavy losses. This caused the enemy to withdraw from contact, but then he spread his troops between the Christians and the sea. This time they were trapped!

Henrique was to blame for that. His camp was pitched much too far from the sea. Duarte's misgivings had been justified. Henrique, though a bold and dashing leader on the battlefield, was not a general.

Duarte's instructions were explicit enough. Either Henrique had not studied them carefully and often as his brother had hoped he would, or else he did not think much of Duarte's views on military matters! "Divide your fleet in three," the *regimento* had laid down; "send one part to Alcacer, one to Tangier, and one to Arzila." In this manner, the King points out, "the enemy's attention would be divided, and the several Moorish towns would be unable to join forces in a combined attack." For reasons best known to himself, Henrique had ignored this sensible advice. The subject of communications also had been stressed: Whatever happened, Duarte enjoined his brother, he must keep open a free passage to the sea, "to receive provisions and reinforcements, and to be able to withdraw if necessary."

But Henrique had never thought about withdrawal! His plans were only for attack. He pitched his camp too far inland, and now the consequence was manifest. The besiegers, in their turn, were besieged. They were hemmed in closely on every side, and between them and the ships which were their sole hope of salvation seethed the countless host of Moors. It was a desperate position, as everyone could see. Better dash for the beach at once, some people suggested. Most of them would be cut to pieces, but a few might still succeed in breaking through.

Henrique might lack generalship, but never calm and resolution. He faced his army cheerfully, as if nothing was wrong. No desperate remedies should be tried yet, he said. The first thing was to improve the defenses of the camp. Then, what about provisions?—What, indeed! Investigation proved there were sufficient for two days. The stores had all remained on board the ships, on the easy assumption that they might be sent for as required.

At this doleful discovery, gloom descended upon the men. Why perish like sheep in a pen? they cried. Better to sally forth immediately, and die like warriors in the field!

It seemed, however, that the Moors left them no choice. They could be seen preparing to attack. The King of Fez was marching forward to the sound of trumpets, followed by the King of Beles and the Vizier Lazeraque. It was ridiculous, the Moors were saying to each other, to be held up by a handful of men. Let them be liquidated without more delay!

Henrique sprang to horse, encouraging his men "with words so sweet and so appropriate that had fear dwelt in any heart, it had been rooted up and fresh courage and energy been planted in its stead."

The battle lasted some four hours. The Christians did not cede an inch. They stood their ground tenaciously, inflicting heavy casualties upon the Moors although their own losses were slight.

This was extraordinary, and it was glorious, but it could only end one way. A few thousand men, short of provisions and equipment, encircled by an enemy well over half a million strong, could not hope to hold out. Some drastic remedy had to be found, if anyone were to embark at all. A rush to the sea under cover of night appeared to be the only solution. There was a chance that the Moors, taken by surprise, might be unable to prevent at least a portion of the army breaking through.

A traitor extinguished that gleam of hope. One of Henrique's chaplains, by name Martim Vieira, suddenly went to pieces and deserted to the Moors. Worse than that, he revealed his master's plan. This black treachery so shocked a renegade, who had been living with the Moors for many years, that seized with repentance for his own sin, he did the other thing, and went to join the Christian camp! From him they learned how they had been betrayed.

It seemed that there was nothing left to do but wait for death. Already they were suffering acutely from hunger and thirst.

The Moorish kings meanwhile took counsel with each other. In spite of the heroic resistance that still held them off, they knew that they were masters of the situation. That being so, it was pure waste of time and lives to go on hacking at their foe until they had destroyed him. There was no profit to be gained that way. Better to take advantage of the Christians' plight by putting through a useful deal.

Accordingly, they flew the flag of truce, and sent messengers to the camp. If Ceuta were given back to Sala-ben-Sala, they said, and all the Moorish prisoners in Portugal released, then the Infantes' army would be allowed to embark, provided that they left their equipment behind.

This was the grimmest choice Henrique ever had to make. Ceuta was as dear as life to him—but his was not the only life at stake. Had he the right to ask his men to stay and to be slaughtered? After all, he had brought them to this pass. His council said that he ought to accept the terms, and he agreed—with what bitterness we can only guess.

He sent Ruy Gomes da Silva—the same man who had written so happily about the crystal cross not a fortnight before—to the camp of the Moors to discuss the conditions for an armistice.

When Ruy Gomes arrived before the enemy, however, he found that the Moors had changed their minds! Sala-ben-Sala and the allied kings might be disposed to negotiate, but the wild tribesmen who made up the number of their troops cried out for battle. Ceuta did not interest them at all—their sole desire was for bloodshed and plunder.

Sala-ben-Sala received Ruy Gomes pleasantly, but told him that negotiations were called off. It was no use for him to return to his side and help defend a hopeless cause. "Remain with us while the battle goes on," the Moor suggested kindly; "afterwards I can land you in Castile."

Ruy Gomes declined politely. He could not stand by while his comrades fought. He rejoined them in time to help sustain a fresh onslaught.

This charge was furious, but the Portuguese held firm, nor did they yield ground when the Moors, enraged by their resistance, tried to set fire to their barricades by means of burning wood and tar.

Henrique on his horse was everywhere at once, helping and cheering all. The baleful armistice was off for the time being, and anything was preferable to that! The Infante Fernando, at his post, was holding every charge, "enduring hardship with very good heart." And the gallant Bishop of Ceuta was a cleric of the old crusading pattern, with carnal and ghostly weapons equally to hand. With the Host borne before him to inspire the living and console the dying, himself clad in full armor, he received and dealt hard blows. And while the battle roared he bent over the fallen to hear their confession, and to bless the departing souls.

The struggle raged for seven hours, during which time the Moors were often reinforced. In spite of all their efforts they could not dislodge the Portuguese from their entrenchments, and when darkness fell they wearied of the battle and withdrew to rest.

There was no rest for the beleaguered army all that night. The Infantes and their men seized hoes and spades and threw up more earthworks around their camp. The enemy, however, did not attack next day, which was passed quietly although in acute discomfort.

Provisions there were none. Already most of the horses had

been killed, and their flesh eaten half-cooked on fires kindled with straw ripped from the saddle-bags. This was unpleasant, but the thirst from which all suffered was far worse. There was no water in the camp. Their sole relief came when some showers fell, and there were many men who sucked the mud.

Still the enemy did not attack. The Moors were sick of fighting with a foe who sold his life so dearly. They renewed their offers of peace—and they meant it this time.

It had to be. Henrique sent his emissaries again, and three days were spent parleying. Sala-ben-Sala would abate nothing of his demands. He must have Ceuta and all the prisoners. He further insisted upon a guarantee of peace for a hundred years—the usual period stipulated in the hopeful treaties of that time!

As was customary in all such negotiations, hostages had to be exchanged; and here, too, Sala-ben-Sala was exacting. He must have one of the Infantes, he declared, though on his side he was ready to pledge his faith with his own son.

Henrique, or Fernando? Either was willing for the sacrifice. Fernando always had the spirit that makes martyrs, but Henrique felt that if he went as the hostage himself, he might be able to prevent Ceuta being given in exchange for him. The general opinion was, however, that D. Henrique must not go. Things were quite bad enough already without the added humiliation of delivering to the enemy the commander-in-chief. It would have to be Fernando; but everybody hoped it would not be for long. After all, the Portuguese would have Sala-ben-Sala's son as guarantee upon their side.

Henrique let himself be overruled. It would no doubt have been less bitter for him to remain a captive with the Moors than to lead his defeated army home. But he was commander, he must see this thing through. He let Fernando go.

That evening Sala-ben-Sala rode up from Tangier, leading a

horse to bear his prisoner away. The brothers locked each other in a last embrace. Fernando then mounted beside the Moor, and rode off with him in the deepening shadows towards the grim walls of the town. Seven of the Infante's faithful servants, by their own choice, followed their master into captivity.

Henrique watched his brother ride away while daylight died. The end of a crusade! Henceforth it would be either Ceuta or Fernando, unless some means could be devised for saving both.

It was a black moment, but darker still next day, when the time came to evacuate the men, and it seemed that the bitter sacrifice had been in vain. Sala-ben-Sala had proposed and given terms. The army under his direct command could be made to respect them—but not his allies. All the wild nomads of the southern desert cared nothing for terms or treaties, plighted faith, or given word. What they wanted was massacre and plunder, and the annihilation of the foemen of their faith. They swarmed about the camp as closely as before. They threw dead animals into the wells outside. They intercepted all provisions sent down from the fleet. Henrique protested to Sala-ben-Sala who shrugged his shoulders and replied that he had no control over these men! He told Henrique which he thought would be the safest way down to the beach. This path was tried, but though a few men did get through, the rest were killed or captured.

Clearly there was nothing for it but to fight their way. The sole advantage gained by treating with the enemy was that what once had been impossible was now no more than difficult and dangerous. It was only the Berbers that they had to face, and not the more organized forces of the Moorish army.

Step by step, and fighting all the way, Henrique moved his barricaded camp towards the sea. They carried all the equipment they could with them, for as the Moors had not fulfilled their undertakings, Henrique no longer felt bound by his. Only what was too

(152)

heavy to be easily transported was left behind, much to the disappointment of the enemy.

The Moors harassed the retreating army all the way, and it was only under a barrage of crossbow shot that the men could embark. A final charge obliged the archers to abandon their position, and the men swam out to their ships, and climbed on board as best they could.

Precipitation such as this was tolerated in the rank and file, but nothing would induce their superiors to show unseemly haste. "After you!" said Alvaro Vaz de Almada politely to the Marshal Vasco Fernandes Coutinho, when having seen their men embark, they stood beside their boat. By no means would the Marshal be so ill-bred as to enter first, and there they lingered on the beach, discussing precedence "with words of great courtesy" while Death stalked at their backs. We are not told whose polite reluctance broke down first, but both embarked safely at last—having been quite correct!

Henrique sent the fleet home with the Count of Arraiolos, and most of the fidalgos. He himself sailed to Ceuta, and thence he sent a message to Sala-ben-Sala: The treaty was of none effect, he pointed out, since the Moors had failed to perform their part. Let Sala-ben-Sala now take his son, and send Fernando back.

The bearer of this message was the Infante D. João. Rumors that things were going wrong already had been heard in Portugal, and the day after Henrique reached Ceuta, his brother arrived there with a fleet from Algarve. He sailed immediately down the coast to Tangier.

Fernando and his jailer were no longer there. The day after the troops embarked, Sala-ben-Sala removed him from the tower above the city gate where he had been confined. He mounted all the prisoners on broken saddles, pack saddles, or else bare back, and drove them before him like cattle out of the town. "Faint with hunger, and half blind with thirst," as one of their number describes it, they reached Arzila, where the population crowded out to stone and spit on them, and there they were placed under lock and key.

Buffeted by the autumn winds, the fleet of the Infante D. João arrived, and anchored in Arzila's unprotected port. Sala-ben-Sala showed no readiness to negotiate; and Fernando had not even heard that his brother was there, when a wild gale from the Atlantic blew the ships away. Struggling for life, they made at last the coast of the Algarve, and there D. João landed with Sala-ben-Sala's son.

Henrique, exhausted and ill, waited at Ceuta eating out his heart.

Fernando, behind prison walls, spent all his days in prayer and fasting while the light of hope grew dim.

The winter storms howled out of the southwest, and moaned across the sea.

XIII

The Price of Ceuta

WHEN Alvaro Vaz de Almada reached Lisbon, he put on all his best and gayest clothes. He dressed his pages in their bravest suits, and with a cheerful smile upon his newly-shaven face he waited on the King.

He found Duarte at the little village of Carnide, near Belem, with the Infante Pedro. The two were seeking some refreshment in a walk, after a most depressing day spent listening to tales of woe.

The army from Tangier was straggling home, bringing the bitter tidings of Fernando's captivity, and one by one returning warriors had sought the King, each with a doleful face recounting his particular misfortune. The royal heart was known to be bountiful, and so the cadgers did not spare their sighs. The appearance of Alvaro Vaz, spruce, colorful, and smiling, came therefore as an agreeable surprise.

Alvaro Vaz declared that he was not downhearted! What reason was there for despondency? Honorable deeds had been done at Tangier—Duarte ought to be rejoiced at that. Nor should he grieve for Fernando's captivity. Some means would certainly be found to have him back. Meanwhile his sacrifice had covered him with fame and glory. To Alvaro Vaz, fame, glory, and honor were all that really mattered—he cared for nothing more concrete than that. The army at Tangier, said he, had fought like gallant

(155)

knights, so why toll church bells for the dead? Rather have a peal rung to cheer the living! All of which was a bit extravagant but went to the right spot. The fate-defying gaiety of Alvaro Vaz was the first ray of comfort to shine into Duarte's stricken soul.

The military disaster of Tangier did not greatly affect the nation's life, but it threw the King upon the thorns of a heartbreaking problem. Should he abide by Henrique's engagements to the Moor? Morally he was not obliged to keep them. Since Sala-ben-Sala had failed to perform his part, Duarte need not stand by his unless he chose. It would have been all very simple if Fernando's liberty were not at stake. The question was, must Fernando be sacrificed for Ceuta? Ought Ceuta to be surrendered for Fernando's sake?

Sala-ben-Sala would not hear of any other ransom. It was useless to propose a mere return of hostages, for the Moor declared it did not matter in the least about his son! He had others that he preferred, and sons, in any case, he added airily, never meant much to him. He once had even put a son of his to death! Clearly, the yearnings of Sala-ben-Sala's paternal heart were not likely to shorten Fernando's captivity. The Moor was interested in nothing but Ceuta.

Give it to him! was D. Pedro's advice, for Pedro more than ever was convinced that garrisons in Morocco were not assets but liabilities. To Duarte the problem appeared more complex. He valued Ceuta, but he cared for Fernando more, and he would willingly have given the town for him. He was not sure, however, that he had the right. Ceuta was not private property—it belonged to the nation. The famous phrase *l'État, c'est moi!* would never have expressed Duarte's theory of kingship. Subjects were members of a body of which the King was head: "they were one substance, and one heart," he told the representatives of the people assembled for the Cortes, and he asked them what they would have him do.

They were not very helpful, for opinions were divided. Give up Ceuta! said the smaller *concelhos*, to whom local affairs were more important. By no means! cried the mercantile and maritime cities of Lisbon and Porto, who already began to think imperially. "Neither for him" (Fernando) "nor for anybody else should Ceuta be surrendered!" The voices of Lisbon and Porto were only two, but they were the only two great cities of the realm. And the Archbishop of Braga—primate of all Spain—supported them. "Without permission of the Pope," he said, "it were a grievous sin to restore to the Infidel a city where the holy Christian rites had been celebrated for more than twenty years."

Others again were for a compromise. Let us gain time, they said. If negotiations are drawn out in length, the Moors may end by accepting a ransom. If, however, no sum can be raised that would satisfy them, then let the kings of Christendom be invited to join in a crusade. Some stronghold might be captured from the Moors, and exchanged for the Infante Fernando. Only after all other means had failed should one consider surrendering Ceuta.

Not only the Cortes, but his own family served Duarte with conflicting advice. His brothers Pedro and João were for returning Ceuta without delay. Their nephew, the Count of Arraiolos, on the other hand, was emphatically against any such proposal. There still remained Henrique to consult, but he lingered at Ceuta until Duarte ordered him to come back home.

Henrique obeyed very reluctantly. He landed in Algarve, and traveled north as far as Alentejo, but refused to appear at court. The King was then at Evora, and Henrique suggested that they should meet at Portole.

Duarte found his brother wearing deepest mourning, but in an unbending mood. He never would return to court, he said, until he brought Fernando back! At the same time, he refused to listen to any suggestion of giving up Ceuta. The Moors had broken their treaty, he said; Ceuta need not, could not, must not be returned to them! He bitterly regretted not having remained as the hostage himself. He would have seen to it that Ceuta was never surrendered. Fernando must be saved, but by some other way. Henrique felt quite sure it could be found. The King of Granada might act as go-between, and negotiate terms of some kind. They might offer all the Moorish prisoners in the Peninsula in exchange for the Portuguese Infante. Better still would be to raise a powerful army to embark for Africa—24,000 men perhaps—all the princes of Christendom ought to be quite willing to help, and together they could easily make up the number.

Could they? And when? Recruiting armies across Europe would take months, or even years. Meanwhile Fernando had been writing desperate letters home, begging to be delivered without more delay. He had been ill all the winter at Arzila, and Sala-ben-Sala was threatening to send him to the King of Fez where he would be handed into the custody of the terrible Vizier Lazeraque.

Duarte returned to Evora wrapped in gloom. A less conscientious ruler or a more indifferent brother would have suffered less. Duarte had been a slave to duty all his life—how was he now to reconcile that which he owed his brother with his duty as a Christian and a King?

He did try writing to his royal colleagues to ask if they would give him any help—and all replied with "sweet and comfortable words" promising to think of him in their prayers! They all agreed that Fernando's example was most edifying—"giving himself into the hands of Infidels to save the Christians!" And all declared that

Ceuta on no account should be surrendered. That would be impious and very wrong! Duarte was left more perplexed than ever.

Meanwhile the nightmare summer went its way on leaden wings. That constant visitor of recent years—the plague—made its appearance in the land again. Already Evora sickened, and from the Alentejo the scourge swept towards the north. Under its approaching shadow the court broke up, and all dispersed like leaves before the storm. The Infante D. Pedro joined his wife at Coimbra, and João went to his at Alcacer do Sal. Henrique did not move from the Algarve.

Fernando, by this time, had already been sent to Fez, and languished in a dark and filthy prison.

Duarte, like a soul in torment, wandered up and down. He came to Tomar at the end of August and there he fell ill. Was it the pestilence that he had caught, as some supposed, or was it the anguish of his heart, as others thought, that sapped his life? Probably both were right. A mortal fever never left him for twelve days, nor, it may be surmised, did he hope that it would.

Pedro was with Duarte at the last. Only this most beloved of his brothers reached his side in time. Henrique, on his rock at Sagres, did not hear until it was too late, and João, who was ill himself, was kept in ignorance by his wife.

On September 9th, 1438, in the twilight of an eclipse, Duarte's short reign of five years came to an end, and all his subjects wept "as if they thought that they would end with him."

More gifted, more sensitive, but less fortunate than his father, Duarte might have been an even greater king if he had lived as long. He had a keen intellect, an enlightened and cultured mind, together with unflinching honesty and earnest longing to do right. It was his anxiety for this that broke his heart, leaving a dismayed nation with a king of six years old.

While the widowed queen "lay wrapped in mourning weeds and tears," the Infante D. Pedro took command, and publicly proclaimed as king Duarte's little son.

Henrique traveled northward from Algarve, pricking full speed across the Alentejan plain.

And all this time, Fernando dragging chains about his ankles, hoed the gardens of the King of Fez, and groomed the Vizier's horses.

XIV

The Barren Years

"IF HE is dead, my captivity will end only with my life!" said
Fernando despairingly, when a rumor of Duarte's death first
reached Morocco. Later, the Vizier cruelly thrust before his
eyes a letter confirming the news, and Fernando fell to the ground
as if under a blow.

"I have lost one who loved me more than I can say!" he told the
servants who had followed him into captivity. What hope was
there left of deliverance? The new king was a child to whom
Fernando was a stranger.

"You have other good brothers still," his comrades reminded
him reassuringly. That was so; but not one of them was king, and
who could say what complications might arise out of a regency?

Fernando's foreboding proved to be better founded than the
optimism of his friends. These naturally supposed that with such
uncles as little Afonso V had, the troubles usually attendant on
a long minority would not occur—but they had reckoned without
the boy's mother!

Queen Leonor lamented, swathed in sackcloth, and dissolved
in tears, and there was nothing insincere about her grief. She
mourned her wonderful Duarte—the best and kindest husband
woman ever had—and one who added to his shining merits that
of unbounded admiration for the talents of his wife! How high
had been Duarte's estimate of her, only Leonor knew—as yet. At

last the time had come when all the world, and more especially her supercilious brother-in-law, would see how Duarte had judged his Queen.

The prospect of her coming triumph over that tiresome Pedro could still have charm for Leonor in the depth of her grief. Her kinsman, the Archbishop of Lisbon, who disliked Pedro, would enjoy it too. Accordingly, the day after her husband's death Leonor sent for both of them, and caused Duarte's will to be opened and read before the Council. It came as a surprise to all—it has not ceased to surprise us today—that in it Leonor was named, not only executrix of her husband's testament besides sole guardian of their sons, but also regent of the realm for the minority. How the sensible Duarte ever came to make such dispositions is a mystery, the more so that his affection and esteem for Pedro never seem to have suffered an eclipse. If this amazing will represents his deliberate thought, and was not tampered with by some intriguing hand during his last illness—then we have yet another proof that love is blind!

The publication of the will aroused a storm of indignation in the land. Were not there three Infantes left in Portugal? All three beloved of the people who had perfect confidence in them? That they should all be set aside—and for a foreign woman—was unendurable!

The citizens of Lisbon spoke their mind with the frankness of free men. What right had any king, they said, to choose a regent for his heir? That was the people's business! If Duarte had died without a successor, "it would be we alone who could elect a king, and it is also for us to appoint a regent."

Leonor did not lack candid friends at court to explain the position: "You are a woman," they pointed out, "and a foreigner. The people will never submit to be ruled by you!" Besides, they added crushingly, the charge was far too heavy for her feminine frailty. The wisest and most graceful thing for her to do would be to retire of her own free will, rather than wait till she was forced to do so. "It is quite enough for you, Senhora, to see to the up-bringing of your children, and care for your husband's soul. These are great, and honorable, and honest things," they concluded firmly. She ought to be quite satisfied with them!

Leonor was impressed. Perhaps she was asking for trouble! Perhaps it would be better to let Pedro take the regency—but here another set of advisers stepped in.

For though the nation was disgusted at Duarte's choice, it must be owned that some people were charmed. A royal minority during the Middle Ages could stir up just those troubled waters in which scheming nobles loved to fish. A king of six years old, for regent a woman whose weak position as a foreigner would make her easily the puppet of ambitious lords—the stage was set for all kinds of pleasing developments! If, however, D. Pedro took the helm, it was certain that there would be no fun. It would be a strong government, with no more scope for stirring spirits on the make than if the King already were of age.

Among those who were seriously weighing these matters was the Count of Barcelos, the Infantes' bastard brother. D. Afonso's relations with his father's lawful sons had hitherto been brotherly and pleasant. They never failed to treat him with consideration, and even—for he was much older—with respect. He was rich and influential, a great power in the land—but still the fact remained that he was his father's first-born, and yet in precedence he ranked after the last! A bastard carries a grievance from birth, and the seeds of bitterness and jealousy are rarely absent from the bottom of his heart. In D. Afonso's case they might have never come to light if Duarte's premature death had not afforded him an unexpected chance of paying off old scores. And he was egged on by his wife, D. Constança de Noronha, whom he had married when a widower past middle age. D. Constança was charming and young —and sister to the Archbishop of Lisbon. Her elderly husband was putty in her hands, and the Noronhas were related to the House of Aragon, so they were cousins to the Queen. All those who hoped to see the reins of government held in Queen Leonor's uncertain hands looked to the Count of Barcelos as their natural supporter.

D. Afonso was not a simple soul. He did not take an open stand against his brothers at this time, preferring to pull strings behind the scene. His henchmen gathered around Leonor, declaring that she must accept the regency. She owed it to her husband's wishes, and to herself—especially she owed it to her children! Had she considered what would be the likely consequence of surrendering the power to D. Pedro? Did she imagine he would be content to be no more than regent? No, no! Human nature was human nature, and the desire to reign the strongest temptation that could assail a man. It was not likely that D. Pedro would resist it. He had sons of his own, and would covet the crown for himself and his heirs.

It was not difficult to make Queen Leonor see Pedro as potential wicked uncle. She began to waver at once and think that she had better keep the regency herself.

Then Henrique arrived at court, in deepest mourning and heartbroken. Though he had ridden furiously all the way from Algarve, he still had failed to be in time to see his brother. His sorrow, says the chronicler, renewed everyone's grief. Duarte's family mingled their tears, and Leonor's mind, which was like a pendulum, began to swing the other way. With Henrique, she always was amenable to reason, and under his influence she began to soften towards Pedro. Pedro himself undid some of her prejudice about this time by having her younger son, Fernando, proclaimed successor to the throne in case the little king should die

•efore reaching manhood. That did not look like the uncle who
s plotting to usurp the throne! Leonor, in a melting mood, told
.im that it had been Duarte's dying wish that Pedro's little daugh-
er should marry his heir.

Pedro was gratified and touched. He thanked her from his heart.
;uch a marriage, he said, would realize his dearest hopes. He sug-
;ested, however, that the moment was not ripe for a public be-
rothal, with all the family in mourning and the little couple still
o young. Leonor quite agreed. She signed a written promise on
.er son's behalf, and there the matter rested.

Everything appeared happy and harmonious. Queen Leonor
sked Pedro for advice on many matters. She even sent him offi-
ial papers to sign, but he politely returned them to her. The ques-
ion of the regency would be decided by the Cortes about to as-
emble, and Pedro would not take command except at their
equest.

That request would be certainly forthcoming, as discontented
idalgos realized with dismay. D. Pedro would be regent, they fore-
aw with gloom, "and we have nothing to expect from him!"
They feared that he was more interested in the welfare of the peo-
•le than in their noble selves or their prerogatives. A meeting
vas called to discuss the matter, presided over by the Archbishop
f Lisbon. Let us unite, they all agreed, and keep D. Pedro out!
They could be certain of the Count of Barcelos' support—and
vhy not, added someone hopefully, that of the Infante D. Hen-
ique?

They were mistaken there. Besides being quite loyal to his
•rothers, Henrique did not care who ruled the land so long as it
vas not himself. All he wanted was to get back to Sagres and his
hips, and study how Fernando might be saved without losing
Ceuta. But until the question of the regency was settled nothing
ould be done. Meanwhile the fact that Henrique had no axe of

his own to grind made the contending factions look to him as arbitrator.

Since he must find a solution, Henrique devoted some weeks to his uncongenial task. Between the nation that demanded Pedro for regent, and those fidalgos who called out for Leonor, he sought to make peace by a compromise. Supposing each had some part in the government? The Queen could be sole guardian of the royal children, and all the court appointments remain in her hands. She would style herself Regent, and Pedro would be Defender of the Realm, and all decrees would have to be approved by both. In case of difference of opinion, the other Infantes might be called in to give advice. The Cortes would assemble every year, and a permanent council would be formed to be appealed to on all weighty matters.

Henrique set forth all this in a carefully thought-out and lengthy document. It was quite sound, but the Queen did not like it much, and Pedro knew her far too well to hope that it would work. All the same he expressed his willingness to try, but Leonor did not meet him half way. She had made up her mind by then— or rather Pedro's rivals had done so for her—that she must rule alone.

D. Pedro shrugged his shoulders. Henrique was impatient and annoyed, Afonso of Barcelos chuckled, but the citizens of Lisbon showed their teeth. If there was to be so much fuss, they said D. Pedro ought to take sole charge at once! The Queen was scared by their menacing attitude. She called for Henrique, and begged him to produce once more his paper of suggestions. She would agree to everything! She signed the document at once, the Cortes gave their blessing to the compromise, and Henrique gladly withdrew from court. He had done what he could to straighten matters—let Leonor and Pedro do the rest!

That would have been all very well if Leonor and Pedro had

been left alone to make friends with each other, but there were many people interested in widening the breach. The ease with which the Queen could be influenced was quite fascinating, and the Count of Barcelos, for one, felt that he would be a fool if he should fail to make the most of it. That the King should be betrothed to Pedro's little Isabel displeased the Count, for as it happened he, too, had a little Isabel—his granddaughter—she was quite as good as her cousin, and why should not she be queen? He did not actually propose such an exchange to Leonor, but made her feel that she had acted rashly. She never should have pledged her son without consulting all the great ones of the land. They were feeling very hurt about it, said the Count.

As usual, Leonor swallowed the bait. What ought she to do now? she asked perplexed. Get D. Pedro to return her written promise, said Barcelos coolly, and if she had not got the face, he would do so himself!

Pedro listened in silence to the ungracious request. Immediately he took the paper from the casket where it lay. He would not dream of keeping back by force, he said, what had been offered of free will. He tore the sheet in two, and gave the fragments to his brother. Let it go thus, he added, as symbolic of broken faith. We are not told if Leonor had the grace to feel ashamed.

It was not a very auspicious beginning to the joint regency. Pedro took up his share of the burden with good will but without much hope; while Leonor, full of more zeal than judgment, plunged headlong into the affairs of State. The partnership was an uneasy one, for Pedro's rivals saw to it that if he pulled one way, she pulled the other. And she tried to take more and more upon herself, which, as foreseen, proved far beyond her.

There is no doubt that Leonor meant well and was conscientious, but she did not know how to work. All day she wrestled with dispatches and decrees, and never seemed able to get through

(167)

them. Each day the pile of unanswered petitions mounted higher; each day the people murmured more at the delay. D. Pedro groaned to see confusion that he could have remedied, while the Queen struggled, drowning in a sea of papers.

Her physical condition made matters worse. Leonor had been left pregnant when her husband died. Her capacity for work was naturally diminished as her confinement drew near, and in March, 1439, everything had to be held up while she gave birth to Duarte's posthumous daughter.

If she had had the sense to relinquish her charge to Pedro at this time all might have yet been well, but Leonor clung desperately to office, however much her family cares might interfere with public matters. Pedro, both chivalrous and loyal, excused her as best he might to anybody who complained to him, but discontent was growing more and more vociferous. Medieval prejudice against petticoat government was not likely to be dispelled by a regent with a small baby on her hands, besides five little children! D. Pedro ought to rule alone, was the popular cry.

The Infante João declared that the people were right. His sister-in-law, he told Pedro, was well-meaning and virtuous, but quite unfit to govern. He always had advised her not to try! "If you think that it would be wrong," he said, "to take over the regency, I don't know what is right!" If Pedro did not want to rule himself, he should ask Henrique to do so—Henrique would not have thanked him for that!—"If I had not two elder brothers," concluded João, "I should insist on governing myself, for it is humiliating for us to be ruled by her."

Pedro was thoughtful. Had he not seen with his own eyes his mother's country torn by factions, while his uncles strove among themselves to wield the power for an infant king? "I fear," he said, "to raise dissensions in the land such as might ruin a great state, and how much more this little Portugal! I would rather die than bring about the perdition of the land where we were born and bred, and which our father won by labor and by blood. Certainly," he added, "if it were the desire of all, and could be without strife, I should gladly accept this charge."

João shrugged his shoulders. "The strife you fear," he said, "is inevitable unless you do accept it!"

So it appeared indeed, as Pedro was forced to admit when the mob chased the Archbishop of Lisbon from the town, and threw one of the Queen's officials out of a window. This man bounced down on to a roof and was unhurt, but the lid had blown off the cauldron of the people's wrath, and it was boiling over. Something had to be done to quiet them. The Count of Arraiolos sent a friar to preach a sermon exhorting the citizens to order. Unfortunately the man overdid it. Carried away by his own oratory, he fulminated condemnations right and left. He told his hearers that they were disloyal, ungrateful traitors—like the townsmen of Bruges who revolted against Philip of Burgundy!

The simile upset his audience. "What has the case of the Flemings to do with us?" an honest barber murmured audibly. "They sought to kill their prince and lord—we would not kill our king, but die for him, because we love him!" At this point, we are told, the congregation "rolled such angry eyes" towards the preacher that, seized with panic, he broke off his sermon in the middle and bolted from the pulpit to his monastery.

Pedro had to come to Lisbon to pacify the people. He reprimanded them roundly for their disorderly behavior. They listened meekly to all that he had to say, and then went quietly home. João was right. The only way to avoid revolution would be for Pedro to take charge himself.

Not only revolution appeared imminent, but civil war, and even foreign intervention. The Queen was urging her adherents to attend the Cortes fully armed, and in Castile the fugitive Archbishop tried to raise support. Near Lisbon the Lord of Cascais fortified his castle on the rocks from whence he hoped to overawe the capital. The citizens of Lisbon besieged the fortress and starved him out, and made him surrender his castle to the Infante D. João. At the same time, they urged Pedro to take the title of regent at once, and presented him with a resolution drawn up and signed by all to the effect that they would have no other ruler. "You take too much upon yourselves," Pedro replied.

Henrique thought so, too. He hated every form of lawlessness, and the Cortes alone possessed the legal right to dispose of the regency. They had approved the joint government scheme last year. No change ought to be made without their sanction.

They were due to assemble very soon. Queen Leonor began to lose her head. Her partisans were noisy, but she knew that the Infantes had the nation at their back. She made a desperate attempt to divide the brothers. She was quite willing to renounce the regency, she said, but to the Infante D. João! And she would like the little king to marry João's daughter.

He smiled at these proposals. "God forbid," said he, "that anyone should sow discord between the sons of the King D. João, who were brought up so lovingly together. I should be ashamed, I do not say to accept, but even to think of accepting the regency when I have two elder brothers both so well fitted for the charge." As for the suggested marriage, "I should prefer to see my daughter on the street—which God forbid!—than marry her that way."

Still unable to understand the family into which she had married, Leonor turned to Henrique whom she had always liked. Let him beware of Pedro, she wrote confidentially—this bad brother was plotting to arrest Henrique and to cast him into prison!

Henrique read the letter, and he laughed. He carried it to Pedro at Coimbra to enjoy the joke with him. "See, brother," he cried,

"what the Queen writes to me! To show you how much I fear
you I have come unprotected to your house!"

"You will find it an honorable prison," Pedro replied, but as he
smiled he sighed. "I am not surprised," he said, "that these times
bring forth such strange fruit!"

Leonor, utterly disgusted, sulked at Alenquer, and refused to
come to Lisbon for the Cortes. Since they were bent on appointing D. Pedro to the regency, she would not bring the little king to
ratify proceedings. They had to send Henrique to fetch her at last,
for he alone seemed able to do anything with her. He persuaded
her to come away with him, but even he could not succeed in
making her polite to Pedro, who rode out of the town to meet
them and kiss her reluctant hand. Leonor was very stiff and cold,
and let him see that she thought he was not an uncle to be trusted.
She would not let him take the King to figure at the opening of
the Cortes without a written undertaking that the child would be
returned to her as soon as his presence could be dispensed with.
Pedro was hurt, but gave her every guarantee she asked, and
faithfully observed them.

Leonor's foolish prejudice recoiled upon herself. If she had
shown herself less hostile to her brother-in-law the people would
have been less anxious to combat her influence over her son. As
it was, when Pedro had been invested with the regency, the delegates from Porto moved, amid general approval, that he should
also be sole guardian to the King and his small brother. The royal
children must not be educated by a woman, they declared. Afonso
and Fernando would grow up effeminate under Leonor's tutelage,
and the nation could not endure a Mother's Darling on the
throne! Besides, added the Portuenses thriftily, it would be too
expensive to maintain the King and Regent in separate households. In that case, Pedro replied, the Queen could share estab-

lishment with him. His nephews were too young to be separated from their mother.

The mother's pride, however, showed itself stronger than her love. Queen Leonor, encouraged by the intriguers around her, refused to share the household of her brother-in-law. Against Pedro's sincere desire for friendly co-operation her obstinacy rose like a blank wall. If Pedro must live with Afonso and Fernando, then Leonor would leave her sons! Her counselors suggested that the separation would not be for long; her partisans would rally and restore her to the regency, and D. Pedro would have to go.

Leonor listened, and as was her wont, acted impulsively. At midnight, her two small boys were wakened from their beds to be embraced by a mother in tears. "God bless you, my son," she sobbed, taking the little king into her arms, "and never let me live bereft of you, as I am of your father!" Afonso, only eight years old, tried to console his mother like a little man. She went away with his three sisters in the night, and we are told that no one saw him cry.

This time even Henrique failed to bring Leonor back, although he tried his best. She saw herself as a much-injured woman, and she still hoped that her supporters would avenge her before long.

The truth was that her supporters were cooling, for the new regent was the idol of the people. The citizens of Lisbon even proposed raising a statue to him to show their gratitude for some of his reforms. Pedro, who had no illusions, refused the honor. "If you made a statue of me," he said, "your sons would no doubt smash it! I look for no other reward for any benefits I may confer upon you."

Statue, or no statue, there appeared no immediate chance of undermining the mob's fickle favor. Leonor vainly did her best to stir up trouble. Proud, bitter, and heart-hungry for the sons she had abandoned of her own accord, she wandered from Lisbon

to Sintra, thence to Almeirim, from Almeirim to Crato, and
eventually into Castile. And wherever she moved she was the center of seditious plots, the puppet of intriguers. She pledged her
word, she gave away her jewels, she made appeal to all her relatives throughout Castile and Aragon. They sent half-hearted em-
bassies to Portugal, and fomented ineffectual unrest in frontier
provinces. Those fidalgos of Portugal—on whom Leonor pinned
her hopes—either deserted her or had to make their submission
to the Infantes. Even the Count of Barcelos, so long the power
that pulled the strings for her, decided that he might be backing
the wrong horse, and flung himself into D. Pedro's arms like a
devoted brother.

After four years of struggle Leonor's obstinacy broke down. Her
partisans had left her, her jewels were gone, her money spent, her
family was bored. From Castile she sent a humble message to
Pedro, begging to be allowed to return home. She asked no longer
to be Regent, nor even Queen, if only he would have her as a
younger sister!

Pedro was not the man to turn down so pathetic an appeal
from Duarte's beloved. Arrangements were set under way at once
for her return to Portugal, but she had stayed in Castile just too
long. She is believed to have been poisoned by the Constable D.
Alvaro de Luna, who suspected her of intriguing with his enemies.

If Leonor spoiled her own life, she succeeded in embittering
those of her brothers-in-law. The period of her widowhood were
sad and weary years for them, especially perhaps for Pedro, strain-
ing every nerve to serve his country and Duarte's son; while Duarte's widow stirred up trouble at home and abroad, and answered
every friendly overture upon his part with distrust and with scorn.
These days were dreary for Henrique too, caught in the whirlpool
of internal politics, obliged to help Pedro to unravel Leonor's con-
spiracies, and to look to the defenses of the land. The death from

illness of their brother João, always a helpful comrade and faithful adviser, increased the burden and enlarged the sorrow. With all these cares Henrique had small leisure for the mysteries of the Guinea coast, nor for the fascinating task of equipping his little ships, and worst of all, till there was peace at home, what possibility was there of organizing a crusade that might have delivered Fernando?

All through the barren years the specter of the prisoner at Fez shadowed his brothers' hearts. Duarte in his will had urged his heirs to give Ceuta for Fernando, if he could be saved no other way. Although the Pope Eugene might write "admonishing that by no means the city should be surrendered, alleging for this holy and catholic reason with respect to God, and to the honor and praise of the realm": upon this subject at least Leonor and Pedro had agreed, and during their joint regency an envoy had been sent to Arzila to negotiate the exchange of the prisoner for the town.

It proved no easy matter. What with the slowness of communications, mutual distrust, besides intrigues among the Moors themselves, discussions dragged on indefinitely. It seems that Sala-ben-Sala was willing to give Fernando for Ceuta; but Lazeraque, who was the Infante's custodian and hoped to reap a ransom for himself, refused to let the prisoner out of his hands. He always had some plausible excuse for not bringing Fernando to Arzila, and in the midst of these delays Sala-ben-Sala died. A brother of the Moor succeeded to his post, and negotiations were held up again while Lazeraque ostensibly discussed them with this new captain, and secretly plotted his overthrow.

Time passed, and nothing was done. So far as can be seen amid this network of intrigue, we gather that Sala-ben-Sala's brother would have abided by his predecessor's terms; but Lazeraque, preferring a financial deal, deliberately drew out the discussions. Henrique would have given money, and Pedro offered Ceuta, but neither Moor would let the other have his way. Even when D. Fernando de Castro was sent to Ceuta with full powers to surrender the city, no agreement was reached. The Moors refused to bring forth the Infante till they were in possession of the town; the Portuguese, who not without reason feared losing both, declared that scraps of paper were not good enough—Fernando must be sent to Arzila where envoys were waiting for him, before the Moors could be permitted to enter Ceuta. The result was deadlock.

And all this while Fernando's life at Fez was hell. His clothes were rags, his food was bread and water, his lodging was a dark and filthy dungeon where twelve men slept in space designed for eight. His companions were driven every day to work, but the Infante Fernando, although he begged to be allowed to follow them, after the first year was kept in close confinement.

His patience was amazing. His faithful secretary, Father João Alvares, who went into captivity with him, says that Fernando's own sufferings moved him far less than those of his companions. Alone among the prisoners, he never railed against the Moors, however they might threaten or torment him. What was the use? he said to fellow captives, who relieved their minds by reviling their jailers. What else but harsh treatment could you expect from infidels? "We ought rather to pray God for our enemies, that they might turn to Him. . . . I have no wish to be honored or praised by them—only," he added wistfully, "I would that God were pleased to deliver me from them!"

But earthly deliverance was not for Fernando, nor any mitigation of his suffering lot. On the contrary. His ingenious tormentors found that he had still one pleasure left: during the long dark days he could look forward to the return of his companions from their work at night. They adored him, and he loved them with all his heart. Evening brought him friendship and sympathy, and

scraps of news from the outside world, so Lazeraque removed
Fernando from his friends, and locked him in a closet all swarming with vermin, and without a window or chink to let in a ray of
light. They let him have a lamp by which to read his Breviary,
also a bench on which to sleep at night, and there was room for
nothing more in his unwholesome cell, in which a man could just
turn round. He was allowed to see his confessor once a fortnight.
Sometimes the porter who brought him his food could be bribed
to admit one of his friends for a few minutes. Sometimes his comrades worked outside his cell, and Fernando discovered a loose
brick in the wall, which left a hole through which he could just
catch a glimpse of them. Such were his only consolations during
fifteen months, at the end of which he was dying.

Three of the captive Christians passing by his prison door,
heard Fernando groaning in mortal pain. He begged them to implore the King and Queen of Fez to intercede for him with Lazeraque that he might not be left in this dark place to die alone.

The captives entreated the King and Queen, and the King's sister, who was Lazeraque's chief wife. "Let the Infante make the
best of it—we can do nothing!" was the cold reply. They went
to all the chief alcaldes of the town—they prostrated themselves
upon the ground, and kissed their feet and hands, imploring them
to have mercy upon a dying man. Some shrugged their shoulders;
some said that they were sorry but they could not help, while
others jeered. "Infidel dogs!" exclaimed the Vizier's Lieutenant,
"get you hence! If God wills he will kill your lord or restore him
to health!"

They tried yet one more official, and he at last consented to tell
Lazeraque. The Vizier still would not bring Fernando out of his
noisome prison, but locked his physician in there with him, and
allowed visits from some of his fellow captives.

It seems that heavenly visions lightened the darkness for Fernando on the day he died, and he was very happy. His friends tried to assure him that God would restore his health, but even to themselves their wishes must have sounded hollow. Death was the only blessing for which Fernando had longed for countless somber days. Released at last, he partook of the Sacrament, and turning his face to the wall, sighed wearily, "Now let me end!"

The fetters were sawn from his wasted limbs only when he was dead.

The corpse, embalmed and disemboweled, was hung head downward from the walls of Fez, but in the secret of the night, Fernando's servants stole his entrails and his heart. They buried them in a jar filled with salt, and marked the spot with a white cross. Every evening as they passed by, returning from their work, they paused a minute there to say their prayers.

After eight years, Father João Alvares, at one time Fernando's secretary, was ransomed with three surviving companions, and he conveyed the precious relics home to Portugal. Enclosed in a casket covered with black damask, they were borne reverently to the great church at Batalha. The Infante D. Henrique, riding out of Tomar one day in June, met the procession on the way, and turned to follow it.

Under the Gothic vault of Our Lady of Victory, where D. João and Philippa, enshrined in stone, lay hand in hand, a sepulcher was waiting ready for their youngest son. In the small hours before the summer dawn the chanting of the Mass of Plurimorum Martyrum awoke the echoes of the sleeping church. The candles burned, the torches flared, the shadows flickered about the effigies of the conqueror of Ceuta and his Queen, while their son Henrique prayed by the open tomb—a tomb that would be empty but for that small casket. A withered corpse still hung upon the walls of Fez—the price at which Ceuta would remain a Christian town.

(177)

High in the echoing space arose the voice of priests chanting the Martyrs' Psalm:

Their blood have they shed like water round about Jerusalem! and there was none to bury them . . .

The black casket lay by the grave upon a crimson pall. Henrique kneeled and kissed his brother's heart.

XV

White Wildernesses

FOOTPRINTS in the sand—figures that fled—nets of birch bark abandoned by the shore—what else was known of those mysterious lands south of Cape Bojador which Henrique had sought for fifteen years? No wonder that to practical persons it seemed that the Infante was chasing a chimera. What labor, and what waste of time, and what expense, for such worthless results! But there was one practical man who never joined in this chorus. The Regent, D. Pedro—clear-sighted realist although he was—had caught his brother's vision. Pedro might not agree with Henrique about crusades in Africa, but when it came to exploration he was with him heart and soul. Pedro had followed the discovery of the islands with enthralled interest; Pedro had taken upon himself the colonization of São Miguel in the Azores, and any time that Henrique wished to send ships to coast down the intriguing continent of Africa he could be certain of the Regent's whole-hearted support.

For five years nothing had been done. The anguish and the turmoil that had followed the tragedy of Tangier and Duarte's death had come between Henrique and his vision. But even through the clouds it never ceased to lure him. No storm could wholly blot out from his sky the light from hidden horizons that had shone on his early youth; no strife could wholly still the call that sounded in his ears from far away, more vibrant with each year that passed, until the time came that it drowned all other voices and Henrique lived for nothing but his quest.

When, in 1441, some measure of peace had been restored at home, two small ships were sent out, rather tentatively.

The first, commanded by a youth named Antão Gonçalves, was commissioned for nothing more than to fetch oil and sea lions' skins from the Rio de Ouro. The second, which followed close after, already was charged with the Infante's accustomed sailing orders—that is, to reach the farthest point that ever had been touched before, and then to pass beyond. Nuno Tristão, a valiant knight, was entrusted with this command, and the Infante gave him a small ship of the newest design.

She was a caravel. This is the first time that we hear of those enchanting pioneers, the name of which was to become a household word, immortalized forever in the epic of Portuguese history. These graceful little ships, with lateen sails, two masts, a single deck, a castle aft, and steamlined bows, have played one of the greatest parts recorded in the annals of the sea. A caravel was swift and light, and easy to maneuver. She could coast dangerous shores, and navigate in shallow seas; her triangular sails could catch the slightest puff of air, and even make headway against the wind—a feat that had been considered beyond nautical art. No fifteenth-century sailor had ever seen a craft so serviceable. "Caravels," observed the Venetian Cadamosto, "are the best ships that sail the sea, and there is nowhere impossible for them to navigate!" In after years a heavier type had to be built to weather South Atlantic storms, but even then the caravel remained the scout of maritime discovery.

It was in Henrique's shipyards that they were first designed—an adaptation and improvement of a type of boat that fishermen had sailed off the Portuguese coast since Moorish times. Built either for coasting or the deep sea, the caravel was born of the necessities of ocean exploration, and that is why Portugal was the country of her birth. The galley was a Mediterranean craft, the *barcha* was of northern origin, the *barinel*, it seems, was also foreign; but the caravel, that came to surpass them all, was a purely Portuguese contribution to naval architecture. So exclusive was the design that at a later date Henrique's canny great-nephew, D. João II, was able to discourage foreigners from poaching on his African preserves simply by circulating the legend that only caravels could navigate those seas!

Thus, in a caravel, Nuno Tristão set forth, taking with him a Bedouin as interpreter, in case he found some means to get in touch with the elusive desert men. "It would be no small thing to me to have some person from those lands to inform me about them . . ." so Henrique had said five years before, and so he repeated again to Nuno Tristão. "He told him, if he met any people, to make peace with them."

Nuno Tristão found that Antão Gonçalves had forestalled their master's orders. He met his colleague by the sandy shores of the Sahara, in proud possession of a pair of prisoners. Antão Gonçalves and his lads had disembarked by the Rio de Ouro, and followed tracks of camels through a hot and starry night. Panting and thirsty, they had beat the desert sands in vain until, returning to their ship, at last they met an aged negress and a naked man. It was not difficult to capture both, and there the adventure had ended. Here was a man to show the Infante! But as no one could understand the language that he spoke, his conversation could not be of great interest. In vain Nuno Tristão produced his Bedouin. The Moor could make nothing of the Berber tongue, and the captive understood no Arabic.

Nuno Tristão announced his intention to seek more human specimens, for profit and for further information. Neither he nor Antão Gonçalves seems to have troubled much about the In-

fante's orders to make peace with the natives—how could you
do that with people who always ran away? It was so much simpler
—and, incidentally, more fun—to stalk, to scuffle, and to catch!
Joining forces, the two captains tracked and fell upon a nomads'
camp by night, and there they took ten prisoners and marched
them to their ships.

Ten Berbers from the western Sahara, of complexions that
varied from brick red to black—poor simple negroids most of
them, attired in leather tunics and breeches, or nothing at all,
the women swathed in capelike veils that hid their faces but left
off where clothes ought to begin—one only of these prisoners was
an impressive figure.

Stately and dignified, the chieftain, Adahu, "showed in his
countenance that he was nobler than the others. Not only in his
countenance, but in his clothes and also in his manners." His
captors all agreed that he must be a knight, and treated him according to his supposed rank. Adahu was a traveled man—"he
had seen more and better things than had the others." And he
spoke Arabic, they found to their delight. He could talk to the
Bedouin, and answer any question. The very type of man that
D. Henrique wished to see! Antão Gonçalves must sail back home
with him at once, while Nuno Tristão continued his voyage.

Before they parted, Nuno Tristão knighted the junior captain.
Had he not taken the first prisoners from these parts? Antão Gonçalves demurred. He was not sure if this would be according to
the rules. His achievement could not strictly be called a deed of
arms, and there was no precedent to indicate if man-hunting in
the interests of ethnology was an exploit by which a youth might
win his spurs! But just because the situation was entirely new,
his companions insisted that he should accept the honor. What
knight had yet been made on such forsaken shores? So Nuno

Tristão knighted Antão Gonçalves, and Porto do Cavaleiro was the name by which the site was marked upon the map.

Antão Gonçalves sailed for Portugal, happy with his knighthood, his prisoners, his sea lions' skins, and Adahu, leaving Tristão by the Rio de Ouro.

There Nuno Tristão beached his caravel, careened and scraped her just as if he were in a home port, and after that sailed southward with the tide.

He sailed for miles over an empty sea, beside league after league of sandy shore, and never saw a sign of life—always a desert earth and desert ocean, under the sky's unchanging blue.

He reached a barren headland after many days, and anchored in the sheltering whiteness of a cliff. The desert showed no sign of ending, still there were no trees and no green thing—nothing but sand reverberating in the light. Once more they found some nets, footprints and camel tracks, showing that men had passed that way, although the world seemed bare and dead. Cabo Branco —White Cape—was the name that Nuno Tristão gave to that sunstricken solitude.

He had obeyed his master's orders. He had sailed to the end of the known world, and some hundred and fifty leagues beyond. He might as well go home before his provisions gave out.

He found Henrique pondering upon the secrets of the heart of Africa, revealed to him in his long talks with Adahu. That son of the Sahara had traveled far and wide across its length and breadth. He told Henrique of the vastness of his desert, of the everlasting sands that roll in waves of desolation from the Atlantic to the Red Sea. He spoke about the silent caravans that crossed the spaces from long leagues away. The merchandise they brought came from so far: it traveled by so many stages and relays that those who first set out with it would never see it to its

(183)

journey's end. He told Henrique of the way to Timbuktu, desert port on the Niger and crossroad of caravans. There Adahu had seen as many as three hundred camels all laden with gold from the mysterious south. No one followed the precious metal to its origin. It was bartered for salt on the edge of the desert by men who never saw each other's faces. The salt was left in piles upon a certain spot. When the heap was considered high enough, one day it disappeared, and gold remained instead. The gold was carried up the Niger into Timbuktu, thence to Tunis, and Tripoli, and Egypt.

Where did the desert end? Far to the south—in Guinea, where the black heathen lived. One captured these as slaves, that was their use! But of the world outside their desert Arabs and Berbers were vague. Sons of the open sunlit spaces, they shrank before the tangle of the tropical forest and seldom penetrated far into the green twilight. Of all that lay outside the Sahara, Adahu told a strange medley of fact and fable. He spoke of inland seas in the heart of the continent, and the Mandingo empire of Mali, of how the Nile flowed westward to the ocean from the Mountain of the Moon, and of the fearsome heights of Abofur, where lived a tribe of dog-headed and long-tailed men.

Henrique tried to unravel the tangled skein of false and true. The African kingdoms interested him, and the problem of communication overland from west to east. That such communication did exist across the continent of Africa from the Atlantic seaboard to India and the Far East was confirmed by all that he heard from Adahu. The trade routes of the Sahara were in Moslem hands, but what about the negro kingdoms farther south? From Adahu he gathered that the land of Guinea lay outside the Moslem world—the black kings of the forest still were heathen. Henrique was rejoiced to be assured of this. Conversions from Islam at all times have been difficult and rare, but the simple pagan has no prejudice against the Christian faith. What a rich harvest of souls might be reaped by the Church in Africa—if only she got there in time! Islam had had a long start certainly, but Henrique resolved that its conquests should spread no more. The northern desert had been won for Mohammed, the green and golden south lands would be claimed for Christ! And there was one ally at least to be hoped for, even in God-forsaken Africa. South of Egypt there lay the land of Prester John—that fabled Christian champion cut off from his brothers in the Faith. If Portugal could turn the Moslem flank, and reach the land of Prester John, from thence the armies of the Cross could pass to India, and attack the distant strongholds of Islam. What greater and more glorious purpose could be set before the knights of Henrique's crusading order?

More determined than ever to pursue his way around the unknown continent, to find the negro Nile, to bring the heathen to the knowledge of the Lord, and make contact with Prester John, Henrique sent an envoy to the Pope. Would the Holy Father grant to the Crown of Portugal those lands which the Portuguese would discover? Might the Order of Christ have the spiritual jurisdiction thereof, and would the Pope concede the indulgences allowed crusaders to those who might be killed in Moslem or in heathen lands? Pope Eugene promptly sent a Bull, conferring everything that Henrique had asked, and the Regent provided for the expense of the enterprise by transferring to his brother the right belonging to the Crown of one-fifth of all profits to be gained from newly-discovered lands.

Meanwhile, the Berber Adahu was wearying of his captivity. Not that his lot was hard in any way. Since everyone agreed that he must be a gentleman, he had been treated as an honored guest. But the amenities of life in Europe, to a wanderer from the desert, were uncomfortable and strange. In a land of trees and water he longed for his dry and empty sands, and the unpopulous Algarve still would appear overcrowded to him. He begged Antão Gonçalves who had brought him here, to take him home again. He promised five or six fine negroes as a ransom for himself, and added that among his fellow captives were two youths who would be good for at least five more blacks.

Antão Gonçalves thought the proposition sound. "Has that Moor told you all you want to know?" he asked the Infante. If Henrique were willing, he would sail back to those lands, taking those three prisoners for ransom. He would bring back at least ten captives in their place—these would be black, but negroes, too, had souls, and how much better to have ten souls saved than only three! And negroes came from lands much farther south. From them the Infante could find out many things.

Souls, and geographical information—were not these Henrique's chief aim in life? He gave a fine new suit of clothes to Adahu, and sent Antão Gonçalves with his blessing. Find out all that you can about that land, he said, and see if you can hear of India, and of Prester John!

Under these comprehensive orders, Antão Gonçalves sailed, taking not three, but all the prisoners with him, and Adahu, and a young German, who had arrived in Portugal to sate his wanderlust.

This traveler's name was Balthasar, and he belonged to the Emperor's household. He had fought at Ceuta and been knighted there, but he felt that his prestige would be still further enhanced if he had made a voyage on the high seas. Especially he hoped to see a terrible Atlantic storm. That would be a fine thing, he said, to talk about when he got home to his untraveled friends!

He had his wish. He did see a tremendous storm, and by a miracle it was not the last thing he saw. The waters calmed down in the end, and then the little ship proceeded on her way. To

Henrique's seamen such episodes were all in the day's work, but doubtless they would make a most effective tale for central European courts.

They reached the Rio de Ouro, where Antão Gonçalves put in to receive the prisoners' ransom. He kept the other captives on his ship, but let Adahu go, on parole, as practised by the best people. It seemed so obvious that he was a gentleman! "Antão Gonçalves trusted him," Zurara says, "thinking that the nobility he showed would more than anything constrain him not to break his faith." As one gentleman dealing with another, therefore, he released Adahu on the strength of his word alone. The Berber walked off happily into the desert and was never seen again, and Antão Gonçalves was left to realize with shocked surprise that the Sahara standards were not those of European chivalry.

His simple faith in human nature somewhat shattered, Antão Gonçalves waited seven days. It seems that Adahu, although he did not mean to pay his own ransom, must have advised the kindred of those prisoners left on board the ship. On the eighth day a Moor appeared, riding on a white camel, followed by other men to negotiate their relatives' release.

It proved a very satisfactory deal. Clearly, the captives were more valuable than first supposed. Altogether a hundred negroes were obtained, and Antão Gonçalves had ten in exchange for his two. Gold dust was thrown in as well, besides a curious native shield, and many ostrich eggs, which were served at Henrique's table in due course. "We may presume," Zurara writes with deepest pride, "that not another Christian prince in these parts could have such food at his table!" We may indeed presume thus far, but it is harder to accept the statement that these eggs were very "fresh and good." Perhaps it was the enthusiasm of the eaters that made them taste new-laid after so many weeks!

All these things would mean more prestige in store for young

Balthasar, now about to leave. What with ships, and storms, white camels, Berbers, and exotic omelettes, his tales must have made him the life and soul of his own set at home!

Antão Gonçalves' trip had been profitable, but Nuno Tristão was the man after Henrique's heart. Wherever Nuno Tristão set out to go, he always made a point beyond. He passed his shining Cabo Branco the next year, and went on to the island of Arguim. There they saw twenty-five canoes, propelled by naked men, who used their own bare legs instead of oars. Nuno Tristão captured fifteen of the poor wretches before proceeding to another island near at hand. No men were there, only a multitude of herons and large flocks of other birds, whose flesh afforded an agreeable change of diet after weeks of ship's rations.

So long as the Infante's sailors opened new horizons he did not trouble much about material gain. With the great public, naturally, it was the other way. Mere names upon the map left the man in the street completely cold, and while D. Henrique had no more to show for his endeavor, the people smiled indulgently at what they considered a princely foible. A prince must have something to do, and Henrique's amusements, though expensive, were innocent, which was more than could be said of those of some of his compeers! With the advent of human cargoes, however, public interest awakened suddenly. Now, here was something practical! The labor problem was acute in an underpopulated land, but now it seemed that Africa might provide working hands for all, with no wages to pay! Slaves? Certainly! Why not? The fifteenth century was not shocked at the idea. The slave trade had been flourishing in Africa for millenniums. Black men enslaved each other, as they still do today, while Arabs and Berbers kidnapped negroes and sold them in the Mediterranean ports. Circumstances had hitherto prevented Europeans from taking an active part in the business—but if the opportunity occurred why keep out of a good thing? The traffic was not only profitable, it was pious as well! How grateful ought the happy African to be—when snatched from his heathen darkness—not to be servant of the Moor, who could but speed him on the path to Hell, but of the Christian who would baptize him and save his soul! Most theologians were agreed on this. Far from regarding slavery as a crime against humanity, they were convinced that it was for the highest good of their black brother.

African expeditions now grew popular. One went "for the service of God and the Infante our lord, and honor and profit of ourselves"—a charming combination! Lançarote of Lagos, with Gil Eanes of Bojador fame, and several other friends, equipped six caravels. Henrique gave to each one the red-cross banner of his Order of Christ, and under that crusading emblem, they hunted from Cape Branco down to Arguim, carrying off more than two hundred slaves.

Lagos never forgot the sensation of their return. From the first hours of a hot August morning, all roads from the outlying villages into the town were congested by a crowd of sightseers that streamed down to the waterside, where a mixed multitude of poor bewildered Africans were being landed from the ships. They were of every type and shade—some "reasonably white and beautiful," and others brown, while others were so ugly and so black as to make the astonished peasants feel that they were looking upon "images from the world below."

"It was a marvelous thing to see!" Zurara says. But it was harrowing, too. The chronicler, a kindly man, admits as much—apologetically. He prays the Lord to forgive him his tears, which evidently he feels would be disapproved in Heaven. But, after all, he says, these blacks are sons of Adam like ourselves, and so he cannot help being sorry for them!

He well might be. Some of the prisoners were weeping, some

(189)

were groaning, others were chanting a lament, and there were some who beat their faces with their hands, and threw themselves upon the ground. Steeling their hearts to so much sorrow, the captors sorted them into groups, to be divided equally as spoil. The tragedy then became still more excruciating, for families were broken up, and separated from each other, amid the shrieks and protestations of the poor victims. Pandemonium reigned all day long on Lagos market place, where the crowds of spectators, mingling Portuguese good nature with medieval callousness, wept for pity while gazing popeyed at the fascinating sight.

Henrique, mounted upon a tall horse, watched the strange scene. We are not told if he was harrowed, too. According to Zurara, he was "considering with great joy the salvation of those souls which had before been lost." One-fifth out of the number of the captives was his share by right, and he picked out the best of them to be presented to the Church. One of these, a small boy, grew up as a Franciscan friar. He lived a holy life in the monastery at Cape St. Vincent, and quite forgot the wilderness where he was born.

"Sons of Adam, like ourselves!"—Zurara spoke the feeling of his nation. In spite of the slave trade—a sin which every European came to share—it remains to the credit of the Portuguese never to have forgotten that a black man is a human being, and our brother. Slavery in Portuguese-speaking countries has always been seen in its mildest form, and as for the first Africans brought over in the Infante's time, theirs was an easy fate. They found themselves the center of attraction in their strange new homes, where everyone was thrilled to think how they had been rescued "from perdition of both body and soul." It was pathetic, all agreed, to see how ignorant they were! Poor things, not only had they lived "without the light of Holy Faith," but "without anything pertaining to reasonable creatures; not knowing bread, or

wine, or clothes, or decent dwelling houses"—in fact, not knowing anything at all! In future, life would be a different thing for
them! And, glowing with benevolent delight, their masters
treated them like pets. Some of them were killed by kindness, we
fear, and being stuffed with unaccustomed food: "Their bellies
swelled," Zurara tells us tersely, "and they sickened . . . and
some who could not stand it, died."

Most of them, however, became acclimatized, and soon cheered
up. Portugal seemed a wonderland to them and, more than anything, they reveled in the clothes! An African loves to disport
himself in brilliant colors, and these negroes were happier than
their modern brethren who conform to European ways, for the
white man's wardrobe in the fifteenth century gave much wider
scope! Even so, they sought to improve upon it. Zurara says that
many made a collection of colored rags to sew as ornaments on
to their suits.

The novelty passed off in time. The captives ceased to wonder
or be wondered at. Their masters made no difference between
them and their freeborn white servants—if anything it seems the
Africans were privileged. Zurara tells us that he often had been
invited to baptisms and weddings of these slaves, celebrated in
the same style as those of their masters' own sons.

"And best of all," concludes the chronicler, "they willingly
turned to the way of Faith. What a reward," he cries ecstatically,
"will the Infante receive from the Lord God for bringing these,
and many more, to true salvation!"

So that was how slavery appeared to pious people in the fifteenth century!

Not all the Africans who came to Portugal were prisoners.
When Antão Gonçalves, in 1445, returned to the Rio de Ouro a
third time for trading purposes, an enterprising old Berber announced his wish to go and visit the Infante. Needless to say that

Henrique received him well, and loaded him with gifts, sending him back home rich and happy.

However much the godly might approve of catching and kidnapping, and though his men thought it great fun to skirmish and to grab, these were not really the methods that Henrique preferred. His wish was to establish friendly commercial intercourse with the tribes of the hinterland. For such a venture mere daring was not enough, patience and tact would be required as well.

The right man was available. João Fernandes, squire of the Infante's household, knew how to ingratiate himself with anyone, was ready to go anywhere, and feared nothing at all. When Antão Gonçalves left the Rio de Ouro with his Berber guest, João Fernandes volunteered to remain with the desert tribes. He had some knowledge of the Berber tongue, it seems, no doubt picked up from prisoners at home. If Antão Gonçalves would promise to come back to fetch him at a later date, he would stay in the Sahara for months and collect information for their master.

João Fernandes made a bundle of his clothes and took a small provision of biscuit and flour with him. The caravel set sail, and he was left alone in Africa, on the edge of the desert by the sea. Alone in one sense, and yet not alone. His Berber hosts took charge of him. They also took charge of his food and clothes, and dressed him in a tunic like their own. They were kind to their foreigner, but firm. If he would go with them, he must adopt their ways. And wheat flour was so rare and delicious that they must have that for themselves!

With truly Portuguese adaptability, João Fernandes shared their tents as to the desert born. These men were Azenegue shepherds wandering with their flocks about the Sahara, feeding the sheep in a few oases. João Fernandes roamed with them over the blighted mountains and the hills of sand—a lunar landscape, like the bottom of the sea dried long ago and quivering in the light, shadowed only by dead valleys along which no rivers flowed, and nothing grew but a few blades of wizened grass.

Somehow the sheep lived on these barren pasture lands, and camels too, and men lived on their milk. It served as food and drink most of the time, though here and there might be a brackish well. When by the sea the diet was varied by fish, dried in the sun and eaten raw for lack of wood with which it might be cooked.

João Fernandes did not stay beside the coast for long. One day two men came riding up, inviting him to visit a great man whose name was Ahude Meymom. "I should be delighted," said João Fernandes, "because I hear that he is very noble, and I should like to meet him and make his acquaintance."

They mounted him upon a camel then and struck inland. For days and nights they rode across a featureless waste, guided by stars and winds and flights of birds, as if at sea. Their water failed before they reached their journey's end, and for three days they had nothing to drink. Weary with heat and thirst and dust, João Fernandes arrived at the Berber's camp. He bowed politely to Ahude Meymom, who welcomed the stranger to his tent and regaled him with milk.

The patriarch Ahude Meymom, with his sons and his followers, could muster a hundred and fifty men. His wealth consisted of large herds of cattle and of sheep, a few horses, some negro slaves, and gold brought from the kingdom of Mali in the Sudan—a region of which all reports were vague. Among these nomads could be found leather and wool, butter and cheese, obtained from their own herds, and from the coast they got amber and sea lions' skins. These goods they bartered on the desert's fringe for merchandise from Guinea and the negro lands.

Not much is known about João Fernandes' life with them. He left no written record of all that he saw and heard, and though the chronicler, Zurara, says he knew him well, he gives only a short account of what the traveler told.

We gather that João Fernandes spent some months with Ahude Meymom, and wandered with the sheep and camels up and down a wide and empty land—a land with neither towns nor villages, nor trees except palms of the oases, or datura, or shrubs whose leaves were thorns. Yet there was life amid this desolation—João Fernandes got to know the fauna of the desert: hares and gazelles, and antelopes, and partridges, and ostriches galore. He found the European swallow wintering over the hot sands, and many other little birds he knew at home; but the flights of storks that he sometimes saw overhead passed without stopping on their way to negro lands.

He made great friends with all his hosts—Moslems although they were—wild nomads, living without "either master, or law, or justice, wandering each man where he would, and doing what he pleased." Uncivilized though they might be, they had a culture of their own. They even knew the art of writing, but João Fernandes noted that their script was not the Arabic.

They never stayed more than a week in any place, so João Fernandes must have covered leagues of country almost unexplored even today. Of his itinerary, however, nothing is known—only that in the end it brought him back to that part of the coast where he had first been left. A solitary figure on a hill, he daily scanned the sea with eager eyes, until a sail appeared on the horizon—an agonizing moment for a man who knows that he is but a dot in space. But Antão Gonçalves was looking out. His fleet of three caravels hove nearer to the shore, a boat was launched, and João Fernandes, after seven months, was greeted by his fellow countrymen. They found him bronzed, and fat, and fit; his diet of milk appears to have agreed with him. He was delighted to return to his own kind, but all the Berbers wept! João Fernandes must have had a way with him, for they hated to see him go.

Ahude Meymom had come to see him off, to do a little trading, and gape at the caravels. Two hostages were then exchanged, as proof of good faith on either side, and negotiations went off most successfully. Ahude Meymom was delighted by all he saw, and bartered negroes and gold dust for trifles of small value. His fellow Berbers gathered round, and wondered, and exclaimed. They fetched their wives, and spent a happy day visiting the strange ships.

The Portuguese hostages, meanwhile, were not so well amused. They were kept sitting in the nomads' tent all day, surrounded by the families who stayed behind, and every time that their lords turned their backs, the Berber ladies gave the strangers the glad eye. The Portuguese could not feel sure if this was owing to their manly beauty, or if it might be merely a decoy. The situation therefore was somewhat embarrassing, and they were happy when their opposite numbers returned at last to set them free.

Instead of putting into Lagos, as was usual, Antão Gonçalves brought his caravel to Lisbon, which caused a great sensation in the capital. He had been skirmishing and hunting around Cape Branco and the islands on the return voyage and had collected there a multitude of prisoners. These hardly could be led to the Infante's palace through the crowds of sight-seers that thronged the streets. The spectacle moved the people to joy, and even those who had condemned African adventures before, now loudly praised "the great virtues of the Infante."

What Henrique, however, would have liked to see, were fewer captives and a longer coast line on the map. It was not always easy to make his subordinates understand this, as was proved by the case of Gonçalo de Sintra. The Infante had sent him out with

(195)

orders not to stop anywhere for anything, but to sail straight on down to Guinea.

Gonçalo de Sintra, a tall young man and "of great heart," thought that mere exploration was a little tame. He told his companions that he would sweep down upon one of the islands as they passed by and pick up a few captives. They pointed out that the Infante's orders were to go straight on, but he replied that orders should not be taken too literally!

Moved by his "desire for honor and profit"—especially the latter, we suppose—Gonçalo de Sintra landed on an island near Cape Branco with his crew. They found it quite deserted, because their interpreter—a captive from these parts—had managed to escape and had warned his friends. Better to go back to the ship and continue the voyage, some people urged; but Gonçalo de Sintra would not hear of it. "If I die on these islands," he exclaimed dramatically, "I will not leave before I have done so mighty a deed that nothing like it ever shall be done again!" The deed he ought to do, his comrades said reprovingly, was to obey orders!

Gonçalo de Sintra waved all that aside and passed to an adjacent islet with twelve men. The tide was out. They left their boat on a sandbank and waded across several creeks.

Everything appeared silent and deserted, with nothing more spectacular to do than scramble on the rocks. Still seeking for his epoch-making deed in these unpromising surroundings, Gonçalo and his men wandered around the coast all night and then, returning to the creek where they had landed first, they found it had filled out into a wide lagoon. Their boat was on the far side, out of reach. They must remain upon the island till the ebbing of the tide.

While they stood there marooned, the seemingly deserted island came to life. Two hundred natives fell upon them suddenly.

All twelve fought desperately, but there was not a hope. Five of their number managed to escape at last by swimming to the ship, but Gonçalo de Sintra could not swim, nor could three of the others. There were three more young men who would have been able to swim, and so might have escaped, but they chose deliberately to stay and die by their commander.

Thus perished the first victims of the African adventure—unnecessarily. The caravel returned to Portugal without seeing the Guinea coast, and poor obstinate Gonçalo de Sintra, who had hoped to amaze the world, did no more than bequeath his name to a forsaken bay.

XVI

The Guinea Coast

W AS it a gigantic sea bird?
Was it a flying fish of a kind never seen before,
that had swum up from depths unknown?

The creature with white wings was drifting slowly from the luminous horizon towards the beach where naked black figures gesticulated, pointing in surprise.

Four valiant souls allowed curiosity to overcome their fear. They launched a canoe made from a hollow tree trunk, and paddled close up to the apparition. Horrible sight! The blood froze in their veins. Here was no bird, nor fish, but something like a floating island, with terrible white faces of strangely dressed men looking over the sides.

Panic-stricken at what must surely be some sort of magic— some powerful ju-ju unheard of yet, the bold investigators turned and fled, much to the disappointment of the men above.

It was the caravel of Denis Dias—"a man who wished to see new things." He was seeing them! From the time of leaving Lagos he had set his course south, resolved not to strike sail until he reached the negro lands.

He left the Rio de Ouro far behind, and the white hills of sand by Cabo Branco's lonely cliffs. He never stopped to hunt among the negroids of the islands about Arguim, nor anchored beside any desert shore. South of all this he saw the coastline broken by two palms against the sky. He turned inland and breathed the off-shore wind. Hot and scented as if blown from the gardens of Paradise, this air was a caress. The long-sought change had come at last! The curse was lifted from the landscape. The burning, barren plains of drifting sands were gone. Behold a green land clothed in forest to the distant hills!

While black men gathered on the beach and wondered, the caravel of Denis Dias glided beside a coast that never had seen a tall ship before. She sailed around the brown cliffs of a great headland, and Denis Dias, feasting his eyes upon the trees above, named it Cape Verde.

The navigators disembarked upon a rocky island over which herds of wild goats roamed—just like the European goat, they said, but with much longer ears. Nothing else looked like Europe there. The size of the trees, as one contemporary has remarked, "has to be seen to be believed!" They measured 108 palms around the trunk, and bore a gourd-like fruit with pips the size of hazel nuts.

No human habitation was found on this island, but the mainland opposite was swarming with black men. All down the coast the passage of the caravel had been followed with wonder and surprise, and native boats put out and rowed as near it as they dared. Some of them rowed a bit too near and, not so lucky as the first canoe full of sight-seers, four of their number were captured and carried off by the white men.

Denis Dias went home a happy man. The new things he had seen had been worth while! The Infante made him happier still when he arrived. The riches he brought back with him consisted of four negroes only, but, says the chronicler, "although the spoil was less than that of others who had come before, the Infante esteemed it very great, as being from that land."

Henrique had no lack of volunteers during the next few years.

Many even equipped ships at their own expense and sailed to Africa to seek their fortune. The trouble was to persuade such to seek it far afield. "The service of God and the Infante," was doubtless a stirring incentive, but "the honor and profit of ourselves" was more attractive still. To ensure this, all that was necessary was to make a landing somewhere near Cape Branco or the islands of Arguim, and there do doughty deeds among the hotchpotch of fierce tribes wandering about those shores. After performing prodigies of valor against any odds, you loaded your ship with all the natives you could catch for ransom or for sale, and set your course homewards again, having enjoyed a new and dangerous kind of hunting—a grand sport!

The Infante was always patient. He was a visionary without illusions, who never showed surprise when others failed to share his distant views. To everyone he said, "Go farther!" but to those whose preference was for the proverbial bird in hand, he offered no reproach, only congratulations for their lesser triumphs. After all, every expedition had its use to fill in missing details on the map.

Thus men became familiar with the creeks and inlets of the coast. The capes and headlands were noted and named. The navigation of those seas which once had filled the stoutest seaman with dismay grew to be such an everyday affair that fishermen of the Algarve cast their nets by the Rio de Ouro.

The islands, one by one, were all explored by seekers after "Moors" to fight and catch: Tider, where there grew cotton trees; Arguim where fresh springs flowed; the Island of Herons close by; and that of Turtles where, in 1445, a tragedy took place like that of Gonçalo de Sintra. A small party was ambushed there and killed, and it is believed that the natives ate them! Such incidents discouraged nobody. It only made the skirmishing the more praiseworthy. And sometimes, when the warriors had had their

fling, and made their catch, they would remember the Infante
and suggest: let us sail farther down the coast, "if but to see the
land and to report upon it, thus adding to our honor!"

But João Gonçalves Zarco, the discoverer of Madeira, was not
of those to whom exploration was an afterthought. He was not
moved by any hope of monetary profit, we are told, when he sent
from his beautiful Funchal "a very noble caravel," manned and
equipped entirely at his own expense.

He gave his nephew, Alvaro Fernandes, the command, with
orders "not to consider any other gain, but to find out some new
thing if he could." No raids upon the way! the uncle insisted. He
must sail straight on till he reached the negro lands, and there
proceed as far down the coast as possible to gather information
that would please the Infante.

Alvaro Fernandes was "a bold young man." He had an energetic and like-minded crew. The caravel was equipped with stores
of every kind. Such an expedition was prepared to travel far.

They reached the Guinea coast without a stop, and disembarked at the mouth of a mighty river. Surely this was the westerly
branch of the Nile which, Moors had assured the Infante, flowed
into the Atlantic Ocean!

Enthralled, they gazed upon "the noblest river of the world,"
whose wondrous course the Ancients had described with a wealth
of detail untrammeled by dull fact. Perhaps, Zurara suggests cautiously, these writers did not speak from certain knowledge! Two
casks were filled from the symbolic stream. Not even Alexander,
the explorers reflected with solemn joy, could have tasted of this
exotic water. Henrique was to have that privilege which, so far as
we know, did him no harm.

Leaving the supposed Nile—or Senegal, as it was called by natives of that coast—the mariners sailed around Cape Verde and
found Gorea, Denis Dias' island of the goats. There they enjoyed

(201)

a good meal of fresh meat, and carved the Infante's armorial bearings on the trunk of the greatest of those giant baobabs that had amazed their predecessors.

A little farther down the coast they saw twelve negroes rowing towards the caravel in a canoe. Alvaro Fernandes, wiser than some of his colleagues had shown themselves, did nothing to scare the wild men away. On the contrary, he invited them by friendly signs to come on board, and fearlessly the negroes came. Alvaro Fernandes entertained them all as best he could, and regaled them with food and drink. His visitors took leave apparently quite happy, and, it was hoped, good friends, but later events proved that this was not the case. Something had roused the black men's suspicions and fears, or perhaps on the contrary, they thought the white men were so inoffensive as to be an easy prey.

Whatever may have been the reason, forty armed men appeared in six canoes and made as if they would attack the caravel. Alvaro Fernandes promptly launched a boat before which the assailants fled. The canoe soon was overtaken, but the natives swam and dived "like seagulls"—or like slippery fish. In the end only two were taken and carried forcibly aboard.

Still farther south another cape was seen—a promontory left desolate by some cyclone that had decapitated all its palms. They stood up gaunt and bare against the sky, like the masts of a ship that had struck sail before the storm, so Alvaro Fernandes named that headland Cape of Masts.

Four black men sat upon the beach with bows and arrows in their hands. They threw these weapons down and fled when the white strangers disembarked. A meal of roast wild pig remained abandoned on the beach until the landing party found and ate it. There, too, was left a muzzled antelope who was so tame that not even those hardened huntsmen had the heart to kill her. It seems that the blacks kept her as a decoy for capturing other game.

Alvaro Fernandes would have followed the horizon farther still, but provisions were beginning to run short. So, having reached a latitude about ten degrees north, he turned his helm and sailed for Funchal and then Lisbon. Henrique welcomed him and all his men with joy and rich rewards, for this, of all the caravels sailing that year, had made the longest voyage.

It was not, however, the only one to touch the Guinea coast, or see the supposed Nile. Gomes Pires, Lançarote of Lagos, Alvaro de Freitas, and three more, had followed close in Alvaro Fernandes' wake. It was one of those supplementary voyages that added to one's honor.

These gentlemen had sailed from Lagos about the time that Alvaro Fernandes left Funchal. They were commanding units of a fleet bent upon chastising those "Moors" who had killed their companions on the Turtle Island. All had gone well. The islands had been safely reached. The enemy showed fight, but had to scatter. Sueiro da Costa—a veteran warrior who had seen Agincourt and every other European battle of that century—chose to be knighted at Tider, having consistently refused the accolade on far greater occasions. Why he felt this one to be more auspicious is not clear, except that to be knighted in outlandish places seems to have become the fashion. Altogether there had been honor and to spare for everyone, while a shipment of captives ensured profit. The captains of the smaller craft decided to go home.

Not so Gomes Pires. "You are aware," he said to his colleagues, "how great is the Infante's wish to hear about the negro lands, and more especially about the river Nile. So I have decided to sail that way, to reach it if I can, and find out as much as I may of everything. . . . I know," he added hopefully, "that the Senhor Infante will reward and honor me for this!"

Lançarote declared that Gomes Pires had taken the words from

(203)

his mouth. He had been just about to make the same suggestion, and—"I am not the man," cried Alvaro de Freitas, "to quit your company, but to go with you as far as you will—even down to the Earthly Paradise!"

Not Eden, but the river Nile—alias Senegal—became their goal. The Infante had given them its bearings based on information supplied by Berber captives. Twenty leagues beyond the first palms it flowed into the sea, and so they followed down the coast, keeping a sharp lookout.

It was not long before a red and muddy stain spread over the blue water miles around. "Here we have a new marvel!" cried the man who was casting the sounding line, for he had brought his fingers to his lips, and found the water fresh although they were two leagues from land. The Nile, of course! they told each other with delight. No lesser stream could make its presence felt with so much power. A bucket was then lowered to the sea, and all refreshed themselves by quaffing draughts of Nile water. Brackish, one would suppose, but such is the prestige of a name that all agreed that it was excellent!

The caravels entered the river mouth and anchored off the bar. Round native huts were seen beside the bank, and eight men went ashore to look inside them. The village seemed abandoned except for two children, a small boy and girl, both black. These urchins were captured—on principle, for the good of their souls! —while the party continued to explore the huts. All were empty, and the sole object of interest found there by anyone was a round shield made of the tough hide of an elephant's ear.

An energetic little man named Estevão Afonso hunted about to find the children's parents, if he could. Guided by the sound of an axe chopping wood, he crawled stealthily through the bush and, peeping through the vegetation, saw a stalwart negro hard at work. Estevão Afonso flung himself on to the bent back and ran his fingers deep into the wooly hair.

Estevão Afonso was a little man. The African was very tall. He stood upright, and ran with Estevão Afonso hanging by his wool, with feet clean off the ground. The more the black giant tried to shake him off, the more the little white man clung. The position was awkward for them both. What could the negro do with some-one hanging like a limpet to his hair, and how could Estevão Afonso let go? He was beginning to regret that he had been so hasty when some of his companions came to his rescue. They seized the negro by the arms, and would have bound him fast, but at that moment Estevão Afonso dropped down. Finding his head released, the negro shook off his captors easily and disappeared into the bush.

Hard on Alvaro Fernandes' heels they reached the island of wild goats. They were surprised to see the reeking hides his men had left behind, and the Infante's arms carved on the tree. Upon the mainland opposite was gathered a crowd of black men. Gomes Pires thought that he would try to make friends. To signify his good intentions he deposited upon the beach a loaf of bread, a mirror, and a sheet of paper on which he had drawn a cross.

Reactions were unfavorable. The natives crumbled up the loaf and threw away the bits. They smashed the mirror with their assagais, and—quite regardless of the cross—they tore the paper into pieces. In the way of friendship, it would seem, here there was nothing doing.

"Since that is so," said Gomes Pires to his crossbowmen, "shoot at them, that they may know that we can do them harm!"

The bowmen shot, but the negroes were archers too, and their arrows were poisoned.

We do not hear of any victims being taken this time on board the caravels. They all returned to Portugal without mishap, and the two Senegalese children were duly delivered to the Infante. Henrique was delighted with the little boy, and set about to have him taught "all the things that a Christian ought to know." The child soon learned to read and write, and say his prayers, and know his catechism. He made such progress in the doctrines of the Church that many Christians, Zurara observes, were not so well-informed or so devout as he. The Infante hoped to make a priest of him to send to Africa as missionary to his own people, but as so often happens to such infant prodigies, the learned little African died young.

His sister, whom we may suppose nobody dreamed of burdening with study, grew up to happy womanhood in Portugal, where she was never treated as a slave.

South of Cape Verde, Henrique's seamen now entered on a new wonder-world—a world where everything was different and intensified, or on a larger scale; a world of taller trees and wider rivers, of sweeter and quite unfamiliar scents, fantastic plants and fruits, and flowers of species never seen before, and impenetrable thickets which poured forth poisoned arrows. The fierce life of the Tropics was revealed to European eyes, and the mysterious continent below the deserts of the North took on a new face, strangely beautiful.

It was beauty with a sting, but none the less alluring. Those sluggish, death-dealing rivers of Africa were like so many open doors inviting to its heart. The valiant Nuno Tristão, breaker of records, was one of the first to follow on and meet his doom.

He sailed for sixty leagues south of Cape Verde, to the mouth of an unknown river. The shining water glided smoothly from the forest shade, and Nuno Tristão, with his crew in two small boats, rowed upstream to explore. Borne by the tide inland beneath a canopy of green, they suddenly were surrounded by twelve canoes. At that same moment from all sides there descended a rain of arrows—light pointed darts that did no more than prick, but every point was steeped in death.

Four of the wounded died before they reached the river mouth, the rest just managed to row to their caravel. Struggling against the poison stealing through their veins, they moored the boat, and hastened to get the ship underway, but no one had the strength to haul the anchor up—they had to cut the ropes.

The caravel drifted to sea, laden with dying men. The only sound persons on board were Aires Tinoco, a very young ship's clerk, two little pages, a black boy, and one seaman. The three lads gathered round this sailor anxiously, asking what they should do. He said that he was sorry but he could not navigate. He would, however, do his best to sail the ship, if somebody could guide him.

Then the boy Aires Tinoco showed himself a man and worthy pupil of the Infante of Sagres, in whose household he had been brought up. Putting together all the theory he had picked up at Henrique's court, he set the course himself and told the seaman how to steer.

It was a strange and tragic voyage. The first day out they had to cast the bodies of their captain and their shipmates to the deep. Only two of the wounded men survived, and for weeks they remained helplessly ill.

Two months on end they sailed, far from all sight of land, manning the ship as best they might, short-handed as they were, and trusting to Aires Tinoco's hearsay nautical science.

They did not trust in vain. Not for nothing had this boy spent his early years beside the navigators' prince. After eight weeks of empty horizon they saw a dim coastline, and for the first time there appeared a sail upon the sea. The apparition was noted with mingled feelings of anxiety and hope, for none could tell if it would prove a blessing or a curse. It might have been one of those

Moorish corsairs that patrolled the north Moroccan coast, and then the painful Odyssey would end in some dungeon at Fez or Tetuan.

The ship approached and hailed the caravel—oh joy! in Christian accents. The captain was Pero Falcão, an honest Galician corsair, and they were off the coast of Portugal, near Sines, of Alentejo! The amiable pirate himself piloted their caravel into Lagos, where they met the Infante, and presented him their spoil —a multitude of poisoned arrows.

Henrique mourned for Nuno Tristão and his slain comrades, "for he had brought up nearly all of them," but the disaster did not slacken enterprise. The very next year, that game little adventurer, Estevão Afonso, took three caravels into a river thirty-two leagues beyond that of Nuno Tristão.

He sailed upstream until one vessel ran aground, and then he disembarked with his companions. They wandered about under cotton trees, and by the native plantations of rice in swamps beside the river, until they reached a stretch of dense forest beyond and found that it rained arrows and bristled with spears. To fight an enemy so armed, protected by his native bush, was quite impossible for fifteen or twenty men. They withdrew to the caravel, but not before five of their number were stretched dead under the trees.

Alvaro Fernandes also made his second voyage to Guinea at about this time. He sailed 110 leagues beyond Cape Verde, breaking the distance record for that year. He won the Regent's prize of 200 doubloons for this achievement, and Henrique gave him a hundred more. But he had not escaped the vengeance of the forest men. He had left Guinea with a poisoned arrow in his leg, and nearly died on his way home.

Henrique ordered no reprisals. He had never meant to carry violence down the coast of Africa, and felt that too much had been

(208)

done already. His earlier orders to bring back men from the newly-discovered lands to give him information had soon been turned to a pretext for constant raids and battles in which combatants on either side were killed. Henrique was sufficiently of his own time and his Peninsula to think that there was always some merit in fighting "Moors," but the farther you followed the said "Moors" from their centers of culture into the primitive wilderness the less he cared for such hostilities. It was all very well for his chronicler, Zurara, to reflect, when the natives took to their heels, that had they known what would be for their highest good they would have rushed to meet their pursuers instead of running away—the fact remained that such perception was denied them, and Henrique did not desire to see his glorious enterprise degenerate into a form of piracy. He had no objection to bringing slaves from Africa, as we have seen, but he preferred to barter them for merchandise and not seize them by force. It may have been about this time—chronology is rather vague in the record left by his old servant, the seaman, Diogo Gomes—that "the Senhor Infante recommended not to fight with the people of those parts in future, but enter into alliances, and trade with them, because he wished to make them Christian."

It took some time for the idea to sink in. During the voyages of the next few years we continue to hear of skirmishes and catches. To establish relations with primitive people of another race needs patience, a quality by which all of Henrique's captains did not shine. Intercourse with the nomads of the Rio de Ouro had started pleasantly, thanks to João Fernandes' enterprise and tact. The natives' friendly confidence was even quite embarrassing, for every time a ship anchored off their coast they climbed on board in crowds and camped there all day long. But Gomes Pires upset everything.

It must be owned that he had provocation. When he arrived to do a little trade the tribesmen of the coast informed him that there were rich merchants not far off inland "with slaves, and gold, and other things with which you well may be content."

"Go and fetch them!" said Gomes Pires happily, and paid them to do so.

When he had waited for some weeks and nothing happened, Gomes Pires saw that he had been deceived, and lost his temper. He cleared all loafers off his ship, and told the natives that they must be on their guard. Hitherto he had granted safe conduct to all in the name of the Infante, but now that they had played him falsely peace was at an end. He sailed away, not to begin by taking an unfair advantage, and then, returning, made a series of raids up and down the coast. He got off with some eighty prisoners but, needless to say, the Rio de Ouro commerce suffered a severe setback.

Henrique did not punish Gomes Pires for his hasty conduct. We gather that Henrique seldom punished anyone. His philosophy of life seems to have been to take men as they were, and not expect too much. He did get angry sometimes—he could even be very angry, as when two of his captains caught Canary Islanders by violating safe conduct. But no mention is made of any Nemesis overtaking the offenders. All we are told is how their victims were compensated by handsome gifts, and were repatriated praising loudly the Infante.

When Gomes Pires upset the Sahara trade, Henrique simply tried again elsewhere—at Meça, higher up the coast. There, things went well, thanks to the useful João Fernandes, who landed and exerted his diplomacy again. He obtained slaves in ransom for some Moorish prisoners—and brought home as well a fine desert lion! Perhaps Henrique found this was an awkward pet to keep, for he soon passed it on. The lordly beast was sent to Ireland to an English friend of the Infante who resided at Galway. It is not likely that the poor thing survived many winters there, but while it lived it was a great success, for "never," says Zurara, "had such been seen in those parts!"

What with the travel stories of wandering knights like Balthasar circulating the continent, and parrots and monkeys carried by Portuguese traders to Bruges, and even lions on show in countries so remote as Ireland, all cultured Europe was commenting on the wonders that Henrique had revealed. Abelhart the Dane, feeling the urge of Viking forefathers stir in his blood, begged King Christian of Scandinavia for leave to visit Portugal, where such exciting doings were afoot. There he appeared one day among the seamen and the savants that thronged Henrique's household, and steeped his spirit in the atmosphere of wonder, and enquiry, and adventure that they breathed. Soon he was asking the Infante for a caravel that he, too, might sail south and see the negroland.

Henrique was only too pleased. Let Abelhart go to Cape Verde, he proposed, upon a diplomatic mission. It had been learned that the natives of that country were subjects of a king. The Regent, D. Pedro, wished to make contact with this African monarch, for it was believed that he might be Christian. If that were so, perhaps he would assist the King of Portugal against the Moors.

Bearing letters to this unknown ruler, Abelhart set forth. Fernandafonso, knight of the Infante's household, went with him to direct the ship and to command the crew, since Abelhart "was foreign, and therefore did not know the character and customs of the men so well." Fernandafonso would also be spokesman to the black king should they chance to meet. Thus, although Abelhart was considered to be the captain of the expedition, his functions seem to have been more or less honorary.

Anyhow, he enjoyed himself immensely. A Dane was bound to be happy at sea, although this voyage took six months, we are told. The delay was partly due to stormy weather, but chiefly because Abelhart, in his eagerness to see all that could be seen, insisted upon coasting all the way.

At Cape Verde they found the usual crowd awaiting on the beach, gathered around the local chief, whose name was Guitanye. This Guitanye seems to have been a gentlemanly sort of person— a *cavaleiro*, Zurara calls him. Upon request, he consented to an exchange of hostages, and sent one of his men on board the caravel. Abelhart's Portuguese not being considered equal to the occasion, it was Fernandafonso who addressed the envoy through the interpreter.

"We are the servants of a great and mighty Prince of Spain,[1] in the far West," he told the African, "at his command we have come here, to speak on his behalf to the great and good lord of this land."

"If you would see our great King Boor," the negro replied, "you cannot do so at present, for he is very far away, fighting another chief who will not obey him." It would take six or seven days, it seemed, for a message to reach the king.

A message must be sent, Fernandafonso said, if Guitanye would render service to his country and his king.

Food was then served. The black man ate and drank, and was given the Regent's letter to show his lord in token of friendship— "The gist of what I said to you is written there," Fernandafonso explained.

It is doubtful if the envoy had any clear idea of what a letter might be. He probably imagined that it was some kind of talisman. The paper caused a great sensation on the beach, where he

---

[1] In the fifteenth century Spain was a geographical term, including the whole of the Iberian peninsula and the several independent kingdoms into which it was divided, just as the name Scandinavia today covers both Norway and Sweden.

and Guitanye were thronged by a curious crowd, all agog to hear about the visit to the ship and struggling to get near enough to see and touch the thing that in some magic way contained the white man's words.

The Portuguese waited all day in a small boat just off the shore, while Guitanye conferred with two colleagues, whose ugliness, they say, was unbelievable. He found it difficult to send an answer back, for the crowd surged about him so that he could scarcely move. He tried to wade out to the boat, but the multitude came after him and closed around. Chief though he was, he does not appear to have had much authority. All business had to be postponed for the next day.

Guitanye showed himself quite friendly. He sent the strangers samples of the country's wealth: a goat, a kid, cuscus, a kind of gruel with butter, native bread, and some ears of local corn, palm wine, and milk, and—to the wonder and delight of Abelhart—a real elephant's tusk!

Parleying continued for several days. Guitanye visited the caravel and made himself agreeable. It was not necessary to send a message to his king, he said, for he was vested with full powers, and they could deal with him direct. Fernandafonso was not so to be put off. He insisted until at last an envoy was dispatched to meet the king. Awaiting this messenger's return, the black and white men exchanged courtesies, and gave each other gifts, and everything seemed to be going well.

But Abelhart was calling for an elephant. Oh, let him see an elephant, alive or dead! He would pay handsomely, he said, whoever brought him one, for he must know what the whole beast looked like, which had teeth like that tusk! He wished to have its skin and bones, and some part of its flesh, to carry back with him to Denmark as a souvenir. "If you can obtain that for us," he told the natives, "you shall be given a canvas tent able to shelter twenty-five to thirty men and yet so light that it may be carried on a man's back."

It was the Africans' turn to be thrilled and dazzled. An elephant was easy to obtain, they said, and Guitanye himself went off to track one down.

That same day, Abelhart saw men signaling to him from the shore. Don't go! advised the more experienced travelers, who had seen something of the natives of that coast. Better to wait until the friendly Guitanye came back.

But Abelhart was confident. He felt that he knew how to deal with the black men. Besides, who knew if they had not already there an elephant for him?

He rowed towards the beach on which a negro stood, seeming to offer him a gourd of wine, or water. Abelhart ordered the boat to be brought farther in, though several of the oarsmen shook their heads.

Abelhart sat at ease in the poop of his boat, watching a group of blacks under a tree. He did not see the interpreter lean forward as if to reach out towards the gourd, and so slip overboard. His companions, however, noticed the maneuver and, suspecting treason, tried to turn about, but the next wave threw the boat on to the beach.

Then suddenly, out of the shadows, rose a swarm of black men waving spears. They closed around the boat—and little is known of what happened next. One man only jumped overboard, and was able to swim back to his ship. He looked around more than once towards the shore, but only saw one of his comrades killed, and every time he turned there was the tall, fair Dane, still sitting on the poop. This man's account is vague, but no other eye-witness returned to add further details.

Nobody ever knew the fate of Abelhart, nor of those men who

had rowed with him to the shore. White men and black—alive or dead—all vanished in the bush leaving no trace behind. Only after long years, some captives brought from Africa told the Infante of four Christians they had seen imprisoned in a fortress far inland. One of them had since died, but three were still alive. From the description they might well have been the missing Scandinavian and his men. But nothing more definite has been heard of them from that day until this.

To make alliance with the wild men of the forest, clearly was not the simple task it first appeared. These fifteenth-century Europeans, bred of progressive Christian culture, unconscious heirs of still older civilizations, were faced for the first time by the elusiveness, cunning, and the treachery of savage man. The experience was baffling.

Almost any other prince of D. Henrique's time would have set about arming military excursions to chastise the heathen in their homes.

But Henrique's orders were not to fight.

XVII

The Ascent of Bragança

A CALM between two storms—so Henrique in after years must have remembered the period of his brother's undisputed regency.

The interval was all too short. Unhappy is the land whose king is a child! Medieval peoples from the depths of their bitter experience, knew this truth, but it did not make things any better to pretend that at fourteen a child already was a man! That seems to have been the accepted convention in most countries, and thus in 1446, King Afonso V of Portugal was ceremonially proclaimed of age.

Awe-stricken and a little nervous, he sat upon his throne in the great hall of Lisbon palace, facing the full assembly of the Cortes—fidalgos, delegates from the Concelhos, and the magnates of the Church. Beside him stood the three surviving uncles who were left in the place of parents to the orphan boy.

Afonso's uncles played unequal parts in his young life. Perhaps Henrique was the favorite at this time. Not that Afonso had seen much of him. The Infante, deeply engrossed in the exploration of his newly-found lands, was more often at Lagos or at Sagres than at court. But uncle and nephew shared an enthusiastic interest in military exploits and knightly deeds, which would provide the theme for many a delightful conversation. Besides, Henrique had the advantage of never being called to exercise authority over his nephew. His rôle was merely that of pleasant visitor—to Pedro fell the more ungrateful task of guardian and preceptor.

To bring up other people's children is often a thorny mission, and Pedro had protested when the Cortes transferred the custody of the two princes from the boys' mother to him. He did not wish to be disliked by his nephews, he said, but he must do his duty, and there might well be moments when "they would deserve correction and reproof rather than praise!"

It is difficult to say if young Afonso liked or disliked his guardian at this time. We gather that the "correction and reproof" had not been overdone; the boy was docile more than otherwise, and the uncle was by nature kind and just—but there were hidden influences at work. While D. Pedro was Regent, and the King a child, these undermining forces were unable to manifest themselves openly. Still, they progressed in secret by suggestions here, insinuations there, and subtle play on the undying memory of a night at Lisbon when Afonso was a little boy, and his mother had kissed him, and wept, and gone out of his life forever.

Which brings us to the King's namesake and third uncle— Afonso, Count of Barcelos, promoted by the Regent to be Duke of Bragança in his old age. This high honor—a title hitherto exclusive to the two elder Infantes, who were Dukes of Coimbra and Vizeu respectively—still failed to blunt the spite nursed by the bastard towards his father's lawful sons. Afonso of Bragança had not much to do with the King's childish years, but in the background, he was waiting.

He was waiting for such a day as this, when his nephew had completed his fourteenth year, and tradition ruled that he should no more be considered a minor.

Afonso V took the symbolic Rod of Justice from the Regent's hand, and listened to the learned discourse of the lawyer, Dr.

Magaancha. The orator admitted that fourteen was rather young —but, he added impressively, such were Afonso's virtues and good sense that the helm of State could safely be entrusted to his care!

Somewhat chastened by this solemn thought, the young king left the Cortes for his own apartments, bolstered by good advice upon the way from his uncle Henrique who walked by his side. In the royal chamber where the court officials were assembled his uncle Pedro gave him a great deal more. When the medieval young went wrong, it was not for lack of proper cautioning from their elders. Pedro held forth upon the art of reigning and the duties of a king. These were many and arduous, it appeared.

Completely shattered, young Afonso begged his uncle not to leave him yet to govern all alone! Could not the regency continue just a little longer—"until he saw what he would be able to do . . . because he feared that by himself with nobody to help him he could not manage so heavy a task!"

It was a reasonable request. A few days later the Cortes were informed that it was the King's wish for the Regent to continue in office.

The delegates had not the least objection to such an arrangement, for the country had prospered under Pedro's guiding hand. He had brought in excellent reforms, reorganized public administration, and at the same time he had revised and brought up to date existing codes of law—the famous "Ordenações Afonsinas" were largely Pedro's work. His foreign policy was equally successful. His influence had turned Castile from a menace to something of a satellite; while Henrique's explorations by sea and land had progressed steadily through the Regent's support. Pedro could look back upon his term of government without remorse, conscious that he had served his country and his nephew well.

Was it any satisfaction to him to have his rule prolonged? That would be difficult to guess. Pedro took up the reins of power or laid them down in the same manner we observe in him through life—that of an open-eyed and slightly disillusioned philosopher. He never seems to have expected to reap anything but thorns. He said as much to Henrique one day when they were leaving Coimbra together. Riding towards the bridge across the Mondego, they looked up at the city's arms carved over the gate: the figure of a woman rising out of a chalice, with a lion at one breast and a dragon at the other. "See, brother!" Henrique remarked, "this figure is like you, for you are nourishing the lion of Castile, and Portugal is the dragon!"

Pedro paused and considered. "Yes," he said presently, "but look again, and see that she is on a chalice, which means blood —and that, no doubt, will be the sole reward for all my pains."

It may have been the young king's character that caused Pedro's misgivings. The boy was lovable enough. He was warm-hearted and enthusiastic, truthful and brave, and though his ruling passion was for arms, he shared the predilection of his family for learning and for books. He was easy to lead—but therein lay the trouble. There was too much of his mother in Afonso; like her he could be swayed by every wind. His guardian knew that there were seeds of prejudice sown long ago. Any determined person could foster them into growth—and all the while the Duke of Bragança was waiting.

After biding his time so long, the old man's rage to see the regency prolonged is easy to imagine. His indignation overflowed. It was a scandal, he declared, for a king to be kept in tutelage when he was old enough to rule alone! The Duke protested to the Cortes, but without effect, and so he wrote and told his nephew what he thought. Let Afonso assert himself, he said, and reign! At his age, and with "the perfect judgment and

understanding that God had given him, he was fit to rule much
greater realms than that of Portugal." To be subject to D. Pedro
as if he were a child was not becoming to his manly dignity.

Men of fourteen are sensitive about their manly dignity, and
Afonso was stung. He told his uncle that he had changed his
mind. He already felt old enough to reign alone, and he would
like to do so.

Pedro did not discourage him. "Of course you can," he said,
"if you want to." However, in view of the fact that the King had
informed the Cortes that he did not propose to govern yet, he
could not decently reverse his own decision without some delay.
Afonso was to be married after his fifteenth birthday. He agreed
to his uncle's suggestion that he should start to rule upon his
wedding day.

The bride-to-be was Pedro's eldest daughter, Isabel—a choice
which the Duke of Bragança disapproved. At this date, however,
he did not actively oppose the match—he knew it was too late.
The marriage, arranged between the parents in the first place, had
now passed from the older people's hands. The two children,
betrothed since babyhood, adored each other, and Afonso, un-
stable though he was, in this at least was certain of his mind.
Duarte's son was a one-woman man. The bride of his childhood
grew up to be Afonso's first and only love, although he was to
be widower for more than half his life.

The date was fixed which was to end the regency, but still the
Duke of Bragança was not content. He with his son, the Count
of Ourem, and D. Pedro's old enemy the Archbishop of Lisbon,
now returned from exile, tried all their wiles on the young king.
The Archbishop especially came to Afonso's bedroom at night
and talked to him for hours. A grown-up person should not have
a guardian, he declared, and when a king had been proclaimed of
age, then the regent must go! It doubtless suited the Infante

D. Pedro to treat his nephew as a minor still, but to the impartial spectator things looked bad. If Afonso did not take a firm line with this uncle of his, he would be all his life in leading strings!

With the skill of a practised hand, the Archbishop thus pricked and prodded Afonso's schoolboy pride. He vowed that he would show the spirit of a man, and peremptorily ordered his uncle to transfer the reins of government to him. At once! He did not mean to wait till he was married. Pedro handed over everything to him without the least protest, and did not sign a single paper from that moment on. Afonso, feeling himself every inch a king, prepared to rule at the dictates of the Bragança clan.

These gentlemen saw their dreams about to come true. To have a king fifteen years old—a born spendthrift at that! A golden opportunity for fortunes to be made, and only one obstacle to be seen on the horizon! The ex-Regent, if he remained at court, might well prove a kill-joy. His influence was bound to count for something with the King. And how could they feel sure that Afonso, once the thrill of emancipation had worn off, might not turn again to his former guide? Pedro must go, decided the opportunists, before the King was old enough to appreciate his uncle.

It would be harder to get rid of Pedro's daughter, but the intriguers noted with delight that for the present she did not seem likely to upset their plans. The little Queen, absorbed in her childish romance, was more or less oblivious of all else. She had a dutiful affection for her father, but she worshiped her boy lover. He was her hero and her king, and whoever might be at fault, it never could be her Afonso! Isabel was a charming child —well brought up, well read, pretty, and accomplished—but she had not in her to become the power behind the throne that her grandmother had been. Her husband loved her wholly, and she never lost his love, but being a submissive little soul she never tried to use her influence upon him.

This was a pity, for Afonso was easily led by anybody who knew how to take him, and there were many of the wrong kind who did that. They gathered around him like a swarm of flies, and battened on his weakness and his youth. They buzzed about him, and they murmured in his ears, they hinted and insinuated and invented calumnies: D. Pedro was ambitious, they repeated constantly; he wished to reign himself, and to promote his sons—he was hatching a plot to seize the power again! It was the old accusation, already tried successfully upon Afonso's mother.

The son proved quite as gullible. Afonso listened, hesitated, half believed—and then the Count of Ourem scored the winning hit. He told the young king bluntly that his subjects all were vexed to see that he was still under his uncle's thumb. It was quite plain that though officially the Regent had resigned, he only had to whistle, and Afonso came to heel!

Afonso, furious at such a suggestion, vowed that he would ask his uncle to withdraw from court. The Count, fearing that the boy would not have the nerve, advised him to send a message of dismissal. Afonso, however, who had some sense of decency, said that it would be more correct if he spoke to the Infante himself.

Pedro saved him that awkward interview. Someone had warned the ex-Regent of what was coming, so he sought his nephew himself, and asked permission to retire to his own lands. They needed attention, he said, having been neglected for many years. Afonso, enormously relieved at being thus forestalled, bade his uncle quite an affectionate farewell.

Then the Braganças and their minions took possession of the court, and enthusiastically made hay while the sun shone. One by one all the partisans of the late Queen made their appearance in Afonso's halls. The tales that they told him were harrowing, of how his wicked uncle had ill-treated his poor mother! She had been persecuted, exiled, robbed, and finally—they hinted darkly—poisoned! Was such a horror possible? Of course it was! The Regent had done things like that before. Did Afonso think that his father had died a natural death? And the Infante D. João? went on the calumniators, warming to their task—he died of fever, people said, but that fever had been provoked by a little dose of something given by his brother! Why D. Pedro should wish to murder his right-hand man and most ardent supporter, they did not trouble to explain.

Whether or not such far-fetched accusations carried weight, the sorrows of Afonso's mother were an easy theme to harp on to her son. He remembered her tears very well, and naturally he never would suppose that her troubles were all of her own making. The tale of a dead mother's wrongs could not fail to rouse the indignation of a chivalrous and warm-hearted boy, and Afonso—who remained rather guileless all his life—was not the one to see through intrigue when he was fifteen. Both he and his young brother Fernando soon found themselves hating the uncle who had brought them up.

The Infante D. Henrique, in the Algarve, contemplating the sky and the Atlantic Ocean, watching his ships return with trophies from Cape Verde and Senegal, caught echoes of the turmoil and intrigues at court. He heard that Pedro was the butt of basest calumniators. Henrique, with a jerk, descended from the stars; he closed his books and put aside his maps. Turning his back upon the sea, he sprang to horse and rode in haste towards his nephew's court to vindicate his brother.

He found Afonso changed, and no longer the gentle and respectful nephew he remembered. The boy listened impatiently

(223)

to what his uncle had to say, and answered rather rudely. His satellites had warned him not to heed D. Henrique's defense of the Regent, for both uncles were tarred with the same brush. Henrique had encouraged Pedro to usurp the regency. He had been party to the persecution of the Queen, which he might easily have stopped if he had chosen. He could have behaved like the Duke of Bragança, and then how differently all things would have turned out! The King had only one uncle whose conduct had always been above reproach!

Prepared thus by his mentors, Afonso received Henrique with suspicion, and discounted everything he said. And no doubt it was fine to be a grown-up king, and able to take a high tone towards one's uncle, who was no more than a subject after all! Surrounded as he was by flatterers, Afonso's youthful head was being turned. Henrique understood that uncles were at a discount, and tried another hand upon his nephew.

Alvaro Vaz de Almada, Knight of the Garter, Count of Avranches in France, hero of Agincourt and of Tangier, the dearest friend and traveling companion of D. Pedro's youth, at a word from Henrique left Ceuta where he was fighting the Moors, and hastened back to court.

His arrival created a sensation, for Alvaro Vaz was a great hero in Afonso's eyes. D. Henrique had often told of his exploits. There was no other realm in Spain, he said, that could boast such a champion. When Alvaro Vaz appeared upon the scene, Afonso ceased to be the young king overwhelmed by his own dignity, and became just a boy admiring a great soldier.

Alvaro Vaz was no courtier. He spoke his mind frankly to anyone and at all times. The Infante D. Pedro was his friend, and he defended him in public and in private. Afonso never contradicted Alvaro Vaz—how could you argue with such a distinguished warrior as that? Had not Afonso's cousin King Henry V

—a connoisseur in deeds of arms, as all men knew—been so impressed by the prowess of Alvaro Vaz that he gave him a title, and the Garter?

All the Bragança faction gnashed their teeth. Until that man removed himself, they could do nothing with the King. They tried to frighten the hero away! The court was no safe place for him, murmured some self-styled friend. His enemies were concocting a plot to have the Count arrested at the next council meeting.

Alvaro Vaz laughed heartily. A likely story! What pretext could be found for such an act? He had never failed to serve his king and country faithfully—"I deserve rather to be endowed with towns and castles than with prison chains." And if some calumniator was at work—"I will show myself worthy companion of the Holy Garter which I have received. I hope to God that those who visit me may see me rather in my grave than in dungeons or chains. . . . Don't you worry about my life," he concluded, "an honorable death will make it highly praised, and honored in the memory of men forever!"

That same day, dressed in his best clothes, Alvaro Vaz swaggered nonchalantly into the council chamber. He went straight to the King and told him of the warning that he had received. In the same breath he challenged his detractors. Let them but meet him in the field, he said, he would be happy to take on the best of them—three at a time!

Afonso was thrilled. It sounded like his favorite books! Nobody came forward, however, to take up the challenge. The King assured the Count of Avranches of his perfect confidence, and the incident closed. Then the intriguers, seriously alarmed lest Alvaro Vaz, backed by the Infante D. Henrique, might undermine their influence over the King, hurried Afonso off to Sintra for the summer, and so the court broke up. The usual dispersal took place, and Henrique with Alvaro Vaz de Almada went to join D. Pedro at Coimbra.

They found him worried and depressed, for even in his retirement the hatred of his enemies pursued him. The King—or rather the Count of Ourem on his behalf—was sending letters to the great ones of the realm, forbidding them to visit the ex-Regent. This was followed by a notice to Pedro himself prohibiting him to leave his lands or show himself at court. Pedro and Henrique sent a messenger to ask the reason for this banishment, but no explanation was forthcoming. The fact was that the self-appointed keepers of Afonso's conscience were afraid that the Infante D. Henrique might bring his brother back to court with him. Uncle and nephew must be kept apart at any price, for if they were to meet it would be easy for Pedro to justify himself and to expose the malice of his calumniators. The plot was therefore to entangle him, and force him to some compromising act before he had the chance of explaining himself.

Having failed to trap him in various ways, his enemies began to circulate the rumor that D. Pedro was arming to the teeth, and fortifying his castles of Coimbra and Montemor. A messenger from court arrived post-haste, ordering the Infante to desist from such treasonable activities forthwith. His answer was to show the envoy over all his castle where not a sign of warlike preparations could be seen.

That was all very well, said the backbiters to the King, but there were armaments at Coimbra! What had happened to those munitions that the regent gathered several years before, when the King of Castile had appealed for help against his enemies, and troops from Portugal had been dispatched? As matters had turned out, this aid was not required, and all the weapons had been returned intact. They had been stored in the Coimbra arsenal.

This was true, and Pedro did not deny it, when he received an imperious command to hand them over. The intimation was purely provocative, for the weapons were not needed for any present purpose, and would only have to be stored elsewhere. In making the demand, however, Pedro's enemies were sure to score, for if he obeyed, then he was disarmed, and if he refused—then he was a rebel!

Henrique's advice to his brother through all this was to be patient to the end. Better obey even the most unreasonable orders than give his enemies any handle against him. The King was very young, and in bad hands, and dizzy with his own emancipation. This state of affairs would not last. If Pedro could bring himself to endure not only the pinpricks but the insults, their nephew would come to his senses presently.

The advice was sound, but particularly hard for Pedro to follow. He had been very patient all the while, but the attitude of humble and obedient subject wilting under the royal displeasure is not easy to assume towards the boy you have brought up yourself. There must have been moments when Pedro would have liked nothing so well as to chastise the arrogant youngster who chose to treat his uncle as a rebel!

At other times he found excuses for him, for he still loved the boy. These persecutions were not really moved by Afonso, he said, but by the intriguers around him. One could not blame the King, he was too young. Such considerations, however, did not make Pedro more inclined to obey orders. He knew from whom they really came, and that his enemies would stop at nothing in their spite towards him. For this reason he did not wish to be unarmed.

He explained himself to Afonso in a letter of great restraint and dignity: "Since the weapons of his innocence," said he, "had not the power to defend him from the assaults of his enemies, he begged to be allowed to keep those material defenses of his life and honor." Since they were Crown property, he was prepared to pay for them, or if they were not to be bought, let him be given time to send for other armaments before surrendering these.

It seems that many letters were exchanged between Afonso and his uncle, and if the correspondence had never been tampered with, some good might have resulted. But we are told that Pedro's rivals cast fuel onto the fire by forging letters for both sides. It was too easy! The King was a child, and though he would have scouted the idea, he was still ruled by grown-up people. They made what use they chose of the royal seal and much was written in Afonso's name of which he had no knowledge. The archivist, Ruy de Pina, was convinced of this when he compared the letters written to D. Pedro in the King's own hand with those ratified by the seal alone. The latter speak the language of an irate monarch to a rebellious vassal, whereas the letters that Afonso wrote himself observe the respect owing to an uncle who is also a father-in-law.

This dual relationship was a bitter pill to D. Pedro's enemies, obliged to bow the knee before his daughter as their queen. They made her suffer for it, too. The young girl was a friendless figure at her husband's court, with critical and hostile faces all around. The campaign against her accompanied that which was launched against her father, but Isabel's detractors were forced to work underground.

That did not discourage them. There was nothing that they did not devise to separate the King from his young bride. When they found that no distraction—not even the pleasures of the chase—could keep Afonso long from Isabel, then they remorselessly conspired to arouse his jealousy, and blacken her fair name.

But here the shafts of malice broke themselves in vain. No slander could prevail against the certain knowledge of Afonso's heart. At the core of his yielding nature ran one fiber like steel. Intriguers might poison his mind against whomsoever they would, but not against his little love. Of her he could believe no evil; towards her he never changed. Between her and the malice of the world his perfect faith was an unfailing shield. When Alvaro de Castro, the King's chamberlain, was arrested upon the charge of having made love to the Queen, Afonso ordered him to be released at once, and showing him marked favor, vindicated his wife's honor.

In other respects D. Pedro's enemies had it all their own way. The Count of Ourem was their ringleader at court, and he was doing all he could to precipitate issues. The Duke, his father, at this time was in the North of Portugal. The Count made the King summon him to court, and secretly advised his parent to come down through Pedro's lands, armed to the teeth and escorted by troops, without so much as asking the Infante's leave. He would regard this as an insult and a provocation, and so it was intended to appear. The Duke and Count desired nothing so much as to goad Pedro into violence of some kind.

The Infante, hearing of his approach in such array, protested to the Duke. If he would travel through his brother's lands, let him come as a brother, with his usual retinue, but not as an invader leading an army. In any case, there was no need to take these men through the district of Coimbra.

The Duke replied that he must pass through Lousã with them all. He was traveling peacefully to court upon the King's business, and could not leave his following behind. He always went about accompanied like that!

"Tell the Duke that I am not a fool!" retorted D. Pedro. "We know each other of old. He has passed through my lands before, and I remember very well what was his retinue." To march around with sixteen hundred men, he pointed out, did not look much like peaceful traveling!

The Duke insisted, and the position grew tense. The Count of Ourem made the King order the Infante to let the army of Bragança through. Pedro did not feel inclined to obey. King's orders at this time, he knew, were no more than his Lordship of Ourem's good pleasure. Many of the Infante's friends advised him to meet force with force. Alvaro Vaz de Almada was emphatically of this opinion. The Duke had chosen to defy Pedro, and honor demanded that the challenge should be taken up.

Henrique disagreed. Violence, he thought, would not improve the position in any way. He sent Pedro a message from Tomar, begging his brother to do nothing until they were able to meet and talk things over. He hoped that would be soon. The next that Pedro heard of Henrique was that he had left suddenly for Santarem, where the King was in residence.

The reason for this change of programme has been much discussed. Uncharitable persons said that D. Henrique had preferred to leave his brother to his fate. Others—and this seems far more likely—supposed that he wanted to try again his personal influence with his nephew on Pedro's behalf. Another version has it that he received an urgent summons from the King, whose satellites desired to keep the Infantes apart. That also is quite possible, but still we are given to understand that Pedro was surprised and disappointed at the apparent defection.

Henrique seems to have done what he could to move the King, but all to no effect. Afonso had allowed his counselors to persuade him that Pedro was a rebel. Henrique protested his brother's loyalty, but at the same time he wrote to Coimbra advising Pedro to submit to the Duke of Bragança's passage through his lands. Unreasonable though it might be, such were the King's

orders, and Henrique—a firm believer in the royal authority—
considered that it was D. Pedro's duty to obey.

Pedro was in no mood to follow such advice. Obedience to
one's lord the King could hardly seem a sacred duty when the
said lord, too young to use his own judgment, was no more than
a puppet in the hands of unscrupulous intriguers. Distressed because Henrique did not come, harassed by the network of slander and intrigue against which he had struggled so long, excited
by the pugnacious Alvaro Vaz, Pedro's serenity for the first time
was wearing thin, and his philosophy was fading. Meanwhile the
Duke of Bragança came on, and Pedro resolved to oppose his
passage.

Everyone expected a big battle, but none took place. The
forces sighted one another, and made ready to engage, but suddenly the Duke of Bragança withdrew. "Pursue him!" cried D.
Pedro's men delightedly, but that the Infante refused to do. The
Duke led off his men into the Serra da Estrela, still knee-deep
in April snows, and there he caught a fearful cold. Everyone
thought that it would be his death, but the old man was tough.
He turned up hale and whole at Santarem by Eastertide, and
was received at the court like a conquering hero.

No word was bad enough in the royal circles for the infamous
Pedro. He was called traitor openly, but D. Henrique put a stop
to that. "I will not have it said," he cried, "that any son of D.
João I would do an injury to his King and lord!" He defended
his brother vigorously, but he was powerless against the forces
of intrigue. How could an uncle move a nephew who had been
persuaded that his were wicked uncles, and whose little sisters
were sent weeping to implore the King's vengeance upon the murderer of their mother? As for the Queen—she dared not speak!
Her one fear was that they would take her from her idolized
Afonso. With the self-centeredness of youth in love, she thought

far more of her own happiness at stake than of the hostile plot against her father. Perhaps she had not quite outgrown the childish view of the omnipotence of parents. Surely her father would know how to overcome his enemeis!

At the same time, she warned him what these enemies were planning. The King was soon to march on Coimbra, she wrote to offer him three punishments from which to choose: prison, perpetual banishment, or death.

D. Pedro read the letter unperturbed. He asked the messenger if Afonso was well, and how he spent his time. He ate his dinner quite calmly, and then summoned a council of his truest friends. To them he spoke at last in vehement and bitter terms of "those injuries and persecutions without justice, reason or humanity . . . I appeal to God," said he, "who is Lord of all, and then to the royal House of Portugal in which I was born and nurtured and which I have always served faithfully, and also to the House of England to which I so largely belong—and finally I appeal to you, my servants and my friends!"

Of the three sentences suggested, he said he preferred death. He did not wish to beg his bread at foreign courts where he had lived before as honored guest, nor could he contemplate the shame of prison. He still insisted that the King was not responsible. Left to himself he never would have done these things. Pedro declared that he would march with all his followers to meet the royal army, and beg his nephew for justice.

Most people raised objections to this plan. Better, they said, to fortify Coimbra, Montemor, and Penela, and so wait for happier days. These places could hold out for a long siege—perhaps for years. Meanwhile the King would grow in age and judgment, so would the Queen. When she became the mother of Afonso's children her position would be very much stronger. Her influence would counteract that of her father's enemies; and the In fante D. Henrique still had access to the court, and he might help to bring the young king to his senses.

That really seemed the wisest course, but Alvaro Vaz de Almada never was for temporizing. "Better to die honored and great," he said, "than live diminished and disgraced. Let us now arm our bodies and our hearts, and so make way to Santarem— not as a lawless, desperate, or disloyal host, but as men united under the command of such a prince and captain, the truest and most loyal servant of our lord the King, going to beg a just hearing against his enemies." If, however, the King refused to listen to D. Pedro, and insisted upon attacking him as a rebel, then they must all defend themselves, "and die upon the field like good and valiant knights."

To D. Pedro, heartsick and weary of the long struggle, this appeared best. Rather than drag on in suspense he much preferred to force the issue, and so cut his way out of the net that was entangling him.

There was one more attempt at conciliation. Isabel, seeing military preparations underway, woke at last to a sense of her father's danger. Weeping, she threw herself at Afonso's feet, and begged him to relent towards her father.

He consented, of course, well pleased to play the part of magnanimous monarch before his beloved's eyes. He would forget the past, he told her loftily, if D. Pedro would show himself repentant, and write to ask forgiveness of his royal nephew!

Overwhelmed by the generosity of her Afonso, the poor infatuated child wrote to inform her father of this kingly clemency. He smiled a bitter smile. The situation might be tragic, but it was absurd. Must he eat dust before yonder misguided boy? Nevertheless he did it—for his daughter's sake. He knew that life was difficult for her, alone among his enemies. He would do anything he could to ease the burden for his child. Resignedly

(233)

he took a pen and begged Afonso's pardon, although he told Isabel that he did not know what for—"I do so rather to please you," he wrote to her, "than because I can see the reason for it!"

Unfortunately Afonso read all his wife's letters, and he demanded to see this one too. The boy was furious. Instead of the great king who in his righteous wrath tempered justice with mercy, it seemed that his uncle only saw a spoilt child needing to be humored! The appeal for forgiveness, he declared, was all hypocrisy. So the Queen's intervention did more harm than good.

The die was cast. The King decided to march on Coimbra, and to besiege his uncle there.

Pedro, too, felt that the die was cast. Except by force, he never would obtain an interview with his nephew. The Prior of Aveiro, and other holy men, had implored him to remain at Coimbra and await events. The Prior even volunteered to see the King on his behalf, and explain everything. Catching at this last hope, Pedro had let him go. His enemies, however, managed to forestall the move, and the Prior was not allowed to see the King. Pedro then resolved to march south with an army at his back, and seek justice or death.

Not to alarm his wife and children, who were with him at Coimbra, he showed a smiling face, and passed a cheerful evening in their company. He called for music and dancing as if nothing were wrong—but afterwards went out into the night, to the Cathedral, and the church of Santa Cruz, and Santa Clara by the river, in each one to commend his soul to God.

Dawn found him in the little church of Santiago, kneeling beside his faithful friend Alvaro Vaz. Companions in arms, and of the Order of the Garter, they took the Sacrament together and vowed that one would not survive the other. Then Pedro returned home, untroubled and serene, to take leave of his wife and family.

Upon May 5th, 1449, D. Pedro left Coimbra and marched south at the head of an army carrying two flags. "Loyalty," was the inscription borne by one, "Justice and Vengeance" were the words emblazoned on the other.

They reached Batalha in the hollow of the hills, where D. João I's still unfinished abbey raised its cream-colored spires to the blue sky. The foreman of the works would have denied the Infante entrance, but the monks opened wide their doors and welcomed in the Founder's son.

"*Whoso dwelleth under the defense of the most High shall abide under the shadow of the Almighty*"—the psalm of Pedro's choice—rose echoing under the soaring vault. All night he knelt beside his parents' tomb in the cold peace of the vast church. Here was his father's chosen tryst for all the family, and here before D. João died, he had prepared a place for all his sons. Pedro rose from his knees and stood a long while gazing at the arch over the empty niche reserved for him. When morning dawned he left the shadows and the dead, and rode away over the shining fields.

At Alcobaça he heard that the King was still at Santarem, preparing his own forces. Pedro refused to lead his men towards that town, not to appear to carry arms against the King. He would advance in the direction of Lisbon, he said. If he were attacked by his enemies, he would resist. If nobody came out to meet them, he would turn around by Torres Vedras and Obidos, and so back to Coimbra. During that time he thought the Queen or D. Henrique might succeed in softening the King. He expected some message soon from either of these two.

None came. It does not follow necessarily that none was sent, but Pedro's enemies would take care that nothing arrived. Amid

the arch-intriguers of the court a simple young girl like the
Queen, and an unpolitically-minded scientist like D. Henrique,
were not likely to score. Meanwhile Afonso marched from Santarem, convinced by all his flatterers that he was a great king
about to quash rebellion.

The forces sighted each other at Alfarrobeira, near Vila Franca
de Xira. It is doubtful if either side really wanted to fight. Some
say that Afonso did not mean to attack his uncle. His orders certainly were only to send heralds to D. Pedro's camp, summon-
ing the Infante's followers to abandon the rebel and to join
the King.

Pedro, we know, did not intend to give battle except in self-
defense. He only sought an opportunity of pleading with his
nephew, although it must be owned that to arrive in so much
force, for one who did not wish to seem a rebel, was unwise.
However that may be, it was purely by accident that the two
armies came to blows.

Certain archers of the royal troops, hidden in a wood, began
of their own accord to shoot off arrows. The knight commanding one of D. Pedro's outposts ordered his men to shoot back.
To stop the skirmishing that naturally ensued, D. Pedro caused
a bombard to be fired at the stragglers. As ill luck would have it,
the bombardier was not a good marksman. The stone ball fell
close to the royal tent, and all the King's guard turned out and
charged at once.

Nothing could stop it now. A fierce fight soon was raging in
all ranks. D. Pedro, lightly armed, plunged into the thickest of
the battle, and almost at the start was seen to fall, pierced by an
arrow through the heart. "Be quiet!" said Alvaro Vaz de Almada
to the page who brought him the news. "Tell nobody about it."

He called for bread and wine, and renewed on the battlefield
the pledge that he had given to his well-loved lord and master.

On foot, he re-entered the fray where already the royal army was prevailing through numbers. Alvaro Vaz fought till he could fight no more, and without being wounded, dropped from sheer exhaustion. "Body, thou canst no more!" he was heard to exclaim. "Soul, wherefore dost thou tarry?" "Come on, Boys!" others heard him cry. "Take your vengeance, villeins!" So he was slain, and they cut off his head. Thus Alvaro Vaz de Almada found the "honorable death" that he desired.

It was six years before D. Pedro was laid to rest at Batalha beside his parents in the place prepared for him. During those years his body lay in an obscure grave in the church of Alverca, disgraced and alone. His rivals battened on his heritage, his widow fled from Coimbra, his gifted children wandered in exile, and shone at foreign courts. We find their names in chronicles of other lands—pathetic, radiant figures wherever they passed, admired and beloved everywhere, and deeply mourned, for all died young.

Queen Isabel appeared the happiest of her family, but her short life also knew bitter moments. Her father's rivals, having made an end of him, determined to bring about her downfall. The King was urgently advised to repudiate the rebel's daughter and take him another wife. This council was backed up by weighty reasoning by the most learned theologians in the land. It was a formidable onslaught, but psychologically unsound, for what young lover in the world was ever yet convinced by arguments of theologians? Afonso's answer was to send for Isabel, to ride and meet her on the way, and take his darling in his arms. That was the last attempt to separate these two for the remaining years of the Queen's life. There were not many left. She died in 1455, aged twenty-three, some months after the birth of their only surviving son.

Did Afonso ever repent his treatment of her father? That is

difficult to say. For one who felt persuaded that he was a justly outraged sovereign the chorus of disapproval that arose from every European court must have been disconcerting. For the Infante D. Pedro was known throughout the continent, and everywhere esteemed. *"Vous estes d'un bon sang,"* Philippe of Burgundy observed to Pedro's son, *"et dont tous ceux qui en sont partis ont esté gens de bien!"* That was the general verdict upon D. Pedro and his descendants, and Alfarrobeira called forth universal censure. The Pope issued a Bull extolling the virtues of the deceased, and Afonso's uncle of Burgundy sent the Dean of Vergy to Portugal to remonstrate with the young man in four tremendous Latin harangues, pages long. All this appeared to leave the King unmoved. The Braganças and their friends had made a good thing out of Pedro's fall and they would not allow Afonso to reverse his judgment.

Where Latin failed, and papal Bulls were powerless, love won at last. Six years after the tragedy, when the country was rejoicing at the birth of the future D. João II, then Pedro's daughter begged her husband to relent towards her father's memory, and lay his bones to rest in the family shrine. So D. Pedro came home at last to sleep in his own place, and the nephew who had wronged him, and the daughter who had feared to intervene, followed the funeral train. Only the young Infante D. Fernando, cold and bitter, refused to do honor to the dead man. To him D. Pedro was the wicked uncle still.

The Infante D. Henrique organized the obsequies of this last of his brothers. With what feelings he did it no one knows. After Alfarrobeira, it appears, he would have withdrawn to Ceuta there to end his days fighting the Moors, but at the last moment the King forbade his departure, so Henrique remained. Had he reason for remorse, as some suggest? The chronicler, Ruy de Pina, seems to think that he had deserted his brother, and modern writers reproduce the charge. It is a tremendous accusation, and not one to be justly taken up today, unless new documents should come to light to prove or to disprove it.

Actually, the only circumstantial narrative of these events is that of Ruy de Pina, and later historians have based themselves on him. Ruy de Pina, writing at the end of the century, considers that Henrique showed himself lukewarm in Pedro's defense, and failed him at the last. Against this, the Infantes' contemporary, Zurara, declares that Henrique did everything he could to save his brother, and that those who would have it otherwise did not speak as "men who knew the whole truth." Zurara says that he has much to tell about the circumstances leading to D. Pedro's death, as his readers will gather in due course. Unhappily the promised account was never written, or has not survived, but all the same this passing reference has its value, coming from one who knew D. Henrique well.

It is difficult, in any case, to know what the Infante could have done against the intriguers at court. The King was wholly under their influence, and they had upon their side his mother's memory, a powerful weapon which they exploited to the full. An honest man is always baffled by intrigue, and Pedro's persecutors stopped at nothing. Pina himself tells us how messages were intercepted, letters forged, and every device used to poison the mind of the King. What pressure could Henrique bring to bear upon a boy who was convinced that both uncles had been the enemies, and one the murderer, of his mother?

Whether Henrique should have joined Pedro at Alfarrobeira is another doubtful question. We know that he thought it was a mistake for Pedro to leave Coimbra at all. Obedience to the royal commands was a matter of principle to him. On the other hand, while he remained at court the ex-Regent would still have one defender near the King.

The whole position is obscure, and we have not the data to pronounce fair judgment. "Certainly," Zurara writes of Pedro and Henrique, "there always was great love between them." Zurara knew both of them personally. Can we, after five hundred years, contest his statement?

One person surely might have saved D. Pedro had she dared to make a determined stand, and that was his own daughter. Afonso loved her more than anyone on earth. He had a pliant nature, and one cannot doubt that she could have led him where she would. But courage failed her to stake her hold upon his heart against the hostile forces around. Her enemies appeared to her so old, and worldly-wise, and terrible. She was a child, she did not know her power.

XVIII

Sagres

HENRIQUE spent more and more time upon his rock.
All his interests were there. The tragedy of Alfarrobeira
had broken the last link that might have drawn him
back into the world of politics. He never had entered it on his
own behalf. Now that his brothers all were dead, he stood apart
and watched with perfect indifference the rise of the Braganças.
They did not interfere with him, nor he with them, and the
young King had soon regained his former esteem and affection
for his uncle. Afonso of his own accord never thought ill of anyone, and once Pedro was dead it no longer was worth anybody's
while to defame D. Henrique to the King. For Henrique crossed
no one's path. He went his way alone over unbeaten tracks
where only daring spirits followed him.

He made an appearance at court from time to time, as duty to
his family demanded. Thus we hear that in 1450 it was he who
received the ambassadors of Emperor Frederick III, who came
to ask the hand of Afonso's young sister Leonor. Henrique figured at his niece's marriage by proxy the next year, and it was
doubtless he who saw to it that the fleet carrying the bride to
Italy was commanded by the most skillful sea captains and accompanied by "master astronomers, well able to set their course
by stars and by the Pole."

The usual feasts and jousts were held in honor of the great

event, and the prize of the tournament was awarded to the King's young brother, Henrique's godson and adopted heir, whom he always refers to as "my son Fernando."

The childless man seems to have deeply loved this boy, though he made no attempt to play the part of heavy father. Perhaps it would have been a good thing if he had, for Fernando at eighteen was apparently a temperamental and rather a spoilt young man. He and his brother Afonso were good friends on the whole, but that did not prevent outbursts of bickering and argument.

Thus Fernando was peeved because Afonso would not let him sail with their sister to Italy, and there was squabbling over things the young man wanted which the King refused. Fernando decided that he was not appreciated at home. He would run away —that would teach them! Either he might cross over to Ceuta and do something wonderful, or else visit the King of Naples, his maternal uncle, who could not fail to be delighted with so promising a nephew. Without saying a word to any of his family, Fernando disappeared. He slipped away from Evora, and secretly embarked upon a caravel.

The sensation that he hoped to create was entirely successful. The next day all the court was rushing around to look for the missing Infante. Search parties beat the countryside in every direction, and messages were sent to frontier towns. When it was discovered that he had embarked, ships were sent sailing after him, and orders were dispatched to the captain of Ceuta to stop Fernando passing through the Straits. The King joined D. Henrique in Algarve, and together they proceeded to Tavira to be near at hand.

While his brother and his uncle waited anxiously for news, the truant pursued his complacent way. He sailed triumphantly into Ceuta, where the old Count D. Sancho de Noronha was prepared to meet him.

D. Sancho handled the situation with much tact. He welcomed the young prince with great ceremony, solemnly offering him the city keys. Fernando, very gracious, waved them aside, and he and the old warrior conversed as man to man. The Count, being in mourning, had allowed his beard to grow— Fernando suggested that he should take it off. D. Sancho promised that he would if Fernando would do the same! Much gratified, we may suppose, that his incipient beard already should excite comment, Fernando for the first time shaved his downy chin. The happy understanding became so complete that D. Sancho took advantage of it to advise the fugitive to return home. When he saw that his counsel appeared to be sinking in, the old man slipped across to Tavira one night and told the King that he had caught his brother.

The runaway by this time was disposed to pardon his ungrateful family, the more so that a delegation of the most important people in the realm was sent across to beg him to return. The King and all the courtiers wrote besides, imploring him to reconsider his hasty decision. Fernando, thoroughly enjoying all the fuss, graciously allowed himself to be entreated. They brought him back via Cadiz, where the Castilian authorities received him festively, and there Fernando spent some happy days, buying all sorts of things and giving and receiving presents.

He crossed the frontier to Castro Marim, where his uncle Henrique was waiting to greet the prodigal. The modern legend that makes the Infante a stern hard man has not contemporary evidence to justify it. Zurara complains of his laxity towards the undeserving, and his reception of this scapegrace nephew seems a case in point. Instead of scolding the naughty boy who had so upset all the family, Henrique proceeded to give him a good time!

Fernando spent a week with this indulgent uncle, having new clothes made for himself, and all the gentlemen who came with him, from the fine cloths of silk and wool he had bought at Cadiz. His wardrobe thus replenished, the young buck traveled north to join the King who rode to meet him "with pleasure and feasting." The brothers were completely reconciled, in token of which the King lavished three towns upon his graceless junior.

But for this mercurial godson and heir, Henrique troubled himself little with the antics of the younger generation. He let the court go its perennial round—Lisbon, Evora, Sintra, Santarem, with occasional excursions north or farther south. It seldom followed him down to Algarve, and there Henrique's kingdom lay, between the windswept Cape of São Vicente and the lovely bay of Lagos where he fitted out his caravels. This kingdom and his quest he would one day pass on to his godson. Fernando was moderately interested.

In Lagos Henrique's pilots and technicians lived; there were his warehouses and his shipyards; in the blue waters of the port there swung at anchor ships of every type that sailed the seas. There galleys from the Levant dipped their oars beside the heavier carracks bound for north European ports, and there, like sea birds poised, floated the light-winged ocean-going caravels. Beside the busy wharves might constantly be seen the unloading of cargoes brought from regions somewhere down beyond the blue horizon: sugar, and wood, and dyes, amber and gum, ivory, and gold dust, and chains of black men.

The sea brought color and life to Lagos, and pungent scents from sandy deserts and green forests far away. At Lagos, Henrique smelled and touched Africa; at Sagres and Cape São Vicente, swept barren by Atlantic storms, watered by spray from wind-borne foam, he reached out towards the empty west, where wave upon wave the ocean surged into shoreless infinity.

Sagres—sacred Promontory of the Ancients—the point to which the ravens had guided St. Vincent's barque—was one of the most desolate on earth. Today the shipping of the world sights it and passes by; but seamen of Henrique's time knew its bleak uplands to their cost. Carracks and galleys sailing from the land-locked seas of the Levant rounded this cape and met the full Atlantic blast hurling itself out of infinite space, and had to fly for shelter under Sagres' cliffs. There, in the rock-bound anchorage, Henrique noted that they were often held up for many days, as cut off from all things, as if storm-driven to a desert shore. There were no resources of any kind. Henrique states that ships there were "without comfort of provisions, or any other necessary things, and with hardly any water!" The nearest hamlet was a league and a half away, over a wilderness of rocks and stunted vegetation. Sometimes—we quote Henrique still—sailors "departed this life and were thrown about these rocks and on the beach." They might as well have died at sea, and had their bodies consigned to the deep. The Infante was "moved with pity" by their plight.

More than the shining town of Lagos, more than the green village of Raposeira, several miles inland, where he often retired to work and think, the desolate promontory of Sagres was destined to be associated for all time with D. Henrique's name. This was the spot that he had chosen for himself. In 1443, during his brother's regency, Henrique obtained the concession of the whole headland, and started building there a town.

The Vila do Infante which arose upon the Cape was designed solely to provide for shipping shelter in the bay. From Raposeira the Infante watched it grow. At the time that Zurara wrote his chronicle it was not yet finished, though already the walls were thick and strong and some houses were built. The spiritual needs of seamen held up at Sagres seem to have been Henrique's chief concern, and so he had a chapel in the town, and just above the harbor stood the church of St. Catherine with a cemetery adjoining—no more need sailors fling their dead like dogs to the wet shifting sands. On the material side the town would always keep supplies of everything a ship might need, and pilots would be constantly on tap for any who required their services.

Buildings, churches, warehouses, and pilot-stations all are excellent, but do not make a town unless you have inhabitants as well. We gather that these were not too easy to find. The cliffs of Sagres were no Eden to which settlers willingly would flock. How this problem was met may be deduced from papers in the chancellery of D. Afonso V where we find sentences of banishment and other penalties commuted into residence in the new Vila do Infante.

Henrique's aim in calling into being such a town was mainly altruistic, but the scheme must have had commercial possibilities. Zurara tells us that the Genoese offered to buy the settlement for a large sum—"and, as you know," he adds, "they are not men to invest their money without sure hope of gain!"

Needless to say, neither the Infante nor the King of Portugal would cede Atlantic bases to the Italian maritime republics. It was quite bad enough to have the Castilians in the Canaries! Henrique never ceased to covet those islands. The state of affairs prevailing there simply invited intervention! The authority of the Castilian crown was nominal, and the various captains of the archipelago seemed to spend all their time in chasing one another on and off the islands. Messire Maciot, heir to the first colonizer, Jehan de Béthencourt, was happy to escape from his island of Lançarote and lease it to the Infante D. Henrique for a yearly rent of 20,000 reis. "Mice Maciote," as the Portuguese called him, took refuge in Madeira. The Infante married the Frenchman's daughter to João Gonçalves' Zarco's son, and undertook to defend Lançarote against all comers. Accordingly, the useful Antão Gonçalves was sent with a thousand men to occupy the island, and in the battle that ensued a hundred Castilians were killed.

Their king protested vigorously. The Infante D. Henrique was meddling with his affairs, he complained, and it was an unfriendly act. Once more the ownership of the Canary Islands became the theme of diplomatic notes. As usual the result was inconclusive; but some years later, when a new king of Castile married Afonso V's sister, he magnificently bestowed Palma, Teneriffe, and the Grand Canary upon the Count of Atouguia who brought him his bride. As none of these three islands had been occupied, or even conquered, this burst of generosity was not expensive to the giver.

Henrique's reasons for desiring the Canary Islands must have been chiefly strategic, for as an advance base for exploration Funchal could not be bettered. Ships on their way to Guinea usually stopped there to replenish provisions and all stores. They could repair there too, and caravels were built at Funchal with wood from the famous Madeira forests. Sometimes, too, expeditions started from the island for exploration of the African mainland, but on the whole it remained more a port of call than starting-point or terminus. The power that sent forth ships over the unknown seas was centered in Algarve, and while Henrique lived the home port of the caravels was Lagos, as Lisbon came to be in later years when the initiative of discovery had passed to the Crown.

Lagos of the Infante's time was not only a busy port and starting-point of all long-distance voyages, but it was the center around which gathered students of the new science of navigation. In the observatory of Lagos astronomy was studied, not as the superterrestrial mystery influencing the destinies of man, expounded by medieval stargazers and fortunetellers, but as a sure guide to accurate navigation. In the same way mathematics and geometry, from abstruse speculations of the sage became a practical science bearing on daily life; and at Lagos expert cartographers drew out new maps—maps that no longer were compiled from guesswork and hearsay, but which showed islands where they really were, and coast lines as they had actually been seen.

The Infante himself was deeply versed in astronomy and mathematics. There had doubtless been princes quite as learned here and there in various countries and at different times, but D. Henrique had the spirit of the modern scientist who makes his observations from nature direct, and applies the rules discovered to practical use.

These things engrossed Henrique more and more, and it was happy for him that this should be so. A solitary man, past middle age, who had to look back many years to recall memories that were not sad, life might have been gray and empty for him had he not this door of escape into a world apart. At Raposeira, "a place remote from the tumult of men, propitious for contemplation and study," he spent long days and nights in the pursuit of knowledge—"knowledge from which all good arises"— to quote his own words—an unmedieval conception, already vibrant with the enthusiasm of the Renaissance, the coming dawn that was to bring man back for a short time to something of the wondering delight that Adam may have felt when first he tasted the fruit of the Tree.

Recluse, Henrique has been called at this period of his life, but the term is not quite exact. He chose out for himself the desolate and solitary places of an abandoned seacoast, but in his wilderness he did not live alone. No prince has ever gathered around him a stranger court. Men from all parts of the known world rubbed shoulders in this isolated corner of Algarve, and many came from regions scarcely known. Such a "variety of nationalities, with customs so unlike our own," Zurara says, that it was marvelous to see. We hear of Genoese, Venetians, Catalans, Englishmen, Frenchmen, Germans, Scandinavians, Arabs, Jews, and Moors. There you might meet Canary Island warriors, black catechumens from Guinea, Azenegue prisoners from the Sahara, and Berber hostages—and there were strangers more intriguing still, whose presence no one has yet quite explained. We know of them only as names on some laconic document surviving in the National Archives, or through some casual reference of a chronicler.

We are left guessing who might be "the Indian Jacob," who sailed to Africa with Diogo Gomes to function as interpreter if India should be reached. Most writers think that this Jacob was Ethiopian, not Indian, but Zurara makes mention separately of Ethiopians and Indians visiting Henrique's court, who received gifts from him. They came, he tells us with tantalizing brevity, "to see the beauty of the world." No chronicler has troubled to refer in more detail to such Oriental tourists, nor explained how, or when, or why they came. In the same way no allusion is found to "Jorge, ambassador of Prester John," beyond a document from which we gather that he was at King Afonso's court in 1452, whence he was sent on to the Duke of Burgundy. Was Jorge another amateur of beauty, and was he a member of the delegation from the Abyssinian monastery in Jerusalem that attended the Church Council at Florence? It seems quite likely; but Zurara's Indians still are unexplained.

Historians hold forth, and the learned argue, but evidence is vague. East and West, the familiar world of fifteenth-century

Christendom, and the barbaric wonderlands outside meet and merge together in an undefined and shadowy borderland some-where beyond Jerusalem and Cairo. Figures loom out of the penumbra and vanish again; voices sound dimly from the dark. We do not know how far Henrique's contacts reached. We only know that figures from the Orient mingled with those of Africa and western Europe at Sagres, and Afonso V, in 1454, invested the Order of Christ with spiritual jurisdiction of the lands of Guinea, Nubia, and Ethiopia. Pope Nicholas, with a stroke of the pen, confirmed the rights of the Infante in all lands to be discovered from Cape Bojador to India; his successors ratified and enlarged the claims of Portugal, and no protest was made by any Christian king. Time to worry about India, if anyone should get there!

Their unconcern about Henrique's quest was balanced by his for their politics. He played no part upon the European stage. It is doubtful if it interested him at all. His face was turned towards a wider, more entrancing world, out of which turbaned camel-drivers came to tell him about commercial markets in the Sahara and the Sudan, while Arab travelers described the course of great African rivers, and merchants from Oran passed on the latest news concerning the upheavals in the negro kingdoms round about Lake Tchad. Traders from Timbuktu and from the desert market of Wadan brought slaves and gold dust to Henrique's factory at Arguim, receiving in exchange wheat and white cloths, and burnooses, and European merchandise, sent out by the In-fante in a ship owned, Diogo Gomes says, by Robert Kerey. Surely the real name of this man must have been Carey, and we have here another of Henrique's foreign protégés—an English-man this time?

The island of Arguim, once the scene of bloodshed and ambus-cade, was now a peaceful trading post. No more assaults were made upon the nomad tribes of the mainland. The up-river explorers no longer attempted to waylay and catch. Henrique had imposed his will at last. The caravels of Portugal, plying their way down the African coast, no longer made their presence felt by violence, but by overtures of friendship and fair barter with the natives of those lands. "The Infante," young Cadamosto noted when he entered his service, "does not permit harm to be done to any of them."

No doubt some people regretted the good old days. Zurara, breaking off his chronicle with the year 1448, remarks a little sadly that "from this year the affairs of those parts were conducted by means of trade and merchandise, rather than force or deeds of arms." He is too loyal to criticize what his Infante has ordained, but you can see he feels it is a pity!

Henrique did not care what firebrands thought. Let them go to Ceuta, and there fight the Moors! To put such hardened Moslems to the sword might be a godly and glorious procedure, but as for the more primitive peoples south of Cape Bojador, he hoped to make them Christian. Contemporaries all agree that this was his first aim and, crusader although he was by education and heredity, he did not really think that spiritual truths were best brought home at the point of a spear. Kindness was far more convincing, and friendly contacts might first be made over material things. The trader could prepare the way, and then the missionary would follow. It was all very well to carry off captives by hundreds, or even thousands, to be catechized and baptized at home—but what happened after? You had gained a few thousand souls, and hostilized a tribe!

The question also had its practical aspect. War only led to ruin and to bankruptcy, and exploration had to be paid for somehow. How to meet the financial burden of his enterprise was the most acute problem of Henrique's life. The Infante was probably the richest man in Portugal—his personal needs were of the simplest and the most austere—yet he was always short of money.

As Master of the wealthy Order of Christ, which had inherited the riches of the Temple, Henrique had command of great resources, nor as administrator could he be accused of fecklessness. Strange though it may seem, this stargazer had considerable business ability, and anything he handled was a financial success. No master of the Order ever farmed its lands more profitably than he did. The Infante seems to have understood agriculture as well as science, and under his control every inch of waste ground was brought into production. He obtained privileges for the workers on his farms. He grazed large flocks of sheep upon the hills around Alcobaça. He erected windmills for grinding corn at Santarem, and dammed fishpools in the river Rodão.

Always on the look out for lucrative side lines, Henrique also tried his hand at industry. He owned dye-works, and he ran soap factories, which made black and white soap! The coral fisheries off the coast of Portugal were his. He obtained the monopoly of tunny fishing in Algarvian waters. All these sources of income were added to the tribute that he levied on the Guinea trade, and revenue that poured in from the islands, especially from the sugar industry of Madeira.

With so many irons in the fire—and all going concerns—the Infante ought to have been rolling in wealth, but he spent every penny.

The sea swallowed the most: shipbuilding, fitting out, repairs, rewards to seamen, pensions for their widows—all this accounted for vast sums each year, to which were added the expenses of the fleet that Henrique maintained off the Moroccan coast to fight infidel pirates. It is true that after the first few tentative voyages to Rio de Ouro and Guinea merchants from Lagos and elsewhere invested capital in ships and trading ventures, but the Infante still sent expeditions of his own, and his captains had orders to seek information more than profit.

Voyages of discovery are never cheap. It is known that Columbus' three ships cost two million maravedis to the Castilian Crown. Henrique's expeditions may not have cost so much, but the expense was constantly renewed. Explorations of the African coast no doubt often brought in some profit, but there were others which could bring no material gain—voyages of inquiry and nothing else, pushed far over the unknown spaces of the sterile sea.

Beyond all this, those "men of various nationalities" who thronged around the Infante must have cost him a pretty penny. Any who did him service could be certain of a rich reward—not for nothing did all the best cartographers, astronomers, and physicists gravitate in his orbit. D. Henrique kept open house for all interesting people; Moslem, Jew or Christian, Portuguese or foreign, and no one, says Zurara, ever left his presence without "some profitable gift." For visitors this must have been delightful, but ruinous for their kind host!

Henrique also spent money on public buildings, not only in his Vila do Infante, but about the realm. He built, or endowed and embellished, many churches in Portugal and on his islands of Madeira and the Azores. Among them may be mentioned a small chapel at Restelo—Santa Maria de Belem—a league from Lisbon, near the river mouth.

Crossing the bar, this sanctuary would be to a returning sailor the first glimpse of home. Here he might disembark and say his prayers; and here it was that nearly forty years after Henrique's death another generation saw his efforts crowned. Vasco da Gama, returning from India, landed at Belem, and Manuel the Fortunate, the son of Henrique's scatterbrained Fernando,

(253)

reaped what his great-uncle had sown. The King enshrined the nation's triumph in a forest of carved stone, and in the great church he erected on this spot, Henrique's modest chapel, like the beginning of his quest, was swallowed up in glory of fulfilment.

All visible traces of Henrique's hand have been lost at Belem, but we may find his mark upon Tomar. This little town, headquarters of the Knights of Christ, was improved and embellished in his time. He built a new house for the Order there, parts of which still remain, though nothing is left of his hospital for the destitute, nor of the fine hostel designed by him for poor strangers passing through the town.

Yet another call upon Henrique's interest—and purse—was the University, of which he was officially Protector since his youth. This was no honorary title. Believing as he did that knowledge was the source of all things good, the Infante took his charge very seriously, and under his influence the system of teaching and curriculum were revised and brought up to date. It was in his time that mathematics and astronomy were introduced alongside of grammar, logic, and rhetoric that had filled the first place in medieval courses.

The University of Portugal, founded at Coimbra by D. Denis, had subsequently been transferred to Lisbon, where it remained until the reign of D. João III. Henrique found it getting on as best it might in hired premises rented from the citizens. He remedied this state of affairs by buying suitable houses with which to endow the University.

Henrique chose the buildings with great care, and had them decorated in accordance with his taste, and he himself decided how the various classes were to be accommodated. Thus rhetoric and science would be taught on the ground floor, where the Seven Liberal Arts were painted all around the lecture hall. The medicine classes were also to be held downstairs, presided over by a portrait by Galen. Theology, philosophy, and canonical law appropriately were lodged up above, in rooms respectively adorned with paintings of the Holy Trinity, a Pope, an Emperor, and of Aristotle. Grammar does not seem to have had any pictures at all—perhaps it did not need them. It must have been a lively class in any case, for Henrique decreed it should be taught in an outhouse "because it is very noisy!"

Besides all that he spent on public service of this kind, Henrique's private charities were on a lavish scale. Beggars were fed and clothed by him, the sick were cared for, monasteries enriched, and numberless captives were ransomed.

No fortune could stand such a racket. Henrique's did not. In spite of his vast revenues, he had to borrow money. The Count of Arraiolos, who although a Bragança had always been friendly to Pedro and Henrique, advanced him 16,008 gold crowns, but it was just like pouring water through a sieve. In 1449, the Count produced another 19,324 crowns—these sums are said to equal £130,000 of today—but still they went nowhere. Henrique borrowed money from the monks of Alcobaça too, and ran up debts with Jewish moneylenders. The Crown had to come to the Infante's rescue, allotting him sixteen *contos* out of the royal exchequer. Even that did not stabilize his finances. Henrique died in debt.

XIX

Alvise in Negroland

UNDER the shelter of Cape São Vicente, young Alvise
Cadamosto waited for the wind to change. A Venetian
galley might be mistress of the Mediterranean, but was
not built to face sterner Atlantic moods. In the teeth of an ocean
gale there was nothing to do but anchor beside the Algarvian
coast, and hope for better weather.

Messer Alvise was twenty-two, and out to seek his fortune. His
health was good, his wits were keen, and he makes no bones of
the fact that his ambition was to spend his youth acquiring
wealth "by all possible means." When he was old and experienced and rich, then, says he, he would settle down and take
"some honorable employment."

Meanwhile the world was wide and very interesting. There
was only to look about and choose where to begin. Alvise first
thought of Flanders, which he had visited before. There were
good openings there for a smart business man. Alvise laid out
his little capital upon suitable merchandise, and embarked with
the captain, Marco Zeno, for the Netherlands. He got as far as
São Vicente, as we have seen, and there he was held up.

It might have been a very boring interval under those cliffs,
communing with the sea gulls. The Vila do Infante was in the
making still, and there were no distractions ashore. It must there-

(256)

fore have been an agreeable surprise when visitors arrived from
Raposeira.

One was Patricio de Conti, "Consul of our nation in Portugal," as he proved by exhibiting his papers. The Portuguese
friend who accompanied him, he introduced as Antão Gonçalves, secretary to the Infante D. Henrique. The Consul added
that he, too, was in the Infante's employ, and drew a salary from
him. The Prince had heard that there was a Venetian galley in
his port, and so had sent down a few samples of Madeira sugar,
dragon's blood, and other "good and useful things" from overseas which he thought they might find of some interest.

They did indeed. Sugar was classed with spices then. It was a
luxury article used only in the kitchens of the rich. There was
some grown in Sicily, but the European market was chiefly supplied by what Venice imported from Egypt and the Levant.
Therefore with the keen eye of connoisseurs, the merchants from
the Adriatic examined the beautiful product of the Madeira
canes, while Antão Gonçalves and Patricio held forth, and young
Cadamosto listened with popping eyes to what seemed like a
fairy tale.

They talked of islands far off in the sea—two decades back
unvisited, unknown, abandoned to the waves and mist—now
colonized and cultivated. Europe had found an Eden in the Atlantic which produced everything needful to man, and Europeans would require no longer to buy sugar at high prices from
the Arab traders. That grown at Madeira was superior to any
yet seen, and the date could not be far distant when the island
production would oust all rivals from the market.

But this was nothing compared to the greater things that the
Infante had achieved. Antão Gonçalves told how he had sent
his caravels over the seas no ship had ever sailed before. They
had discovered wondrous lands, full of strange plants and fruits,

and birds and beasts, and even stranger men. Antão Gonçalves knew what he was talking about. He had made many of these voyages himself. As an eyewitness he described the marvels and riches to be found in Africa. Great fortunes were to be acquired in those lands, he declared, and any capital invested would be multiplied tenfold.

Cadamosto was entranced. This was the El Dorado of his dreams! How gray and uninteresting Flanders seemed! How muddy the canals of Bruges, how boring the fat Flemings. Give him the glittering South where palms waved on the beach, and mighty rivers flowed out of the heart of the green forest, where black men brought in gold dust from an unknown hinterland, and spices grew as common garden herbs! His mouth watered to hear Antão Gonçalves' tales. Could anybody go? he inquired longingly.

It seemed that anybody could. The Infante welcomed all those who were interested. He liked to have Venetians in his service, added the secretary, because they knew more about spices than any other nation. The terms on which permission was granted to private enterprise depended upon who provided the ship. If a merchant fitted out an expedition for himself, a tax of one-fourth of the profits must be paid at Lagos upon his return. When it was the Infante who supplied the ship, then profits were divided equally. If Messer Alvise liked, Antão Gonçalves went on to say, he would take him to Raposeira to talk with the Infante himself.

Cadamosto jumped at the opportunity, and Henrique received the young man very kindly. He confirmed all that Antão Gonçalves had said and "promised to honor and reward me should I decide to go."

That settled it! Flanders was off for Alvise Cadamosto, Marco Zeno could proceed without him. The youth rushed back to the galley, and consigned to a kinsman of his the goods that he was taking for the Flemish market. He bought from the Venetians what he needed for his voyage, and so returned to Raposeira while the galley sailed north. "The Lord Infante showed great pleasure," Cadamosto writes, "that I remained at Cape São Vicente."

A young man who thirsted "to see new things"—that was a recruit after D. Henrique's heart! He seems to have had many talks with Alvise Cadamosto and set him all afire "to see the world and things that no one of our nation had yet seen before." The stay at Raposeira cannot have been dull, but to the young Venetian's eagerness it seemed like "many, many days" before the Infante gave him a brand new caravel, commanded by Vicente Dias of Lagos. She was a noble forty-five tonner. Henrique equipped her with all things necessary, and Cadamosto spent what money he had left on merchandise for the African coast. With a heart full of hope, eyes open wide, and ears alert, provided with a notebook to record all that he saw and heard, our young adventurer set sail for the wonderland of Guinea.

Two days later the caravel arrived at Porto Santo, whence Madeira was reached in a few hours. Like every tourist to the present day, Cadamosto grows lyrical over that island paradise. "The whole place is a garden," he cries with delight, "and everything grows there!"

Madeira was by then a prosperous colony with a rising population that had reached eight hundred. The sugar industry brought wealth to all, the sunny climate and the fertile soil made the whole year a succession of crops. Cadamosto admired the rocky hills, reminding him of Sicily, "but it is never cold there as it can be in Cyprus or in Sicily," he says. Neither was it ever too hot. The crystal streams that flowed down from the mountains never dried. A skillful network of irrigation channels guided them to water the sugar canes, and the rushing torrents turned the wheels of sawmills in the forests where wild peacocks roamed. Although the richness of the soil was not what it had been when first it knew the plough, still even at this later date a head of wheat would bring forth thirtyfold.

What abundance of food there was in Madeira, and what good things to eat! Cadamosto speaks feelingly of the excellent sugar preserves made by the islanders "with great perfection." The fruit also was beautiful. All the European kinds grew there, besides many exotic species, and nowhere had the Venetian seen such lovely grapes! The wine was very good also, he observes appreciatively, considering that the vines were recently imported.

The barren Canary Islands were a come down after this, and the white deserts of the mainland even worse. The island of Arguim had springs of water, it is true, but little else to recommend it. The Portuguese had made of this forsaken spot a port for the Sahara trade which their advent had deviated from the old camel routes to the seaboard. The Infante was building a fort at Arguim, and there merchants from Lagos bartered wares with tall, thin, dusky Azenegues who made their presence felt afar by the fish oil anointing their long hair.

The river Senegal was more interesting. Here suddenly the desert sand gave place to luxuriant vegetation. The great river also marked the ethnological divide—north of it roamed the odorous brown Azenegues; to the south, in the green bush, lived the negroes. These were tall powerful men, Cadamosto observes, who never left off talking, and who constantly told lies! In their persons they were very clean, he says, "for they wash all over four or five times a day," but he disliked their table manners.

The young man had time to study their ways, for he spent some weeks near Cape Verde, in the land of Budomel.

This personage was a great negro lord, already known to Portuguese explorers. He was a safe man to deal with, they told Cadamosto; not only was he friendly to white men, but he paid handsomely for anything he bought. That sounded just like what the Venetian wanted. He was out for adventure and to see the world, but profit figured large on his program. He lost no time in sailing to the spot marked by the tree the Portuguese had named the Palm of Budomel. It was no port, but ships could anchor there, and Cadamosto sent a messenger ashore to say that he had brought horses for barter.

That was a sure bait for a Senegalese chief. Horses were greatly in demand among them. They were supplied by Arab and Berber traders from the Sahara, but the poor beasts never lasted long. Neither the climate nor the food agreed with them. They grew enormously fat, and soon died—hence the constant demand for more and more.

When Budomel heard that horses had arrived from Portugal, he rode up to the beach at once, with all his henchmen clattering after. There was a friendly meeting and a lengthy palaver, at the end of which Cadamosto had disposed of all his horses. Horseflesh was far more valuable than human life. Budomel promised to send him a hundred slaves for seven steeds with their harness, and as a bonus gave him then and there a negro girl twelve or thirteen years old. Cadamosto thought she was "very pretty for a black," and "I accepted her," he tells us happily, "and sent her to the ship."

The other slaves had to be fetched from Budomel's village, twenty-five miles inland. The chief issued a pressing invitation to the stranger to accompany him there. "I went," writes Cadamosto, "quite as much to see and hear new things as to receive my payment."

The visit was a great success. Budomel put up his guest at

the house of his grandson Bisboror, and there the foreigner stayed several weeks collecting his impressions.

He did not think much of his host's standard of living. A negro lord, he tells us, has neither castles, nor towns, nor treasures, nor money of any kind, and he eats "bestially, sitting upon the ground." He may own several villages, and half a dozen wives in each, but all the buildings are no more than palm-thatched huts, and his own residence is not remotely like a palace. The only thing in fact, that seemed to make a negro lord, was the length of his following and the ceremony with which he was constantly surrounded. In this respect he left his European colleagues far behind! No prince of Christendom was so aloof from his subjects, or hedged about with such ritual as was a chief of Senegal. His residence might be a hut, but it was isolated from the vulgar herd by seven palisaded courtyards, each one of which marked a step up in the social scale. Shaded by a great tree that grew in the center of each, the hierarchy of Senegal was grouped in separate pens. Only the outermost enclosure was accessible to lesser fry, while the sacred seventh—where Budomel lived with his wives—was closed to all except a few among the very great. Alone, the irreverent white men disregarded such a taboo, "for they," says Cadamosto, "walk freely in and out." This liberty was shared in some degree by Moslem Azenegues, who were religious teachers to the recently converted tribes of Senegal.

To all others the chief remained invisible, except for one hour in the morning and another in the afternoon when he showed the sun of his countenance at the entrance of his courtyard. Anyone who would speak to him at such a time must first strip to the waist—should he be wearing clothes—and bend upon his knees until his forehead touched the ground, while with one hand he threw dust on his head. Dragging himself in this posture, still flinging earth over his hair, the suppliant laboriously crawled near. Two paces off from Budomel he could begin to speak, but the chief would not deign to look at him, and went on talking to others as if he were not there. When the vassal had said his piece to his master's averted face, then Budomel "with haughty aspect" answered in two words. The proudest tyrant of medieval Europe could not have exacted such abject submission from his lowest serf. "If God Himself had been there," gasps the amazed Venetian, "I don't think He could have been treated with greater respect!"

The Italian trader got on well with the black prince. Although their conversation must have been conducted through interpreters it seems to have covered a variety of topics. Religion was a fruitful theme for many talks, and Budomel took his white friend with him to the building he called his mosque to watch him say his prayers under the supervision of his Moslem mentors.

Certainly Budomel was no fanatic in matters of religion. He did not mind the stranger telling him that his beliefs were false and his teachers were ignorant of the truth; in fact, he seems to have enjoyed seeing these discomfited in an argument, but needless to say the Moslem pundits did not like it! They foamed and fumed while the white man—an ardent polemist like all medieval Christians—tore the Moslem tenets to shreds, proclaiming that "ours was the True Religion." And their disciple Budomel listened and laughed! His interest seems to have been purely academic, and he closed the controversy with a soothing pronouncement of his own. No doubt, he said, the white men's faith was good. God would not have blessed the white race with so many things, and made of them such knowing fellows, without giving them a good religion too. But the Moslem faith also was good, and Budomel thought that the blacks would find it easier to save their souls. The inference was logical: God had given all the best things in

(263)

this world to the white man, and little to the negroes. Since God is just, observed the black philosopher, and He has made the white men lords of the earthly Paradise, that of the next world must be for the negroes!

These Senegalese certainly owned few worldly goods. Cadamosto was convinced of that through frequenting their fairs. The markets were held once a week, and he went hoping to be offered gold, but found little except native textiles, wooden basins, cooking-pots, and local fruit.

He liked to go there all the same for the sake of "seeing new things." In this wish he was not alone. The blacks were keen sightseers, too—the sight for them was Alvise Cadamosto! A white man in those parts was still an object of curiosity that some people had never seen before. Wherever the Italian went he drew a crowd, gaping at so extraordinary a creature. His color seems to have intrigued them more than anything—could such a complexion be natural? We have heard of European children thinking that a negro might wash white, but these negroes supposed a white man possibly washed black! Accordingly they rubbed his hands and arms to see if such a strange veneer did not come off.

They were also astonished at his clothes. We should be, too, but for another reason. Our stouthearted Venetian faced the sun of Senegal attired in a black damask doublet covered by a woolen cloak! To the natives, who knew of no textile but cotton cloth, such fabrics were exotic wonders.

This was nothing compared to their amazement when Cadamosto invited his black friends on board the caravel. They thought the ship must be a living creature—had she not a wide open eye upon the prow with which to see her way? But even with a seeing ship, the negroes said, the white men must be great magicians to guide her right across the pathless sea, and not be lost! "They do not understand the art of navigation by compass and chart," Cadamosto informs his readers rather unnecessarily.

He terrified his guests by firing off one of the ship's bombards. This artillery could kill a hundred men at one shot, he explained. "Such are inventions of the devil!" said the Africans with perfect truth.

A very different verdict was passed upon the bagpipes which Cadamosto ordered a sailor to play. The blacks declared that they had never heard such heavenly music. What divine creature could it be that sang so sweetly? How beautifully it was dressed! Cadamosto handed to them the instrument, beribboned and with silken fringes in true Celtic style. Clearly it was no animal, as they could see, but it was a celestial thing, they said, made by the hand of God!

Among the marvels of civilization that impressed them most was a candle burning on a candlestick. Artificial illumination was unknown in their villages, and they thought this was a wonderful invention. Cadamosto, a handy youth, showed them how to make candles for themselves. Material was not lacking, for in these forests there were swarms of bees. The natives ate their honey in the comb, and never thought of separating the wax. The Venetian, who perhaps kept bees at home, taught them how to extract the honey. "Now what is that?" he asked didactically, pointing to the remaining wax. "That is a thing," they said, "which is of no use at all. . . ." "Then, in their presence, I made several candles and lit them, at which they were amazed." There was nothing that the white men did not know! they cried.

Did they profit by the lesson? Perhaps not, for we gather that they were a feckless race. They were too lazy even to till the soil more than was necessary just to avoid starvation. That did not mean much work. There was only to scratch the soil, and something grew. They did a little hoeing now and then, flinging the earth away from them, and not towards themselves after the man-

(265)

ner of a European husbandman. They sowed and gathered showy-looking beans with parti-colored stripes. Their food consisted of such beans, and millet bread, fish from the river and lagoons, and strange tropical fruit. They drank milk, water, and palm wine, which beverage Cadamosto thought very good. "It is sweet and rather sparkling," he says, "and I liked it better than our wines."

The vegetation and the fauna of the land all find their place in the Venetian's notes. He speaks of the rich pastures and the beautiful, enormous trees, and the wild beasts that hunted in their shade. He tells of elephants, leopards, and lions, and the deadly serpents that native magicians charmed, and he admired the parrots' nests, swinging ingeniously out of the reach of snakes at the tip of a palm leaf. Having a keen eye for all profitable side lines, Cadamosto took home with him over a hundred and fifty green and yellow parrots. These sold at half a ducat each, he says, so that was not too bad!

The Venetian rejoined his ship at the mouth of the Senegal. The open roadstead, where the caravel had anchored first, proved inaccessible when the November cyclones blew. Cadamosto wrote a letter to the ship's captain, asking to be picked up within the bar, towards which he would proceed overland. This message was delivered at great risk of life by a stout negro who swam out through surf and swell to earn two pewter majolica jars. "They are the finest swimmers in the world!" Cadamosto exclaims.

With a shipload of slaves and green parrots, and other items of interest or profit, the young adventurer began to wonder—what next? He did not want to go home yet—he wanted to see more. His thoughts turned to the Gambia river of which he had heard the Infante speak. Somewhere above the Gambia mouth there lay the negro city of Cantor, where Arabs from Timbuktu traded with the Mandinga tribes for gold. Cadamosto says frankly that

he coveted that gold—he had seen hardly any gold so far—besides
which he still thirsted for new things.

He would make for the Gambia, he resolved, and while his ship
was getting underway, beheld two sails appear on the horizon.
Rejoicing in the hope of meeting friends, and hearing news from
home, Vicente Dias and Cadamosto watched the caravels draw
near. One, we are told vaguely, was commanded by "some of the
Infante's squires," the other—more interesting to an Italian—
was that of Messer Antonioto, "a Genoese gentleman, and great
navigator."

The new arrivals welcomed the Gambia idea—it may be that
they had instructions to go there. In any case, they all agreed to
seek for the river in company, and together they rounded the
Cape Verde, some thirty miles ahead.

South of this cape they sailed down an enchanting coast where
dense forest rose straight up from the beach. Gigantic trees out-
lined their leafy tops against the sky and mirrored green reflections in transparent streams. "I have traveled east and west," Cadamosto exclaims, "but never have I seen a land more beautiful
than this!"

It was a coast that few travelers had visited before, perhaps no
one since Nuno Tristão and his crew, some years ago, had sailed
into this paradise and met their death. It was the bush where the
wild black men stalked, whose poisoned arrows could kill with a
scratch.

They sailed south of Cape Verde for seventy miles, always
within sight of the coast, casting the line by day, and anchoring
at night some distance out to sea. Reaching the mouth of a small
river, they decided to send a messenger ashore to gather information of the land.

Each caravel was provided with an interpreter—the Infante had
seen to that. He had a trained staff of such men, all Africans who

had been sold into captivity by their own native lords. They all had learned to speak good Portuguese and had been baptized in the Christian faith. Each slave had a slave of his own in payment for his services, and when he had earned four of these he would be a free man.

One such interpreter was landed on this unknown coast to parley with the naked men who had assembled there in log canoes. He talked with them for a long time, but what he said or what they answered no one ever knew. It was the natives who broke off the discussions by killing the unfortunate envoy!

The white men, watching from their caravels, were surprised and dismayed. They never thought he would be slain by his own fellow blacks. "We understood that these men must be very cruel!" was the obvious conclusion.

However that might be, the servants of the Infante were not allowed to fight except in self-defense. Their mission was to open up relations with these people "in good peace and concord, with their consent, and we had to establish that peace by tact, and not by force."

The caravels sailed on, and still the coast grew lovelier with every league. At last they reached the mouth of a great river—seven or eight miles wide across the bar. This surely was the Gambia, and they told each other hopefully that there must be some town or village not far off "where perhaps we may find much gold, or other treasure!"

They sent the smallest caravel ahead to take the soundings. If sufficient depths were found to float the larger ships, she must turn back and signal to the others.

Finding a fathom and half above the bar, the caravel anchored and waited for her sister ships. Meanwhile, two boats were sent some miles upstream between forest-clad banks.

Silently, sinuously, the glassy river wound its path out of the wilderness; the murmuring of the bush filled the motionless air, and there was not a sign of human life. All of a sudden, noise-lessly, three canoes darted out of the green shade and bore down in pursuit of the two boats. Not to be involved in a fight, the white men rowed back towards the river mouth. The negroes fol-lowed all the way until, rounding a bend, they suddenly beheld the caravel, and stopped short, staring blankly at a sight that "neither they nor their forefathers had ever seen before." The white men signed them to approach and to make friends, but all their blandishments were vain. The canoes vanished as swiftly as they had appeared—once more the whisperings of the forest were the only sign of life.

Next day, when the sea wind arose, the three ships sailed into the Gambia "in the name of God." The tide bore them four miles upstream, along a shining road, monotonously beautiful, with forest hanging like a curtain on each side. Then, suddenly, as on the day before, the river was alive with armed canoes. They closed in round the foremost caravel and then stopped dead. A hundred and fifty tall negroes, "very fine men," in cotton shirts, and wear-ing headdresses adorned with white plumes, paused with uplifted oars to gaze up speechlessly at the pale-colored strangers looking down. Europe and Africa—two branches of the human family separated for millenniums—stared silently into each other's eyes. "So we remained for a long time, and neither did they attack us, nor did we make any movement against them."

Then slowly, round the bend, the other two ships glided into view, bearing down towards the petrified black men. That broke the spell. The negroes dropped their oars and seized their bows, but before the deadly arrows left the string the silence of the for-est was rent by a fearful roar. Great stones, hurled in the air by four bombards, splashed the water all around the canoes. The black men let their bows fall by their side, and gazed upon the eddies, thunderstruck. They were brave warriors, however, for they shot again. A Genoese then took his crossbow and sent an arrow through a negro's heart. This started a real battle, but the bombards soon dispersed the blacks. They fled to a safe distance where they lingered, watching still, which gave a chance to the interpreters to hail them.

Why had they attacked peaceful men who only came to barter merchandise? he shouted across the water. The white men had good friends in the kingdoms of Senegal, and wished to be on good terms with them too. These ships had been sent from far distant lands with presents from the King of Portugal to the King of the blacks. Let them approach, said the interpreter, "peacefully and lovingly, and take our merchandise, and give of theirs in exchange—as much or as little as they liked, or even none at all, we would be quite content!"

The negroes answered sulkily that they believed the Christians were man-eaters! The slaves they bought in Africa were merely butcher's meat. "They would have no truck with us of any kind," they said; "but kill us all, and then give all we had brought to their chief!"

At this moment the sea breeze rose and blew upstream, filling the sails of the three caravels. Gracefully gliding, the gigantic birds bore down towards the African canoes, and all the black men fled in terror.

Shall we sail a hundred miles or so up river? the captains then proposed, haunted by visions of Cantor and the gold markets of Mali. But the sailors were weary of the prolonged voyage. They did not care about Cantor when they were overdue for home—and sailors, Cadamosto observes, are very obstinate!

The seamen had their way. The caravels trimmed sail and crossed the bar, leaving the mystery of the Gambia still unsolved. Over a widening gulf the wanderers watched the skyline growing dim astern while the swift twilight fell. The darkness blotted out the unknown continent. The Polar Star hung very low down on the sea. New constellations swam up from the southern skies, pointing to hemispheres unseen.

A young Venetian had set out for Flanders, and his voyage had ended here! The pursuit of "new things" had led him far. All his familiar world had been left leagues behind—further, it seemed, the sky itself was strange.

On the three caravels the steersmen turned their bows about and followed the Northern Star.

XX

The Diplomacy of Diogo Gomes

I WAS the first Christian to make peace with the Gambia blacks!" Diogo Gomes proudly told Martin of Bohemia.

The traveler from Nuremberg listened in wonder to the old man's tales. Diogo Gomes, Sheriff of Sintra, had spent the best years of his youth on the Infante's ships, and later in the service of King Afonso V. "I have seen a great part of the world," he told the stranger.

It was a different world, reflected Diogo Gomes, than what the Ancients had supposed. Believe it or not, it seems that even Ptolemy—the most illustrious Ptolemy—had not been always right! The sage of Alexandria wrote that the frozen North was uninhabited, and that man could not live in equatorial climates—"and we have found the contrary of all this." Men had been seen living within the icy regions near the Pole, and as for the Equinoxial line—"the multitude of peoples there can hardly be believed."

So Diogo Gomes talked, a little bit confused sometimes regarding names and dates, but always interesting. Martin listened and drew him on, and wrote down the old man's reminiscences in Latin, that the world might read and understand.

Diogo Gomes recalled how, in the fifties, he had sailed in command of a caravel owned by a certain Piconço, of Lagos. The Infante had sent two other ships under his captaincy, with orders to go as far as they could. Did Alvise Cadamosto take part in this voyage? From his memoirs it seems quite likely that he did—the second voyage that he describes sounds very similar. He was the leading spirit by his own account, but Diogo Gomes does not mention him at all—no more than Cadamosto mentions Diogo Gomes!

However that may be, the three ships sailed south of all latitudes that had been crossed before, until the current forced them in towards the coast whence natives rowed to meet the ships in their canoes. These did not shoot at the strangers, but offered merchandise barter. Their wares were silk and cotton cloths, ivory, and malagueta pepper in the pod—"just as it grows," which, Diogo Gomes said, "greatly rejoiced me."

The swell at high tide dragged the anchors of the caravels, obliging them to seek the open sea. Against the current that flowed up the coast the navigators could make little progress.

They landed by a cape of broken palms and saw a pasture-land upon which grazed five thousand antelopes that showed no fear of man. Five elephants—three big, two small—emerged out of a narrow watercourse half smothered in the bush, and on the beach were holes of crocodiles—and that was all: "We returned to our ships."

Heading towards Cape Verde they reached the Gambia mouth to sail with wind and tide upstream, seeking the negro city of Cantor. Everywhere that they passed the natives fled in their canoes—fearing vengeance, doubtless, for Diogo Gomes says that it was these who were responsible for Nuno Tristão's death.

Regardless of their predecessors' fate, Diogo Gomes led his three ships up the river. A crowd of blacks took courage and gathered on the right bank—and "we approached, and we made peace with them." How this was managed he does not relate.

The lord of this land was named Frangasick; he was nephew of

Farisangul—"a great prince of the blacks." He gave Diogo Gomes one hundred and eighty pounds of gold in exchange for cloths and bracelets and other merchandise.

Frangasick had a servant named Bucker, "well acquainted with all the negro land," and Diogo Gomes promised him a cloak and shirts, and everything that he might want, if he would guide him to Cantor.

One caravel was ordered to remain at Ulimays—Olimansa, Diogo Gomes calls it further on—the second ship he left at Animays some distance above, "and I," he adds, "sailed up the river as far as I could, and found Cantor."

Cantor, on the edge of the Mandinga country—a meeting-place of many races where the trade routes crossed from distant parts of Africa—was less fiercely distrustful of the foreigner than the more isolated tribes beside the coast had shown themselves to be. From caravan to caravan, a tenuous chain, seemingly lost at times but still continuing unbroken through the jungle and across the desert, linked Cantor to other lands. The men about here knew that there were worlds beyond the Gambia forests, and when the news had spread of the latest arrival by their river, the Africans streamed in from far and wide to see the strange white men. They came, says Diogo Gomes, from northern deserts, about Timbuktu, and from the mountains to the south, "and people came from Kuka, which is a great city encircled by brick walls."

Diogo Gomes was interested in Kuka. They told him that it was a city full of gold, brought there from the mountains of Futa Djalon. The far side of those ranges, Diogo Gomes informed his listener, "is called Sierra Leone." Camels and dromedaries streamed constantly into Kuka with merchandise of the Saracen lands. They came from Carthage, Tunis, Fez, and Cairo. "And all the rivers great and small flowed from those mountains westward to the ocean; but on the other side, the natives said, there were some mighty rivers that ran east. Eastward there was also an inland sea traversed by canoes as large as ships; and eastward still, beyond that sea, there lived white men. What monarchs reigned in those countries? Diogo Gomes inquired, and he was told of Sandoguy and Samanaya, who lived on each side of the lake, and made war on each other. "I told the Lord Infante of all this when I returned." But it appears that he knew it already.

The Lord of Kuka was the King of Boormali, and all the right bank of the Gambia came beneath his sway. He was the lord of all the mines; his courtiers wore gold ornaments in their nostrils and he tethered his horse to a great rock of gold that twenty men could hardly lift, which stood before his palace gate.

All the lands to the east were rich in mines. Men dug the sand out of the pits and gave it to the women to wash out the ore. These miners all died young, it seemed, poisoned by the gases that exuded from the depths below.

What was the way to Kuka? Diogo Gomes asked, and he was told a string of barbarous names he soon forgot. Meanwhile, "my men were worn out by the heat." They had to turn their faces from the golden Empire of Mali and sail back towards the life-giving sea.

They found the other caravel with only three sound men aboard—the captain and the crew were down with fever, and nine men had died. The second caravel was hardly better off—five of its men were dead. Gladly they sailed out of the steamy forest shade towards the sand dunes and the breakers.

Diogo Gomes gave his black guide the promised reward, but did not yet dismiss him. Bucker had told him of another chief—Batimansa by name—who ruled the land on the Gambia left bank. "I desired to make peace with him," said Diogo Gomes, and so he sent his go-between.

The black chief, curious but distrustful, came to meet the white captain close to the shelter of a tangled thicket by the waterside. He had an armed host gathered around him, all carrying poisoned arrows, spears and shields. Diogo Gomes walked boldly up to Batimansa, "bringing my offerings and biscuit and some of our wine, for they only know that of the palm."

The chief drank and approved. "He was very pleased," says Diogo Gomes, "and very grateful." The two became good friends. Batimansa gave Diogo Gomes three negroes, two women and a man, and he swore "by the living God that he would never fight the Christians any more."

It is here that Diogo Gomes speaks about "the Indian Jacob," his interpreter. Whether Indian or Abyssinian—East Africa and India looked much the same thing to fifteenth-century geographers—this enigmatic personage seems to have known all about the west coast. To test Batimansa's good faith, Diogo Gomes sent Jacob with him to visit and report upon a place called Alcuzet. Jacob had passed there once already, it appears, in company with an unnamed Portuguese knight who had trekked from the Gambia forests up to Timbuktu!

Alcuzet was a fair land, Jacob said, "with a river of fresh water, and many lemons," which fruit he carried back to Diogo Gomes. The chief of Alcuzet also sent down a gift of elephants' tusks, one of which was so great that it required four men to bear it! These blacks came fearlessly on board the caravel, and Diogo Gomes went himself to visit Alcuzet. The chief welcomed the stranger to his house—a shanty built of cane and thatch—and there Diogo Gomes was entertained three days on end.

He says that he saw many parrots there, and leopards too, and his host gave him half a dozen leopards' skins. An elephant was also slaughtered in his honor, and its meat sent down to the caravel.

Diogo Gomes makes no comment upon the eating quality of

such a novel dish. "Tough and tasteless!" was Cadamosto's verdict. That young man liked to try everything once, so he sampled elephant's meat, only to say that he had eaten it. He adds that he had some salted for the Infante too, and brought him back an elephant's hoof that measured three palms and one finger across, besides a tusk eight feet long. Henrique was delighted with them all, Cadamosto declares, and sent the hoof and tusk to Flanders as a present for his sister.

Diogo Gomes had made friends on both banks of the Gambia, but still did not feel that his mission was accomplished. He had been informed at Alcuzet that the ringleader of all hostility against the white men was the chief Nomymansa, lord of the lands about the river mouth. Therefore, "I worked hard to make peace with him, and sent him many gifts."

Nomymansa proved coy, though willing enough to accept the offerings. Having sent out many shooting parties against the white men, he hardly could feel easy in their presence. Before risking his precious person in an interview, he thought that he would try it on his subjects. "He sent many men and women to me," says Diogo Gomes, "to see if I would do them harm."

The test was reassuring. All messengers were pleasantly received, and soon returned unscathed. The cautious Nomymansa decided then that he might grant the white captain an interview.

Supported by a host of braves, the black king sat upon the beach and graciously motioned Diogo Gomes to draw near. Diogo Gomes approached with all the ceremony that became a perfect diplomat, and he and Nomymansa talked together.

Religion was the subject of their conversation, it appears, and also the Infante D. Henrique. Nomymansa was Moslem, and by him stood what Diogo Gomes calls "a bishop of his church." This personage—*imam*, or *mullah*, or whatever he might be—questioned the stranger captain concerning the Christian faith—"and

I replied according to the understanding that God had given me."
When Diogo Gomes finished his discourse he tactfully gave the
"bishop" his innings: "I questioned him about Mohammed."

Nomymansa seems to have been more easily influenced than
was Budomel, or perhaps Diogo Gomes preached more power-
fully than Cadamosto, for the black king declared himself converted! He gave his "bishop" three days to clear out of the country, and ordered under pain of death that no subject of his should
venerate Mohammed any more. He was a Christian now! cried
Batimansa. There could be no God other than the one in whom
his "brother the Infante D. Henrique believed." Nomymansa
must be baptized forthwith, and all his courtiers, and all his wives,
and let everybody call him Henrique now, he cried, for he would
have no other name but that.

With one accord the notables around him chose their Christian names—Diogo, Nuno, etc., after their new-found friends—
and they begged Diogo Gomes to baptize them on the spot.

Gratified though he was to see his lightning success as a missionary, the captain did not dare to perform the sacred rite, "because I was a layman." Instead, he invited his converts to dinner
on his caravel—the King, eight wives, and the twelve oldest courtiers.

The banquet went with a swing. The bill of fare consisted of
"chickens and meat prepared in our manner," and "red and white
wine, as much as they would drink." With increasing conviction
all the guests "said and repeated that there were no better people
than the Christians!" Even more fervently the chief begged to be
baptized, but Diogo Gomes remained firm. "I said that I had not
the powers for this, but I would ask the Infante to send a priest
who would baptize them."

Nomymansa—Henrique now!—implored him so to do. He
himself would send a letter to the Infante, he said, asking for a

priest to instruct them in the Christian faith. And could he have a falcon, too? he added wistfully, since it appeared that white men had birds trained to perch upon their wrists, and to catch other birds. He also wanted sheep, ducks, and a pig—and he would like two men as well, to teach him to build houses and a wall of masonry around his town! Diogo Gomes promised that all this miscellany would be duly sent, and their old enemy wept bitter tears to see the Portuguese depart.

Diogo Gomes sailed away from the Gambia shores bearing a tragic trophy. It was the anchor of Nuno Tristão's caravel, cut adrift years ago by men whose poison-stiffened arms refused to haul the chain. Nomymansa had found, and proudly treasured it, but now in token of his change of heart he gave it up to his new friends.

One more errand of peace remained to be accomplished. On his way home Diogo Gomes put into shore beside Cape Verde to seek out the chief Bezeguiche—"a bad and treacherous man."

It so happened that Bezeguiche himself, with thirty-eight men in two canoes, rowed up incognito to meet the ship. The interpreter recognized him however, and whispered to Diogo Gomes that this was Bezeguiche. The captain said nothing, but made the men all come on board. "Is this land owned by Bezeguiche?" he asked innocently. "That is so," the chieftain himself replied. "Why does he treat Christians so ill?" Diogo Gomes went on; "it would be better for him to have peace with them and barter merchandise. He would have horses then, like Budomel and other negro lords! Tell him that I captured you at sea, and out of love for him I freely let you go ashore."

All smiles, the negroes left the caravel for their canoes, and Diogo Gomes, up on deck, watched them embark. "Bezeguiche, Bezeguiche!" he called dramatically when the last man had left the ship, "do not imagine that I did not recognize thee! I could have done what I chose to thee. Since I treated thee well, do thou likewise to our Christians!"

We hear no more of Bezeguiche, which looks as if he gave no further trouble. He lingers on the page of history only as the name by which during the next two hundred years the Portuguese called that port, known as Dakar today.

"The Senhor Infante," Diogo Gomes adds, "was very pleased with our arrival home." And so he well might be. A good new stretch of coast had been explored, the Gambia trade was opened up, and peace was made with nearly all the chiefs from Cape Verde down to the Rio Grande.

Was it on this voyage that the Cape Verde Islands were discovered? Some say they were. Others place the discovery a few years later. And who discovered them? Diogo Gomes affirms that he was the man—in 1460—but Cadamosto speaks of them as "the islands that I discovered." Nevertheless, the person who was rewarded for the deed was the Genoese, Antonio de Noli! There is documentary proof of this, and Diogo Gomes feels bitter about it. He admits that Noli was with him upon this voyage, but says that the Italian stole a march upon him. He had a faster ship and got home first, and "asked the King to make him captain of the Island of Santiago, which I had discovered—and the King gave it him, and he kept it until his death."

It was no Eden that Diogo Gomes had lost—the Cape Verde Islands were the contrary of Paradise. Desolate rocks rising abruptly from the sea, the color of cinders out of which the fire has died, they were rather a vision of some primeval extinct inferno. The best of all the group was Santiago, which the prudent Antonio de Noli had claimed for himself. There was fresh water and good pasture-land, wild fig trees of a sort, and multitudes of birds so tame, Diogo Gomes and Cadamosto say, that they could be caught in the hand.

The archipelago was uninhabited. Duarte Pacheco, who was grandson of one of the Infante's captains, says that D. Henrique began to colonize them. To say he planned to do so seems more probable. He hardly had time to begin. It is not even certain if the whole group came to light before his death. As usual, official records are lacking here, references scanty and casual, narratives few and contradictory. Island fog again! How, when, and by whom were any of these ocean archipelagoes discovered? In the case of the Cape Verde group, at least, the choice of dates is limited. We know that between 1457 and 1462 all ten islands had been explored and named.

The Infante had many better islands, and the mainland at the time was more exciting than a few volcanic rocks. Already the long coast of Africa showed signs of curving east—the passage to the Indian Ocean might be near at hand! No indication of a change yet lay upon the landscape—nothing to suggest the approaches to the culture and the kingdoms of the East. Only black savages plied their canoes upon the silent waterways. Unending forest rolled across the land to somber mountains where far-off thunder like the roaring of a lion rumbled among the rocks.

"A harsh country, and wild," it appeared to Pedro de Sintra who discovered it. Serra Leôa—Sierra Leone—the Lion Mountains—he named those grim peaks shadowed by the storm.

XXI

Lost Atlantis

THE monsters of the South had vanished before the Infante's caravels. The Sea of Darkness had become a path of light which no one doubted could be followed on until the end of Africa should be turned round at last. But what about the empty West? The ocean surged away into blank space—an abyss which no voice had ever crossed within memory of man. "We come from the western shore where the sun sets, and we know not of any land beyond—nothing but water!" So the English pilgrims, Willebald and Wunebald, had told the Caliph of Damascus in the eighth century. When, seven hundred years later D. Henrique was born by that same western shore, geographers had added nothing useful to the pilgrims' statement. Ptolemy's *Almagest* was still the student's oracle, and he spoke of no land west of Europe.

Arab learning did not contribute to the subject: "The ocean itself is the only limit of the ocean," declared the Moslem traveler, Ibn Khaldun, and that was the opinion accepted by most. Aristotle indeed suggested that there might be lands beyond the sea to act as make-weight to the eastern hemisphere, but he supposed they were Asiatic lands. The world is very small, he said, and the Pillars of Hercules not very far from India. There, Seneca agreed with him. A few days should be quite enough, he said—given a good wind—for a ship to cross the ocean; and the medieval Gilles de Bouvier wrote that, if a ship sailed straight ahead, in the end she would reach the land of Prester John. All this was theoretically speaking. Neither Aristotle, nor Seneca, nor their more modern disciples admitted the practical possibility of crossing the ocean.

Yet there were legends—vague rumors recurring down the centuries—of lands lying far to the west. Sometimes it was the tale of a lost continent—Plato's Atlantis, submerged in the waves—or the enchanted Island of the Seven Cities, where seven bishops and their flocks had sought refuge from the Moslem invasion. The Island of the Seven Cities never could be found, because the Bishop of Porto, who was a necromancer, had hidden it by magic in the seas. And nobody was ever able to return because the seven bishops had burned their boats! Besides these there were many other stories, all more or less miraculous and fantastic.

Henrique was not the man to be legend-led, neither did he blindly accept the verdict of the Ancients. But outside fancy or conjecture were the historic voyages of the Vikings, who had sailed round the Arctic circle and down a western coast to Vinland long ago. Their discovery was lost, but tradition remained—and King Eric of Denmark had been married to D. Henrique's cousin. The Infante D. Pedro had visited that northern court, and Henrique seems to have been interested in keeping up the intercourse. We have seen how he welcomed to his service Abelhart the Dane, and certainly he would discuss with him the geographical traditions of the Scandinavian lands.

"The Infante," says Diogo Gomes, "desiring to know the distant regions of the western ocean, if there were islands or continents beyond those that Ptolemy described, sent caravels to search for lands." Seeking, they had found the Azores—but was that all? Had the immense Atlantic only those lost mountains to reveal?

Some people think that D. Henrique, like Toscanelli, and Co-

lumbus later on, toyed with the idea of a western route to India.
While he may quite well have considered the theory—it certainly
was discussed in his time—it does not seem that he accepted it
as the most practical solution of his problem. Though there are
indications of Atlantic exploration moved by him, such voyages
never were his chief preoccupation. His first purpose was to sail
round the continent of Africa, from the Atlantic to the Indian
Ocean. All wanderings to the west were parenthetical—an outlet to a scientific curiosity that he had not the time or means fully
to satisfy.

Such voyages were made none the less, some accidental, others
pre-determined. They are not recorded by chroniclers, uninter-
ested in sterile gropings after shadowy coasts seen dimly beyond
weary leagues of sea. We know of them through hints and traditions, passing reference in documents, and from the fact that by
the middle of the fifteenth century all sailors were convinced that
west of the Azores were other lands.

The colonization of this island group in mid-ocean made almost inevitable that voyages should be tried still farther west.
From the time of their discovery, the Azores had become a port
of call for homing Guinea ships, but compared with that of Madeira, their settled population increased slowly. Henrique stocked
all the islands with cattle from the first, and in 1439 Gonçalo
Velho was authorized to colonize Santa Maria. The Infante D.
Pedro settled São Miguel with Moorish agriculturists, and there,
in spite of earthquakes and seismic upheavals, they seem to have
done well. Isabel, Duchess of Burgundy, also lent a hand in the
family endeavor. Many of her Flemish subjects were sent to Portugal to obtain grants of land and go to live in the Azores.

They were lovely islands, these gardens of green above volcanic
fires. They easily became a granary exporting wheat, and their

fat cattle and dairy produce were soon justly renowned. No cows gave so much milk as the Azorean cows, nor milk so rich in butter; no sheep so succulent as those fed on the island pastures, or producing better wool.

Such great natural advantages were balanced by forbidding isolation. It is not everybody who would care to settle on an island cut off from the world by nearly a thousand miles of sea. The human population of the Azores therefore remained small, and for some decades was confined to Santa Maria and São Miguel. Pico, Graciosa and São Jorge for many years had few inhabitants; nor had Terceira, though it was a frequent port of call for ships on their return from Africa.

Faial was a window towards the west. It was from there that D. Henrique's squire, Diogo de Teive, set sail one day to seek the Island of the Seven Cities. Accompanied by his son João, and the Galician pilot, Pero de la Frontera, he sailed a hundred and fifty leagues southwest over an empty sea.

Finding no sign of land, the mariners set their course to northeast until they saw large flocks of birds. These were land birds, it seems. They followed after them, and so they found the two outer islands of the Azores—Flores and Corvo—which were so isolated from the rest that they were still unknown. This was a discovery, no doubt, but not the one they sought. Diogo de Teive and his crew left Flores and Corvo behind, and sailed to the northwest.

They reached a latitude of 50° north, where boisterous west winds raged although the sea was calm. By every token it appeared that land was not far off—but the air had turned most strangely cold though they were still in August. They feared the northern winter would soon be upon them. Unequipped as they were, they dared not sail still farther west and seek the unknown land. So Diogo de Teive returned to the Azores and Portugal, having just missed discovering Newfoundland. This may have been in 1450 or 1451. In 1453, we know, the King gave the island of Corvo to his uncle of Bragança.

Another seeker was Vicente Dias of Tavira—the man who piloted Cadamosto on his first voyage to Africa. Vicente Dias, returning from Guinea to Portugal *via* the Azores, swept a great circle out into mid-ocean, far to the west of Madeira. He thought that he saw land still farther west—island or continent, whatever it might be. Later, he sailed again to look for it, but *terra firma* or mirage, the land was lost.

Was this the same land that Gonçalo Fernandes saw on his way back from the fisheries of the Rio de Ouro? He saw it on the high seas, it appears, to west-northwest of the Canaries and Madeira. He tried to steer towards it, but the wind was contrary, and though a ship was sent again to seek, the island was not found.

Tales such as these are probably quite true—they are not exciting enough to be invented—but there are other island stories of Henrique's time, founded on fact perhaps, but decked with fantastic detail beyond all verisimilitude. As is usual with legends of the kind, it is to writers of a later date we owe their preservation. Thus the sixteenth-century historian, Antonio Galvão, tells how in 1447 a ship from Porto was blown far out of her course. She reached an island whose inhabitants were Christian. These even took the sailors to their church. They begged them to remain until their absent prince returned, but the Portuguese feared treason and escaped by stealth at night. Bursting with news, they arrived home expecting the Infante to reward them. But he was angry, it appears, that they returned with such scanty information. He sent them back to their island at once, and this time they did not return.

Not a convincing tale in many ways, but the Infante's attitude is quite in character. No one need hope to win rewards from him by spinning travelers' yarns; all that you would get for your pains were orders to return and verify your facts!

Perhaps it is another version of the same story that tells of the adventures of a ship struck by the tempest upon leaving the Gibraltar Straits. She was blown to the Island of the Seven Cities, on to a beach the sands of which were mingled with gold dust. On returning to Portugal, the quartermaster sold some of this sand for a good price to a goldsmith in Lisbon, and the Regent D. Pedro caused the marvel to be written in the national archives. Whether anyone has ever seen this document we are not told!

Such stories may be brushed aside as legendary—though a persistent and recurring legend rarely grows except around a fact—but evidence derived from maps is not so easy to dismiss.

There is the wandering island of Antilia. On every map drawn after 1462 we find Antilia west of the Azores. Its latitude is variable, but generally it hovers on the parallel of Lisbon or Cape São Vicente, or sometimes where the Indies of Columbus later on were found. Guesswork? Coincidence? Actual discovery? Historians argue, and no proofs can be brought forth for any hypothesis. Toscanelli, writing to Portugal in 1474, mentions "the island of Antilia which is known to you," and when Columbus returned from his famous voyage, imagining that he had reached the outer islands of Japan, in Portugal they only said: "He has been to Antilia!"

Besides Antilia there is the "Authentic Island," southwest of Cape Verde, drawn by Andréa Bianco on a map of 1448. Andréa Bianco came to Lisbon just before that date, and then went on to London where he made this map. The "Authentic Island" there depicted is a stretch of coast inscribed as being 1500 miles west of Africa. That brings us to Brazil!

(287)

The mystery of the transatlantic shore lured the romantic imagination of the Infante Fernando, D. Henrique's adopted son. Of all the varied legacy his godfather bequeathed to him, it was the islands of the west that thrilled him most. The coast of Africa did not mean much to Fernando. He seems to have done little to promote its exploration, but he sought for the lost continent with unabating zeal all the remaining years of his short life.

He never found it, so far as we know, and to contemporaries it might seem a sterile quest. Riches were not expected from that side—spices, and slaves, and gold already had been found abundantly in Africa. The seamen navigating towards the misty west were drawn by nothing but the lure of the unknown.

Their labor was not wasted. Little was learned about the lands across the sea in D. Henrique's or Fernando's time beyond the certainty that land was there; but, meanwhile, to the Portuguese seamen the ocean became a familiar book. Sailing from Finisterre to the Sargasso Sea—from the cold Banks of Newfoundland down to the steaming Gulf of Guinea, they came to know the doldrums and the trades, the seasons, currents, and prevailing winds. They learned to steer their little ships along the latitude, or down the meridian, to sail in curves, and tack before the wind, and not lose their true course.

The generations following discovered more lands than Henrique's seamen did, but they owed to them their knowledge of the sea. Other travelers might explore the mainland—the elder seamen did what was more difficult: they explored the Atlantic Ocean. In relative obscurity they cleared the way for those great names who later reaped the laurels. Columbus as a sailor knew nothing that he had not learnt from them—perhaps did nothing that they had not done before.

And their skill and tenacity prepared the way for the far greater feat with which Vasco da Gama crowned the closing of the century. That amazing voyage around the Cape—sailing for ninety days far from all sight of land and crossing sixty degrees in mid-ocean—could only have been possible after experience gained in countless unrecorded voyages of the years before.

XXII

Last Crusade

WHILE the cross was carried southward on Henrique's caravels, Constantinople fell before the Turks, and Mohammed II laid siege to Belgrade. A spasm of terror quivered across Europe from east to west, and the Pope called for a general crusade.

For a moment it appeared that his appeal would meet with some response. The crusade was discussed by all princes in every court, and Philippe of Burgundy, for one, solemnly took the Cross amid great feasts and junketings. It was all very exciting and spectacular, but nothing happened. Each monarch waited for his neighbor to make the first move. Meanwhile, the Turks had not progressed beyond the Balkans, and so long as they stayed down there, the western rulers were not seriously alarmed.

In Italy the position was more disquieting. Pope Sixtus, looking uneasily towards the lands across the Adriatic Sea, continued to cry out for help.

Afonso V, chivalrous and young, vibrated to the summons. It made no difference to him that Portugal was not threatened at all. He longed to draw his sword in the defense of Christendom. He promised to serve overseas for a whole year with a force of 12,000 men, and sent out invitations to his brother kings to come and join him. Full of enthusiasm and heedless of expense, he plunged into his preparations, though "not without the lamentations of the kingdom." His subjects did not share their lord's crusading fervor. Constantinople was too far away for anyone to feel the urge for sacrifice.

Coldly the people watched the King building his ships, raising troops, and buying arms and—since he feared that his own depreciated currency would find no acceptance abroad—minting some fair new golden coins to be known as *cruzados*.

If his subjects showed an unpraiseworthy apathy, the brother kings were not more satisfactory. "Neither by words, nor works," Ruy de Pina says, "did they give him to understand that they would help him."

The more hardheaded of Afonso's counselors suggested that, before going further with all this trouble and expense, it would be well to find out if there was any assistance to be counted upon. Italy, for instance, ought to be more interested than Portugal in defeating the foe of the Levant. Let an envoy be sent to the King of Naples to find out what the Italian princes meant to do.

The answer was nothing at all! The Portuguese ambassador "did not find in Naples nor in Italy that preparation and desire needful for such an enterprise."

Afonso's counselors told him that this was not good enough. Why should he go out of his way to defend the Mediterranean from the Turks when those Christians who lived upon its shores would not exert themselves? He could not hope to take Constantinople with 12,000 men! The best thing for the King to do, they said, was to remain quietly at home and rule his realm in peace and justice. When Portugal was threatened by some foreign power, then it would be time enough to go to war!

Sound advice, but lacking in appeal to an ardent young man. It was not by the arts of peace that D. Afonso hoped to distinguish his reign. Having assembled his men and his ships, he would not send them tamely home! He must do something, even if it were

(291)

no more than to chastise the French pirates who harassed his merchantmen. But there were other more inviting possibilities. Instead of a crusade in aid of kings a thousand miles away—why not one nearer home, that might combine with spiritual uplift some material advantage to the Crown? He would sail with his fleet to Africa, and make fresh conquests from the Moors.

This project roused Afonso's aging uncle. The Infante D. Henrique, already sixty-four, had watched without much personal interest the preparations of the fleet for the Levant. He never had felt moved to a crusade against the Turks, but all his life, for good or ill, Morocco haunted him. The conquest of Ceuta had been the dream of his boyhood, and the glorious achievement of his maiden sword. Tangier had been the longed-for prize, causing the tragedy that wrecked his middle age. The island paradises of the sea, the splendors of the Guinea coast had never blotted out from his mind's eye the tawny mountains of North Africa where the blood of his brother cried for vengeance still. The knife had been turned in the wound when Father João Alvares had been ransomed out of captivity. Henrique ordered this faithful servant to write all he remembered of his master's martyrdom at Fez. The narrative makes grim reading for us today. It must have been a book of horror to Fernando's brother. If King Afonso would chastize the Moors in Africa, Henrique could die happy.

He threw himself into the preparations heart and soul. It was he who organized the fleet of the Algarve, while the King and his cousins mustered theirs in the more northern ports. When Afonso sailed south, he found his uncle ready and waiting for him at Sagres. The Infante greeted the King and all his following with what the chronicler says was "a very perfect speech."

It was a great moment that moved him thus to oratory. He saw at last what he had longed for since 1438—a strongly armed expeditionary force prepared to sail against the King of Fez. The fleet consisted of 220 ships carrying 25,000 men. That was double the force Afonso meant to take to the Levant, but operating so much nearer home his expenses were halved.

It had been decided that Alcacer Ceguer would be the main objective. Afonso V had had larger ideas. He would have liked to try his fortune at Tangier, but this was overruled as being for the present too ambitious. Even Henrique had admitted as much. He had cried out for Tangier twenty years ago, but since then he had learned his lesson. Tangier behind its powerful walls could not be taken by a landing party. The smaller town of Alcacer upon the Straits of Gibraltar to the west of Ceuta was far more likely to be assaulted with success, and its capture would help materially in defending the former conquest.

The expedition left Lagos on October 14th, 1458. Like that against Ceuta long ago, this was a family enterprise, but Henrique alone remained to represent the generation which had sailed that July morning in 1415. Instead of his brothers, Henrique saw round him his brothers' sons—Afonso and Fernando in Duarte's place, and D. Pedro the younger, the late Regent's son, just recalled by the King after eight years' exile. The old Duke of Bragança—over eighty now—had stayed behind, but his son, the Marquis of Valença—a veteran already past middle age—had sailed with his young cousins.

Upon October 19th, Henrique once again beheld Tangier. For two days the fleet rode at anchor underneath those walls, associated with so much bitterness. Afonso looked with longing at the splendid town. That would be a much fairer prize than little Alcacer! Why not assault Tangier instead? But his counsel said no. Let him first try his strength at Alcacer Ceguer—Tangier could not be taken without a long and costly struggle.

The siege of Alcacer was short, although the Moors fought well. Henrique led his troops to the assault with something of his youthful fire. Urged on by his inspiring words, all did great deeds of valor in his sight. At midnight he sent for a heavy bombard to be placed up against the wall, and proceeded to shoot it down. The stones crumbled before the cannon balls; soon the defenders had appealed for terms, and Afonso left it to his uncle to make them.

They were not hard. Henrique told the Moslems that the King had come there only to serve God. No one desired their money or their goods. They could depart, taking their wives and children, and all that they possessed, only leaving the Christian prisoners behind.

The Moors asked for an armistice to consider these terms, but that the Infante refused. They must take them or leave them, he replied, but if they would insist on fighting to a finish, then the Christians would massacre the lot!

The Moors did try further resistance for a day or two, but finding the defense was hopeless, they capitulated. Henrique gave them just the same conditions as he had proposed before, and sent his godson, D. Fernando, to observe that they were carried out.

Fernando watched the Moors withdraw in good order with all their families and their belongings. Not one of them, declares the chronicler, received injury of any kind. As they filed unmolested from the conquered town, did Henrique remember those grim days of 1438, when the position was reversed before Tangier?—his brother riding off in the twilight to martyrdom—the victor's broken faith—the desperate fight to reach the shore? Vengeance for which he had waited so long was in his hand at Alcacer, but he was satisfied with victory. Beside the King he kneeled down in the mosque, now consecrated as a Christian church, and thanked the Lord that he had seen this day.

King Afonso, elated by success, proceeded to hand out rewards wholesale. Such were great moments for all needy noblemen. Afonso was open-handed at any time, but get him in a glow of enthusiasm like this, and he would fling his patrimony to the winds. "He has left nothing but the highways for me!" his son was to say gloomily upon succeeding to the throne.

D. Duarte de Menezes, son of the first defender of Ceuta, was given the command of Alcacer. The Infante D. Henrique urged his nephew to leave the town well fortified and with all necessary supplies, for a siege was certain and imminent. The young man listened absently to his uncle's advice, but was too engrossed distributing honors and largesse to trouble much about it.

Leaving Alcacer, the royal party came to Ceuta, which Afonso had never seen before. It rather staggered him. Here was a large and splendid town—much larger and more splendid than his recent conquest. His grandfather had done better than he—a chastening thought! Afonso soon cheered up, however, resolving that he would do far greater things than that, and he would take Tangier one day! Meanwhile, the King of Fez, from Tangier, came to besiege Alcacer—and as Henrique had foretold, supplies were short.

Afonso did his best to get them in, but without much success. The Moors were encircling the town. He then defied the King of Fez to come and fight him in the field, outside Ceuta. The canny Moor ignored the challenge, however, and sat down before Alcacer instead. Afonso's subjects told him firmly that he must go home. The country could not keep up the expense of such an army overseas. The garrison of Alcacer must carry on, as that of Ceuta had done before. From the Algarve it would be easier to send an armed fleet with supplies. The King set sail for Portugal, therefore, and D. Duarte de Menezes, left at Alcacer, made good. He held the fort for fifty-three days with great spectacular success, and though the King of Fez withdrew only to try again next year, still D. Duarte was more than his match. The captain's wife was as daring as he. She came to join her husband—in the middle of

(295)

the siege—with their daughter and all the ladies of her household. The joy of every young knight of the garrison is easy to imagine, the more so that these enterprising girls made charming nurses for the wounded. With such romantic stimulus it was a light thing to defeat the King of Fez!

A second stronghold of Morocco was firmly in Portuguese hands. The conquest of that kingdom had begun. When, in November, 1458, Henrique looked for the last time upon those shores, he felt that his work there was done. Accounts were not yet settled with the King of Fez, but he had lived to see the day of reckoning. His nephew had sworn not to rest until he took Tangier, and Afonso the African could be trusted to square the balance.

In the dark lands south of the Senegal there remained a task for Henrique still. On his return from Alcacer, Diogo Gomes reminded him that the chief Nomymansa still was waiting for a priest to preach the Gospel. On no account would Henrique disappoint his black brother. He sent a learned and distinguished priest to "remain with that King and to instruct him in the Faith." He also sent his young squire, João Delgado, to teach Nomymansa the European ways, and bring him all those things which he had requested of Diogo Gomes.

The ships sailed—Henrique remained at Sagres, at his Vila do Infante, which by now he rarely left. There, in the town that he had built upon the wild promontory, he could review his lifework and prepare to pass it on. It was an unfinished quest, he knew, but it was well begun. "The Lord has pleased," he wrote, "to give me certain information and knowledge of those parts from Cape Non to beyond the land of Barbary and Nubia, and also quite three hundred leagues of the land of Guinea. . . ." The term Guinea, as used then, was rather imprecise, sometimes including all the coast south of Cape Bojador, at others limited to those countries below the river Senegal. We are not certain in what sense Henrique used the word, and around the starting-point of his three hundred leagues controversy rages. We know at least that in his lifetime his ships reached Sierra Leone, but some would have it that they went still farther.

A strip of coast from the Sahara to Sierra Leone, or perhaps to the Gulf of Guinea—a small result, some critics say, for forty years' endeavor! It is true that within the next two decades the same distance was doubled, but we should not forget that in the efforts of a pioneer the first steps are always the slowest and most costly. Henrique set to work in conditions that never were repeated, with neither sailing-charts, nor handy ships, nor knowledge of the winds and currents of the ocean, neither had science been perfected yet to guide a mariner far from all sight of land. The Infante began with all these problems to be solved, and prejudice and superstition to be overcome besides. The beginnings were bound to be no more than gropings in the dark.

He persevered and won through to the light; therein is his glory. He set a nation's steps upon a path that led to the world's end. The difficulties and dangers that still remained were none so great as those that he had overcome. This much of fulfillment he knew, though final triumph would not be for half a century.

Henrique dreamed great things, and realized some of his dreams—a joy not given to all men—but had his really been a happy life? Hardly, one fancies, during the last twenty years. He had seen his four brothers die, and three of them in tragic circumstances. In fact the dark cloud that descended on the family with the disaster of Tangier had only lifted when Henrique was the sole survivor.

The strongest tie remaining was Fernando, his adopted son—married now to Henrique's niece, Beatriz, daughter of the Infante D. João, who had died seventeen years ago. There were Fernando's children, too—"my well beloved grandchildren," Henrique calls them in official documents. He looked to them for the continuity of his life work, so he was delighted when Fernando asked him for islands to colonize. In August, 1460, he made over Terceira and Graciosa to his beloved son—"for there is every reason that I should do all that in me lies to fulfil his good pleasure."

September, the same year, found him at Sagres still—still giving away islands. This time he transferred to the King the temporal power that had been his over the islands of Cape Verde, reserving spiritual jurisdiction for the Order of Christ. Santa Maria and São Miguel of the Azores were to belong entirely to the Order, which was also to hold spiritual sway over Madeira, Porto Santo and Desertas. Henrique had endowed churches on all these archipelagoes, and he ordained that in each one masses should be said for his soul.

The luminous days of autumn passed. The equinoctial gales began to boom across the sea. Still the Infante lingered on his wind-swept rock, making his will and watching summer die. What had warned him that his own end was near? We are not told if his health was failing. We only know that all that autumn he was setting his affairs in order, and in November he fell ill and died.

No record has been made of the last scene. An enigmatic figure all his life, Henrique died inarticulate as he lived, wearing a hair shirt girded to his flesh, and the fragment of the True Cross that his mother gave him on his breast. His will was to be buried at Batalha in the family vault, but he would be carried there simply, without pomp—and without any mourning, he further enjoined, "for I will have none made for me, only let me be simply and decorously commended to God."

The night of November 13th, on which he died, his body was borne to the church of Lagos where it lay for a month, watched by his servant Diogo Gomes, who ordained the prayers and vigils.

In December his "son" Fernando escorted him to his last resting place at Batalha, where the King waited to receive his coffin.

His effigy was carved in stone upon a stone sarcophagus adorned by his emblem of acorns and oak leaves. The foliage twines about three shields, one of them bearing the Infante's arms, another with the collar of the Garter of which he was knight, and the third with the cross of his own Order of Christ. Along the frieze we read his motto: *Talent de bien faire.*

Henrique lies between his brothers Pedro and João—a grave-eyed knight in armor waiting in the shadows for the Resurrection. It is a face that tells nothing at all—a mask from which all is wiped out but the serenity of death.

The soul of the Infante must be sought elsewhere. A glimpse of it has been illumined for all time by Nuno Gonçalves in his wonderful triptych which shows the knights and seamen of King Afonso's court kneeling in prayer before St. Vincent. Among the worshipers Henrique may be seen—a man no longer young—severely dressed in black. He had a deeply furrowed brow, a sad mouth firmly closed, and eyes that see beyond.

That is as near as we can get to the Infante of Sagres. Of all the great men who have changed the course of history, Henrique is the most strangely aloof. What he achieved is written in letters of light—his personality alone eludes us.

Around that sphinxlike figure controversies rage—historians argue, and psychologists cannot agree. Henrique has been extolled to the skies, and criticized venomously, from his day to the present time. The theorists can say their say, for he has never spoken for himself. Wrapped always in his impenetrable reserve, he passed by indifferently, while some burn incense and others throw stones.

No public figure ever sought the limelight less. As king's son, brother, and uncle successively, he could have played a leading part in politics. Consistently, he always stepped aside, and made his life apart. He helped his brothers when duty required; he gave his nephew such assistance as he asked; but his appearances upon the public stage were always brief. At the first opportunity he turned his back upon the court and concentrated on his chosen task.

Even in this he seemed to seek no glory for himself. His passion was purely objective, and while others did the deeds, he was content to be the power behind. To read the story of Henrique's life is to read of what other men achieved, inspired by him.

He is always in the background, but we always feel him there. His seamen felt that driving force that would not let them rest till they had found. Year after year he saw the fleets depart, bound for the hidden lands below the blue horizon; and year after year the homing caravels sailed into Lagos bay, and sailors disembarked with glowing tales and strange trophies—or a report of failure—for the silent man at Sagres. And he listened serenely to them all, and never failed to praise where praise was due, nor ever had a harsh word for the unsuccessful. But whether they had come from radiant lands, or fruitless wanderings on the bitter sea, to each his exhortation was the same: "Go back," he always said; "go back, and go still farther!"

A hard man, cold and stern—some modern writers say—but was he that? Contemporaries do not seem to think so. "His speech was gentle," Zurara tells us, and "he never bore ill will to anyone, however deeply he might have been wronged." "He never spoke evil of anyone, nor wished anyone harm"—is the testimony of D. Gonçalo de Sousa, who was a member of Henrique's household all his life; and "he was affable to all," adds the Italian, Mateo Pisano, who was tutor to young Afonso V, and must have known the Infante quite well.

As for his alleged coldness—the Frenchman, Antoine de La

Salle, who followed the Infantes to Ceuta in 1415, seems to have seen Henrique in a very different light! If La Salle's story can be taken seriously, the young prince wept for days and nights unceasingly over the death of Vasco Fernandes de Ataide, his preceptor and dear friend. Allowance must be made for fifteenth-century journalese. La Salle was a popular writer of his day, and public taste required to have emotion laid on thick. Like the "great dole passing all measure" in which Malory's knights indulge so unrestrainedly, Henrique's tears as described by La Salle are no doubt partly literary effect. But discount as you will, the fact remains that to the stranger at his father's court he did not look like a callous young man.

From all accounts it seems that those who served Henrique were deeply attached to him, and there is no discrepancy in their opinion of his character. We may choose to reject Zurara as a panegyrist, but what about D. Gonçalo de Sousa? When a man orders to be inscribed about his own tombstone, not his virtues but those of the master whom he has served—a master who died many years before he did—we cannot put that down to flattery or time-serving.

The trouble with Henrique's personality is that a formula cannot be found to fit it. This is distressing to historians who like to show great figures of the past each with his own label like museum exhibits. No two of them seem to agree how the Infante D. Henrique ought to be defined. He was a crusader—a scientist—promoter of commercial enterprise—a dreamer—a reactionary—a modern—each of these attributes is defended ardently, as if one excluded the rest. Henrique seems to have been all these things. Born in an age of transition, his spirit faced two ways. The flame that lit the soldier of the Cross was kindled in his heart in early youth, and to win back Morocco from the Moors was his ambition all his life. He never drew his sword in any other cause. He was

(301)

therefore a crusader, and a medieval warrior, in love with knightly feats and deeds of arms, as practised by the heroes of his times. He shared the mystic ideals of his age, and its unshaken faith, but at the same time he sought scientific knowledge—illumination of the mind as well as of the soul. His patient inquiry into facts was wholly unmedieval, so was the practical realism that kept him from all imaginings. Henrique was a visionary who presaged worlds unseen, but no fantastic dreamer. He did not, like Columbus, hope to find rivers flowing from Paradise. He neither expected monsters, nor miracles, nor El Dorados. His horizons, though vast, were always circumscribed by sober fact. Slowly, patiently, tenaciously, he sought the unknown regions of the solid earth, and when he found, he ploughed and sowed, and turned them to good profit.

Yet this sense of all practical values did not exclude a higher aim than mere material gain. The new lands were not to be considered only as profitable farms. Though much could be got out of them, much also must be given back. The heathen lands were kingdoms to be won for Christ, and the guidance of their backward races was a duty that must not be shirked. Henrique shouldered this responsibility. If he had the spirit of a crusader, he had that of a missionary as well. Where he explored his aim was to evangelize, to civilize, and educate the simple savages with whom his seamen made contact. He sent out teachers and preachers to the black men of Senegal. He brought up negro children to become evangelists to their own people. He treated their chiefs, not as vassals but as brother princes and allies, and did his best to show them a higher standard of life. It is the glory of Portuguese expansion overseas that it continued on the lines that Henrique laid down.

The world owes the Infante more than it often remembers, for he inaugurated a new age. The end of the medieval period is commonly supposed to coincide with the fall of Constantinople. With far more truth it could be put back thirty years, to the date when Henrique first sent forth his caravels. The finding of the unknown world has modified civilization far more profoundly than could the revival of classical learning. A revival, after all, is but the resuscitation of what has already been—the movement started by Henrique brought about conditions that had never yet existed upon earth. In all the millenniums of human history, only during the last four hundred years has there been intercourse amongst all races of mankind around the globe. Civilizations have been born and died, great empires have risen and crumbled, and all passed on without knowing the earth on which they lived except in some small part. Henrique was the first to find the key that opened wide the gate of man's inheritance.

There had been voyages before his time—quite certainly to the Canary Islands, probably to Madeira, and perhaps to the Azores, not to mention the problematical wanderings of Phœnicians in Antiquity—but nothing permanent or useful came from these; they were spasmodic and not followed up. The image of the regions seen by isolated travelers flashed through the nations' consciousness, like dreams that come to us at night, and were not remembered more clearly. All pre-discoveries had to be re-discovered—but Henrique's stand for all time. Since his day there has been no looking back. Deliberately, with study and with patience and with system, he set in motion forces that could never be arrested while a land remained unknown on earth.

So the Infante brought about the greatest change the world has seen, or has seen yet. To be convinced of this we have but to compare the first years of the fifteenth with those of the sixteenth century. In 1400 the picture of a world of self-contained civilizations and cultures, some of which overlap on their confines, but most of which wholly ignore each other. Though they may trade and fight upon their outer fringe, Europe and Asia live apart; and south of the Sahara, in steamy forests unreached by the Arab caravans, the naked savages dream of no worlds outside their wilderness. And all around surges the sea, uncrossed by any ship, circling about the hidden desert islands, and washing on its farther shore an unknown continent where other races live, as ignorant of another world as that world is of them.

A hundred years later we find all changed. The farthest East has been reached by the distant West, the barriers of the world have broken down, Europe is everywhere. Throughout the world nations are making new contacts and finding out new things about each other. Europe is learning standards of luxury undreamed of before, Asia is jostled from her age-long isolation, while the astonished African sees wonder-working white men show him marvels, and learns from them new ways, acquires new needs, is taught a new and better faith—and picks up some new vices!

The ocean is no longer the impassable abyss. It has become the highway of the earth, traversed in every sense by many ships. Its desert islands are inhabited and cultivated, the hidden continent has come to light—a vast new field of opportunity is found. All the doors of the earth appear to have opened at once. It is the Infante D. Henrique who has brought this about.

For good or ill he introduced the modern world. A blessing or a curse? Either, or both? Nothing is gained in life unless something is lost, and fulfillment often brings disillusion. Till all the world had been revealed imagination always placed somewhere some perfect place—some Island of the Blest, some golden city, some righteous realm where innocence still lived. With every voyage the utopias receded further as bit by bit man found the world but lost the Earthly Paradise.

Chronology

Birth of the Infante D. Henrique. March 4, 1394.

Peace with Castile. 1411.

Preparations for the conquest of Ceuta. 1411–1415.

Death of D. Philippa. July 18, 1415.

Fleet sailed for Ceuta. July 25, 1415.

Conquest of Ceuta. August 21, 1415.

King and Infantes embarked for Portugal. September 2, 1415.

D. Henrique is nominated Governor of Ceuta. 1416.

Returned to Ceuta with the Infante D. João. 1418.

The Infante D. Pedro goes abroad. *About* 1419.

Discovery of Porto Santo by João Gonçalves Zarco and Tristão Vaz Teixeira. ? 1419.

Discovery of Madeira by the same. ? *Between* 1420 *and* 1423.

Expedition against Canary Islands under D. Fernando de Castro. 1424.

Marriage of the Infante D. João. 1424.

Colonization of Madeira. *Began about* 1425.

Discovery of the Azores. 1427–1432.

Return of D. Pedro. 1428.

Marriage of D. Duarte to D. Leonor of Aragon. September, 1428.

Marriage of the Infante D. Pedro to D. Isabel de Urgel and that of the Infanta D. Isabel to Philippe le Bon of Burgundy. 1429.

Voyage of Gonçalo Velho to Santa Maria in the Azores. ? 1432.

Death of D. João I. August 15, 1433.

Passage of Cape Bojador by Gil Eanes. 1434.

Gil Eanes returns there with Afonso Gonçalves Baldaia. 1435.

Discovery of Rio de Ouro by Afonso Gonçalves Baldaia. 1436.

D. Henrique adopts his young nephew, D. Fernando, as his son and heir. March 7, 1436.

Papal Bull advising D. Duarte to respect the Castilian claim to the Canary Islands. July 12, 1436.

Discussions at Leiria regarding the proposed Tangier expedition. August, 1436.

Crusading Bull issued by Pope Eugene IV. September 8, 1436.

Preparations for Tangier expedition. 1436–1437.

Infantes Henrique and Fernando sailed for Morocco. August 22, 1437.

Their army reached Tangier. September 13, 1437.

The Moors attacked in overwhelming force . . . . October 1st, 1437.

Capitulation. October 13, 1437.

D. Fernando handed over to Sala-ben-Sala. October 16, 1437.

D. Henrique re-embarks his troops and proceeds to Ceuta. October 20, 1437.

Returns to Portugal. February. ? 1438.

Cortes at Leiria. January to February, 1438.

Death of D. Duarte. September 9, 1438.

Troubles of regency. 1438–1441.

Document authorizing the Infante to colonize the islands of the Azores. July 2, 1439.

Voyages of Antão Gonçalves and Nuno Tristão to Rio de Ouro; capture of Adahu and other Berbers; discovery of Cape Branco by Nuno Tristão. 1441.

Death of Infante D. João. October, 1442.

Bull of Pope Eugene IV granting spiritual indulgences to all those who died fighting in heathen or Moslem lands of Africa. January 5, 1443.

Royal decree granting the Infante D. Henrique the exclusive right to send ships south of Cape Bojador, and reserving him a fifth of all profits to be obtained from those lands. October 22, 1443.

Concession of promontory of Sagres for the Vila do Infante. October, 1443.

Second voyage of Antão Gonçalves to Rio de Ouro to repatriate Adahu. 1443.

Voyage of Nuno Tristão to Arguim. 1443.

Death of Infante D. Fernando at Fez. July, 1443.

Discovery of Cape Verde by Denis Dias. 1444.

Death of Gonçalo de Sintra. 1444.

Slaves are brought to Lagos. 1444.

João Fernandes is left on the mainland near Cape Branco. 1444.

Voyage of Antão Gonçalves to fetch João Fernandes. 1445.

Voyage of Alvaro Fernandes from Funchal to Senegal and Cape of Masts. 1445.

Voyage of Gomes Pires, Lançarote, and others from Lagos to River Senegal and Cape Verde. 1445.

Death of Nuno Tristão off Guinea coast and tragic return voyage commanded by Aires Tinoco. 1446.

Voyage of Abelhart the Dane and his death or capture at Cape Verde. 1447.

Lease of the island of Lançarote in the Canaries by Maciot to the Infante D. Henrique. 1447.

End of D. Pedro's regency. 1447.

Disgrace of Regent. 1448–1449.

Alfarrobeira. May 20, 1449.

Building a fortress at Arguim. *After* 1448.

Armed expedition to the Canaries. 1450.

Building of the Vila do Infante. ? 1450–1454.

Voyage of Diogo de Teive to Banks of Newfoundland. ? *Between* 1450–1452.

Bull of Pope Nicholas V confirming Portuguese rights to all the newly-discovered lands. January 8, 1450.

Second Bull of same Pope granting the Infante the monopoly of exploration as far as India. January 8, 1454.

First voyage of Cadamosto to Gambia. ? 1455.

Voyage of Diogo Gomes to Gambia and beyond. ? 1456.

Discovery of Cape Verde Islands. 1456–1460.

Preparations for conquest of Alcacer Ceguer. 1456–1458.

Fleet sailed for Morocco. October 3, 1458.

Return to Portugal. November, 1458.

Mission sent out to Nomymansa. *End of* 1458.

Donation of Terceira and Graciosa to Infante D. Fernando. August 22, 1460.

Donation of the other islands to D. Afonso V, and to the Order of Christ. September 18, 1460.

Last Will and Testament of the Infante D. Henrique.

Death at Sagres. November 13, 1460.

Bibliography

THE following list has no pretense to be exhaustive. So much has been written about the Infante D. Henrique, especially during the nineteenth and the twentieth centuries, that to compile a complete bibliography would be a herculean labor. I understand, however, that the Comissão do Infante D. Henrique of the Lisbon Geographical Society have undertaken the task, and their work should prove invaluable to all future investigators.

These are the principal authorities I have consulted in the making of my book:

CONTEMPORARIES OF THE INFANTE

FERNÃO LOPES (? 1370–1460): *Cronica de D. João I, Parte II.*

D. DUARTE (1391–1438): *O Leal Conselheiro.*

GOMES EANES DE ZURARA (? 1410–1473 or 1474): *Cronica da Tomada de Ceuta; Cronica do Descobrimento e Conquista da Guiné; Cronica de D. Pedro de Menezes.*

MESTRE MATEUS DE PISANO (Tutor and Secretary to D. Afonso V): *Livro da Guerra de Ceuta,* translated from the original Latin into Portuguese by Roberto Correa Pinto.

ANTOINE DE LA SALLE (1388–1462): *Réconfort de Madame de Fresne,* translated into Portuguese by General Carlos du Bocage under the title of *Consolações dirigidas a Catharina de Neufville, Senhora de Fresne.*

FRANCISCO ALCOFORADO (Squire of the Infante D. Henrique): *Qual foy o Azo com q̃ se descobriu a Ilha da Madeyra escritto por my Franc° Alcoforado q̃ fuy a tudo presente.* Published by João Franco Machado in *Arquivo Historico da Marinha*, 1936.

João Alvares (Dates uncertain. Served the Infante D. Fernando from the age of ten, and in 1470 was still alive): *Cronica do Infante Santo D. Fernando.*

Cadamosto (1432–1477): *Navegação de Luiz de Cadamosto, traduzida pelo academico Sebastião Francisco Mendes Trigoso.*

Diogo Gomes (Servant of the Infante D. Henrique. Still living in 1480): *Relações do Descobrimento da Guiné e das Ilhas dos Açores, Madeira e Cabo Verde.* Translated from the Latin by Gabriel Pereira and published in the *Boletim da Sociedade de Geografia de Lisboa*, 17° Serie, No. 5.

Alguns Documentos do Arquivo Nacional da Torre do Tombo. Publishes a number of documents concerning the Infante D. Henrique.

Documentos das Chancelarias Reaes, published by Pedro de Azevedo (chiefly connected with Ceuta).

Provas à Historia Genealogica da Casa Real Portuguesa, published by Sousa.

Colecção de Documentos relativas ao Descobrimento e provoamento dos Açores, published by Manuel Monteiro Velho Arruda.

ALMOST CONTEMPORARY

Ruy de Pina (1440–1521): *Cronica de D. Duarte; Cronica de D. Afonso V.*

Duarte Pacheco Pereira (1460?–1533): *Esmeraldo de Situ Orbis.*

LATER HISTORIANS

João de Barros (1496–1570): *Decada I.*
Damião de Gois (1502–1574): *Cronica do Principe D. Joam.*
Gaspar Fructuoso (1522–1591): *Saudades da Terra.*
Gaspar Dias de Landim: *Cronica do Infante D. Pedro.*

BIBLIOGRAPHY

MODERN WRITERS

OLIVEIRA MARTINS: *Os Filhos de D. João I.*

FORTUNATO DE ALMEIDA: *O Infante de Sagres.*

MARIO GONÇALVES VIANA: *O Infante D. Henrique.*

VIEIRA GUIMARÃES: *Tres Mestres de Cristo.*

JAIME CORTESÃO: Many articles of great interest published from time to time in Lusitania, *Boletim da Agencia Geral das Colonias, Arquivo Historico da Marinha* and other learned periodicals, besides some valuable chapters in the *Historia de Portugal Ilustrada, Edição Monumental de Portucalense Editora, Barcelos.*

DAVID LOPES: The chapters relating to Morocco in the above-mentioned *Historia de Portugal,* and on the same subject in the *Historia da Expansão Portuguesa no Mundo.*

FRANCO MACHADO
JORDÃO DE FREITAS
JOÃO DE CASTRO OSORIO
QUIRINO DA FONSECA
ANTONIO BARBOSA
} All have made valuable contributions concerning the Infante's life and times to the *Historia da Expansão Portuguesa no Mundo,* and elsewhere.

MAURICIO DOMINGOS DOS SANTOS: "As responsabilidades de Tanger." *Revista Broteria,* 1931.

GAGO COUTINHO: "Passagem do Cabo Bojador." *Boletim da Sociedade de Geografia de Lisboa,* 1934.

VISCONDE DA LAGÔA: "O plano infantista e a passagem do Bojador." *Idem.*

LUIZ SCHWALBACH: "Uma fase da epopeia nacional." *Idem.*

DUARTE LEITE: *Acerca da "Cronica dos Feitos da Guiné."*

CARLOS ROMA MACHADO DE FARIA E MAIA: *Apontamentos para um novo Indice Cronologico das primeiras Viagens, Descobrimentos e Conquistas portuguesas.*

And many other articles by different writers that have appeared at intervals in the Bulletins of Lisbon Geographical Society, or that of the Academia das Ciencias, as well as the papers read at the Historical Congresses held in Lisbon in 1937 and 1940.

ENGLISH WRITERS

HENRY MAJOR: *Prince Henry of Portugal.*
RAYMOND BEAZLEY: *Prince Henry the Navigator.*
EDGAR PRESTAGE: *The Portuguese Pioneers.*

Index